Prentice Hall LITERATURE

PENGUIN EDITION

Unit Three Resources

Grade Nine

PEARSON

Upper Saddle River, New Jersey
Boston, Massachusetts
Chandler, Arizona
Glenview, Illinois

BQ Tunes Credits
Keith London, Defined Mind, Inc., Executive Producer
Mike Pandolfo, Wonderful, Producer
All songs mixed and mastered by Mike Pandolfo, Wonderful
Vlad Gutkovich, Wonderful, Assistant Engineer
Recorded November 2007 – February 2008 in SoHo, New York City, at
Wonderful, 594 Broadway

ISBN–13: 978-0-13-366452-2
ISBN–10:   0-13-366452-X

3 4 5 6 7 8 9 10   VONA   12 11 10

CONTENTS
Unit 3

For information about the Unit Resources, assessing fluency, and teaching with BQ Tunes, see the opening pages of your Unit 1 Resources.

"Carry Your Own Skis" and "Libraries Face Sad Chapter"

"Libraries Face Sad Chapter"

"I Have a Dream" by Martin Luther King, Jr.

"First Inaugural Address" by Franklin Delano Roosevelt

"I Have a Dream" and "First Inaugural Address"

Knowledge Understanding, performed by Tavi Fields

We're hit with **statistics**, (numbers) created from patterns of some knowledge
Are we equipped with
The tools to **interpret**, convert it to understanding?
To understanding . . .

In life we learn many lessons
Obtain different **information** then we make **connections**
So we can see the relations and we gain perspective
Gotta read between the lines gotta play detective
And there's a process between taking something in as a **concept**
And making it a **feeling** you can touch like an object
Except it's a trigger that's inside that's your **instinct**
That's your **senses** on automatic you won't sink
If you trust that anchor in happiness and in anger
It's your guardian angel when you're safe or in danger
Like the difference in leaving a mark or branding
I guess knowledge ain't the same as understanding

(C'mon now help me out)
Well, knowledge plus understanding equals wisdom
And it can come from many different places
I believe in many truths don't think there is one
And that's because I've been in many different spaces (×2)

Please let me **clarify** let me make it clear
You gotta analyze what goes in your ears
Eyes nose mouth and what you touch
East west north south yo listen up
Everything in a textbook ain't always **fact**
You gotta do your **research** from front to back
Don't rely on just one source use many **sources**
Relying on one force? Use many forces

Continued

Power is endless remember these words when you feel defenseless

The more you know the less you gotta ride the fences

And when you understand that's focused lenses

Nod with your head if you **comprehend** this

(Yeah, Yo . . .)

Knowledge plus understanding equals wisdom

And it can come from many different places

I believe in many truths don't think there is one

And that's because I've been in many different spaces (×2)

I like being a nerd love reading and writing words

I live for nouns and verbs some say it's for the birds

And yes I wanna fly so I can touch the sky

I may not get as high but first I gotta try

We all got a light inside let's get bright

Let's share some advice let's give some **insight**

I'm serious don't fear ask questions if you're curious

Unlock the code it ain't gotta be mysterious

I ain't even being specific it's **ambiguous**

To what kind of knowledge that I'm referencing you figure it

Out for yourself and relate it to your experience

And sometimes you'll have to sacrifice your innocence

(C'mon)

Knowledge plus understanding equals wisdom

And it can come from many different places

I believe in many truths don't think there is one

And that's because I've been in many different spaces (×2)

Song Title: **Knowledge Understanding**
Artist / Performed by Tavi Fields
Lyrics by Tavi Fields
Music composed by Mike Pandolfo, Wonderful
Produced by Mike Pandolfo, Wonderful
Executive Producer: Keith London, Defined Mind

Unit 3: Types of Nonfiction
Big Question Vocabulary—1

The Big Question: Is knowledge the same as understanding?

Most people have had the experience of not fully understanding something. Sometimes this happens even when you have knowledge of facts.

ambiguous: unclear; having more than one meaning

clarify: to make something clearer and easier to understand

comprehend: to understand something that is complicated or difficult

concept: an idea of how something is or how something should be done

information: facts or details about something

DIRECTIONS: *Your teachers might as well be speaking a foreign language. You just do not understand! Use all of the vocabulary words to ask your teachers to explain their statements again and in more detail.*

The compounds combine to form a chemical reaction and ignite spontaneously.

1.

The health of the ecosystem is critical to the health of each species living within the ecosystem.

2.

The longest side of a right triangle is *always* directly across from the 90 degree angle. This side is called the hypotenuse.

3.

Name _____ Date _____

Unit 3: Types of Nonfiction
Big Question Vocabulary—2

The Big Question: Is knowledge the same as understanding?

Most students have had the experience of gathering data and ideas for a report or project. In the case of a complicated topic, students often must pore over the data they have gathered in order to gain understanding.

fact: a piece of information that is known to be true

interpret: to understand something to have a particular meaning

research: to study or investigate something in detail

sources: people, books, or documents that supply you with information

statistics: a set of numbers that represent facts or measurements

DIRECTIONS: *Write some guidelines for a young friend who is doing his first research project and is unsure how to research his topic. Use all of the vocabulary words in your instructions, and feel free to explain them to your young friend.*

1.
2.
3.
4.

Name _____ Date _____

Unit 3: Types of Nonfiction
Big Question Vocabulary—3

The Big Question: Is knowledge the same as understanding?

One way of getting information is experiencing it for ourselves. The only way to know if you like chocolate is to taste it. Similarly, we should pay attention to feelings, or "vibes," that we get about situations or people.

connection: the process or result of joining two or more things together

feeling: an opinion or a belief about something that is influenced by emotions

insight: clear or deep perception or understanding of something

instinct: the natural ability to think, behave, or react in a particular way without learning it or thinking about it first

sensory: involving one or more of the five senses: taste, touch, hearing, sight, and smell

DIRECTIONS: *Write your thoughts in a situation where you had a strong feeling about something but couldn't really explain why. Use all of the vocabulary words.*

Name _____   Date _____

Unit 3: Types of Nonfiction
Applying the Big Question

The Big Question: Is knowledge the same as understanding?

DIRECTIONS: *Complete the chart below to apply what you have learned about knowledge and understanding. One row has been completed for you.*

Example	What facts and information the author had	What knowledge the author gained	What the author came to understand	What I Learned
From Literature	In "On Summer," the author's friend has cancer.	Her friend faced life courageously.	We understand life better when others share their knowledge and experience.	Taking the time to understand others gives life more meaning.
From Literature				
From Science				
From Social Studies				
From Real Life				

Name _____

Unit 3: Types of Nonfiction Skills Concept Map—1
Is knowledge the same as understanding?

Literary Analysis:
Types of Nonfiction

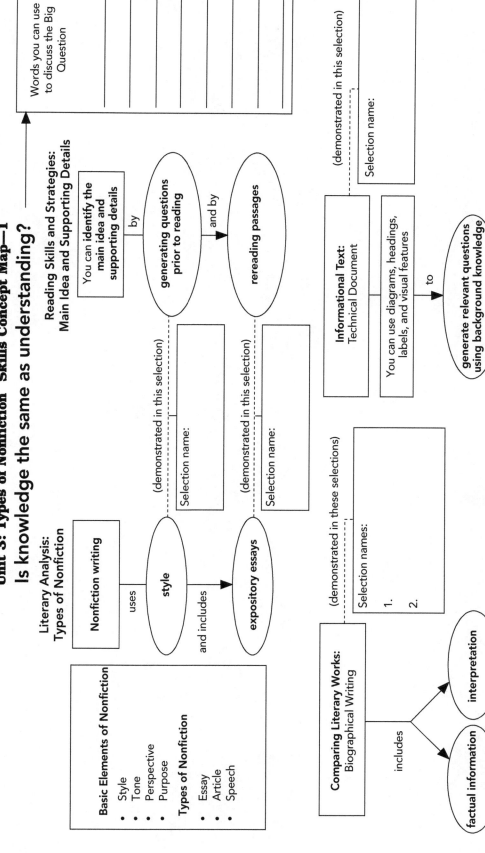

Nonfiction writing → *uses* → style → *and includes* → expository essays

(demonstrated in this selection)
Selection name: _____

(demonstrated in this selection)
Selection name: _____

Basic Elements of Nonfiction
- Style
- Tone
- Perspective
- Purpose

Types of Nonfiction
- Essay
- Article
- Speech

Reading Skills and Strategies:
Main Idea and Supporting Details

You can identify the main idea and supporting details → *by* → generating questions prior to reading → *and by* → rereading passages

(demonstrated in this selection)
Selection name: _____

Words you can use to discuss the Big Question

Informational Text:
Technical Document → You can use diagrams, headings, labels, and visual features → *to* → generate relevant questions using background knowledge

Comparing Literary Works:
Biographical Writing → *includes* → interpretation / factual information

(demonstrated in these selections)
Selection names:
1.
2.

Student Log

Complete this chart to track your assignments.

Writing	Extend Your Learning	Writing Workshop	Other Assignments

5

Vocabulary Warm-up Word Lists

Study these words from "Before Hip-Hop Was Hip-Hop" by Rebecca Walker. Then, complete the activities that follow.

Word List A

communicate [kuh MYOO nuh kayt] *v.* to express oneself so others understand
A smile and a frown <u>communicate</u> opposite moods and emotions.

cultural [KUHL chur uhl] *adj.* relating to customs, behavior, and way of life in a society
The computer has created many <u>cultural</u> changes in today's world.

formula [FOHRM yoo luh] *n.* set method used to do or achieve something
The <u>formula</u> for success in school is to work hard.

local [LOH kuhl] *adj.* relating to a nearby place or area, especially where one lives
A <u>local</u> bus makes many stops in and around a town or city.

rotation [roh TAY shuhn] *n.* regular or planned sequence of events that repeats
The <u>rotation</u> of drivers in the car pool is the same every week.

sagging [SAG ing] *adj.* hanging down; drooping
My eyelids are <u>sagging</u> because I am so tired.

significant [sig NIF i kuhnt] *adj.* important or major
Today's sunshine is a <u>significant</u> change from yesterday's rain.

united [yoo NYT id] *adj.* closely joined by sharing feelings and aims
My friends and I are <u>united</u> by our love of baseball.

Word List B

apiece [uh PEES] *adv.* each
We have two sandwiches for four of us, so we get one half <u>apiece</u>.

approximate [uh PROKS uh mayt] *v.* to become similar to but not exactly the same
For the display, we used cotton balls to <u>approximate</u> snowballs.

bravado [bruh VAH doh] *n.* behavior that is a real or a pretend show of courage
We were all frightened except Sammy, who was full of <u>bravado</u>.

creativity [kree ay TIV uh tee] *n.* ability to use the imagination for new ideas
<u>Creativity</u> is necessary in order to have great art or inventions.

dynamic [dy NAM ik] *adj.* interesting, exciting, and full of energy
A concert is a <u>dynamic</u> event and exciting to attend.

outrageous [owt RAY juhs] *adj.* very shocking or unreasonable
We could not afford anything because the prices were <u>outrageous</u>.

realm [RELM] *n.* area or place for a particular kind of interest or activity
In the <u>realm</u> of sports, star players are the kings and queens.

violent [VY uh luhnt] *adj.* using force to hurt others or showing destructive behavior
I do not like <u>violent</u> movies because they show people being hurt.

7

Name _____ Date _____

Vocabulary Warm-up Exercises

Exercise A *Fill in each blank in the paragraph with an appropriate word from Word List A.*
Use each word only once.

Clothing is one way that people [1] _____ attitudes and feelings.

Take someone who wears a team name on shirts and caps. The person is

[2] _____ with other fans in loyalty for the team. If it is a hometown

team, wearing such a shirt or cap shows [3] _____ pride. Styles

tell whether fashion trends are important to the wearer, such as having

[4] _____ pants or a certain brand of jeans. Styles can also identify

[5] _____ background, such as wearing clothing that is typical of

another country. There is no set approach or [6] _____ for choosing

what to wear. Some people have a regular [7] _____ of outfits that they

wear in a continuous cycle week after week. For others, comfort is all that matters and

is the most [8] _____ factor in how they dress.

Exercise B *Decide whether each statement is true or false. Circle T or F. Then, explain your*
answers.

1. To exercise your <u>creativity</u>, give your imagination a workout.
   T / F _____

2. To <u>approximate</u> the sound of a siren, you must use an actual siren to make the
   sound.
   T / F _____

3. If you need $10 <u>apiece</u> to go to the movies, each ticket costs no more than $10.
   T / F _____

4. <u>Bravado</u> can be dangerous when good judgment is more important than courage.
   T / F _____

5. A <u>dynamic</u> game would keep fans on the edge of their seats.
   T / F _____

6. You need a passport or birth certificate to enter the <u>realm</u> of science.
   T / F _____

7. An <u>outrageous</u> error may have serious consequences.
   T / F _____

8. Self-control is usually not a problem for someone with a <u>violent</u> temper.
   T / F _____

Name _____ Date _____

"**Before Hip-Hop Was Hip-Hop**" by Rebecca Walker
Reading Warm-up A

Read the following passage. Pay special attention to the underlined words. Then, read it again, and complete the activities. Use a separate sheet of paper for your written answers.

Breakdancing was a fascinating dance form when it widely appeared in the early 1980s. It was very athletic and took unusual coordination. It was also unplanned. There was no <u>formula</u> or set approach to dancing that was followed every time. That made it exciting to perform and thrilling to watch. <u>Local</u> kids who mastered the art of breakdancing could use their neighborhood street as a stage.

Breakdancing is part of a rich tradition of young people's dance styles. For instance, in the 1920s, the popular dance the "Charleston" was all about flapping your arms, wobbling your knees, and kicking up your heels. Young women called "flappers" wore short dresses with ruffles and fringe that were a <u>significant</u> change from the long skirts and plainer looks of the decades before. Although their shift in clothes was not as major as that of the flappers, breakdancers did introduce their own signature clothing. Loose, <u>sagging</u> nylon pants and jackets made it easier to do the flips and slides in a breakdancing routine.

Breakdancing can be traced to a dance called the "Good Foot" from the early 1970s. It featured drops to the ground and spins of the body in a routine done by a single dancer. Breakdancing used those moves and added the excitement of having a team of dancers in regular <u>rotation</u>. One dancer performed and then another took over. The "freeze" was used to <u>communicate</u> that a routine was done. A dancer would hold his body perfectly still in an odd pose for a few seconds. That sent the message for the next dancer to step in. The individual dancers might compete in performing complicated and daring moves. However, as a group, they were <u>united</u> in their efforts to put on a great show.

By the late 1980s, breakdancing was no longer the <u>cultural</u> sensation it had been earlier. The music world and society in general moved on to new styles, such as rap. However, to this day, some fans continue to breakdance when the beat is right.

1. Circle words that are a clue to the meaning of <u>formula</u>. Underline the reason why there was no **formula** to breakdancing that had to be followed.

2. Circle a word clue for <u>local</u>. Describe a **local** activity where you live.

3. Circle the word clue for <u>significant</u>. Give an antonym for **significant**.

4. Circle the word clue for <u>sagging</u>. Give a synonym for **sagging**.

5. Underline the sentence that explains the <u>rotation</u> in breakdancing. Explain why **regular** is also a clue to the meaning of **rotation**.

6. Underline the phrase that is a clue to <u>communicate</u>. Describe something that music and dancing **communicate**.

7. Circle the word that relates to the opposite of <u>united</u>. Explain how a group that is **united** would act.

8. Underline the phrase that is a clue to the meaning of <u>cultural</u>. Describe a **cultural** sensation today, and explain why it is one.

Name _____ Date _____

"Before Hip-Hop Was Hip-Hop" by Rebecca Walker
Reading Warm-up B

Read the following passage. Pay special attention to the underlined words. Then, read it again, and complete the activities. Use a separate sheet of paper for your written answers.

In the <u>realm</u> of the music world, music videos are a crowning achievement. For a performer in the area of music, a strong video of a song can skyrocket sales. The <u>creativity</u> of recording artists and the genius and imagination of production companies are key to the success of current music videos. However, the music video is not just a modern development. The idea of a short movie that visually represents a song dates back to the beginning of sound films.

Movie audiences in the 1920s enjoyed animated "visual music." This was a series of shapes and patterns that appeared onscreen in time to a musical recording. It might not seem very exciting or <u>dynamic</u> by today's standards, but sound was just coming into movies. Any use of sound and images together was a revolution. Later, movie studios that produced cartoons began showing animated clips of characters singing songs. While not exactly the same, these could be said to <u>approximate</u> a music video. They were used to attract audiences to full-length cartoon films.

The popularity of these animated musical short films soon interested live musicians. They appeared onscreen entertaining crowds with their hit songs and ballads. There was no <u>outrageous</u> and shocking behavior by the human or cartoon performers. The tone was light, to be enjoyed by all.

The musical short film took a step outside of theaters in 1941, with the invention of a visual musical jukebox. It played a type of musical film called a "Soundie." Soundies featured one song <u>apiece</u>.

Inexpensive videotape and hand-held cameras in the 1970s and 1980s opened the way for the explosion of music videos. Explosive also describes the far more <u>violent</u> content of some modern videos. Often, performers show <u>bravado</u> in dangerous settings that, if real, would demand real courage. The breezy musical short is more and more just a note in music film history.

1. Underline the phrase that explains the <u>realm</u> *of the music world*. Circle the word that would describe any *realm*.

2. Circle the words that are clues to <u>creativity</u>. Underline two groups identified in the passage that are known for *creativity*.

3. Circle a word that is a clue to <u>dynamic</u>. Give a synonym for *dynamic*.

4. Underline a phrase that gives a clue to the meaning of <u>approximate</u>. Explain why the clips could be said to *approximate* a music video.

5. Circle a word that is a clue to <u>outrageous</u>. Give a synonym for *outrageous*.

6. Circle the meaning of <u>apiece</u>. Compute how many "Soundies" would be viewed if you and two friends saw three *apiece*.

7. Circle the word that is a clue to <u>violent</u>. Give an antonym for *violent*.

8. Circle the word clue for <u>bravado</u>. Describe how someone might show *bravado*.

Name _____ Date _____

Rebecca Walker
Listening and Viewing

Segment 1: Meet Rebecca Walker
- What early experiences with literature inspired Rebecca Walker to become a writer?
- What is your favorite piece of literature, and why is it important to you? Explain.

_____

_____

_____

Segment 2: Types of Nonfiction
- How can music influence other art forms, especially literature?
- How do you think the emergence of hip-hop has influenced the nonfiction literature that people write today and will write in the future?

_____

_____

_____

Segment 3: The Writing Process
- Which method in Rebecca Walker's writing process would you most likely adopt? Why?

_____

_____

_____

Segment 4: The Rewards of Writing
- What does Rebecca Walker want to convey to young people who read her writing?
- Why do you think it is important for young people to be well-informed about current events?

_____

_____

_____

Learning About Nonfiction

Three important types of nonfiction are essays, articles, and speeches. An **essay** examines and discusses a focused topic, often including the writer's personal viewpoints. In an **article,** a writer gives information about a specific topic, person, or event. In a **speech,** a speaker addresses a topic in front of a live audience. Like essays and articles, speeches may be informative, persuasive, or entertaining.

In nonfiction, just as in fiction, the author's style and tone are important elements. A writer's **style** is the particular way that he or she uses language. Here are some factors that contribute to a writer's distinctive style:

- level of language (formal vs. dialect or slang)
- use of figurative language (simile, metaphor, personification, hyperbole, symbol)
- diction, or word choice
- sentence patterns (long or short, variety in types of sentences, repetition)
- sensory imagery

The **tone** of a work is the author's attitude toward the subject matter, the characters, or the audience of readers or listeners. A work's tone can often be summed up in one word: *playful, solemn, mysterious, ominous, personal,* or *enthusiastic.* Be alert to shifts in tone. Different parts of a single work may deliberately exhibit different tones.

DIRECTIONS: *Circle the letter of the answer that best matches each numbered item.*

1. the style of a letter you write to your local school board
   A. formal   B. chatty   C. slangy

2. the tone of a birthday card you write to your little sister
   A. playful   B. scholarly   C. pessimistic

3. the tone of a speech urging support for a candidate for public office
   A. relaxed   B. persuasive   C. hesitant

4. the style of an essay focusing on one of your childhood experiences
   A. formal   B. informal   C. neutral

5. the tone of an after-dinner speech at an awards ceremony
   A. solemn   B. entertaining   C. poetic

6. the style of a descriptive essay focusing on a field of sunflowers in bloom
   A. sensory   B. persuasive   C. narrative

7. the style of a letter to a childhood friend who now lives in a foreign country
   A. complex   B. remote   C. conversational

8. the tone of an article summarizing the Civil War for high school students
   A. reflective   B. factual   C. humorous

"Before Hip-Hop Was Hip-Hop" by Rebecca Walker
Model Selection: Nonfiction

An **essay** is a brief work of nonfiction that discusses a focused topic and often includes the writer's personal experiences and opinions. An essayist's **style,** or distinctive way of using language, often reflects his or her personality. The **tone** of the essay, or the writer's attitude toward the subject matter and the audience, is also key to understanding an essay.

Essays can be classified by the author's **purpose,** or reason for writing. A **narrative** essay tells a story of actual events or the life experiences of an individual. A **descriptive** essay builds an overall impression of a person, an object, or an experience by using images that appeal to the senses. An **expository** essay provides information, discusses ideas, or explains a process. A **persuasive** essay attempts to convince readers to take a course of action or adopt the writer's viewpoint. A **reflective** essay expresses the writer's thoughts and feelings in response to a personal experience or to an idea.

DIRECTIONS: *Read the following passages from "Before Hip-Hop Was Hip-Hop." In the space provided in the chart, comment briefly on the style, tone, or purpose of each passage.*

Passage from the Essay	Comments on Style, Tone, or Purpose
1. I noted what they wore and how they wore it: the razor sharp creases of their Jordache jeans, the spotless sneakers with the laces left loose and untied.	
2. Intuitively, kids were making a community where there was none; we were affirming our sameness in a world that seemed to only emphasize our difference.	
3. I hope they will marvel at the fact that in the early days of hip-hop, young people were making it up as they went along, following their hearts, following what felt good. I hope they will think about what it takes to create culture that is unique and transcendent and honest, and I hope they will begin to dream about creating a new world for themselves.	

"Before Hip-Hop Was Hip-Hop" by Rebecca Walker
Open-Book Test

Short Answer *Write your responses to the questions in this section on the lines provided.*

1. Three types of nonfiction are the essay, the article, and the speech. In one type of nonfiction, the writer examines a topic and might express his or her personal point of view. What type of nonfiction would that be?

   _____

2. You are reading a work of nonfiction, and you realize that the author's attitude toward her subject is sarcastic. What aspect of the work are you focusing on?

   _____

   _____

3. You are reading a work of nonfiction, and you are trying to figure out the author's purpose. What purposes might you consider? List at least three.

   _____

   _____

   _____

4. How could you tell the difference between a descriptive essay and a reflective essay?

   _____

   _____

   _____

5. In "Before Hip-Hop Was Hip-Hop," Rebecca Walker writes of "entrenched cliques" at her school in the Bronx. Would it be easy or difficult to join an entrenched clique? Explain your answer based on the definition of *entrenched.*

   _____

   _____

   _____

6. On looking out a bus window in New York City, Rebecca Walker thinks the world is divided. According to "Before Hip-Hop Was Hip-Hop," how did Walker's personal experience differ from the world she saw from the bus window? Cite one detail from the essay to explain your answer.

   _____

   _____

   _____

7. In "Before Hip-Hop Was Hip-Hop," Walker writes of an "ever expanding lexicon." How does she demonstrate that ever expanding lexicon in her essay? Base your answer on the definition of *lexicon*.

   _____

   _____

8. Toward the end of "Before Hip-Hop Was Hip-Hop," Walker writes that "I learned how good it could feel to move with a 'posse,' a group of friends who had my back no matter what." What character trait is Walker praising in this passage? Explain your answer.

   _____

   _____

   _____

9. What can you infer about Rebecca Walker's likes and dislikes when she was young? Cite two details from "Before Hip-Hop Was Hip-Hop" to support your answer.

   _____

   _____

   _____

10. In "Before Hip-Hop Was Hip-Hop," Rebecca Walker describes a year in her life. She also describes her thoughts about how her experience of hip-hop compares with the experience of mass-marketed hip-hop. Based on that description, how would you classify Walker's essay? Is it narrative, descriptive, expository, persuasive, or reflective? Explain your answer.

    _____

    _____

    _____

Essay

Write an extended response to the question of your choice or to the question or questions your teacher assigns you.

11. Writers of all works of literature have at least one purpose for writing. In your opinion, what is Rebecca Walker's main purpose for writing "Before Hip-Hop Was Hip-Hop"? In an essay, identify Walker's main ideas about hip-hop. Then, explain how those ideas relate to her purpose for writing. Support your ideas with specific details from "Before Hip-Hop Was Hip-Hop."

12. In an essay, discuss "Before Hip-Hop Was Hip-Hop" as an example of the essay form. Begin by identifying the topic that Rebecca Walker has chosen for her essay. Then, discuss two examples of the way in which Walker uses personal viewpoints and experiences to consider her topic. Finally, discuss the lessons that Walker feels she learned by participating in the creation of hip-hop. Use the following chart to help organize your thoughts.

Topic: _____

Personal Viewpoints	Experiences

13. An author's style can strongly affect the reader's reaction to the work. In an essay, analyze the style of "Before Hip-Hop Was Hip-Hop." Consider the essay's level of formality and Walker's use of figurative language, word choice, sentence patterns, and methods of organization. Consider, for example, the last two paragraphs of the essay, which contain a series of sentences beginning with the words "I hope." Then, write an essay of your own in which you describe how the style of Walker's essay contributes to your feelings about it. Cite aspects of the style to explain what you like or dislike about Walker's essay.

14. **Thinking About the Big Question: Is knowledge the same as understanding?** What understanding about life and human nature or human behavior does Rebecca Walker want readers of "Before Hip-Hop Was Hip-Hop" to recognize and accept? In an essay, discuss how Walker uses details from her personal experience and from the development of hip-hop to shape and present this understanding.

Oral Response

15. Go back to question 6, 8, or 9 or to the question your teacher assigns you. Take a few minutes to expand your answer and prepare an oral response. Find additional details in "Before Hip-Hop Was Hip-Hop" that support your points. If necessary, make notes to guide your oral response.

Name _____   Date _____

"**Before Hip-Hop Was Hip-Hop**" by Rebecca Walker
Selection Test A

Learning About Nonfiction *Identify the letter of the choice that best answers the question.*

_____ 1. Essays, articles, and speeches are all works of nonfiction. Which of the following is an accurate statement about the authors of nonfiction?
   A. They are always real people.
   B. Their style is always full of figurative language.
   C. They usually focus on retelling historical events.
   D. Their tone is always objective.

_____ 2. Some works of nonfiction examine and discuss a focused topic and include the writer's personal viewpoints. This type of nonfiction is known as which of the following?
   A. speech
   B. essay
   C. lyric
   D. short story

_____ 3. In a work of nonfiction that includes the writer's viewpoint, why does the author's style deserve the attention of readers?
   A. The author's style helps readers to understand the topic.
   B. The style of the writing is often more important than the topic.
   C. An author's style often reflects his or her personality.
   D. Style can lead to bias, and readers need to be alert.

Critical Reading

_____ 4. When Rebecca Walker began her seventh-grade year at Public School 141 in the Bronx, what made a vivid impression on her?
   A. the teachers' enthusiasm for their classes
   B. the winning record of the athletic teams
   C. the broad variety of courses being taught
   D. the diversity and energy of the student body

_____ 5. According to Rebecca Walker, hip-hop today is which of the following?
   A. a swiftly passing fad
   B. a global industry
   C. on a long, slow decline
   D. much better than it used to be

___ 6. From details in "Before Hip-Hop Was Hip-Hop," which of the following can you conclude about the author?
   A. She loved popular music when she was young.
   B. She had a special interest in classical music.
   C. She preferred dance to any other art form.
   D. She wanted to study painting and sculpture in school.

___ 7. Read the following excerpt from "Before Hip-Hop Was Hip-Hop."
   The "breakers" moved in "crews" that competed against each other. Standing in a circle we watched as members of the different groups "moonwalked" into the center, and then hurled themselves to the floor. . . .

   Which of the following terms correctly describes the words in quotation marks in the passage?
   A. figurative language
   B. symbolism
   C. slang
   D. sarcasm

___ 8. In "Before Hip-Hop Was Hip-Hop," what did the author's friends Loida and Diane teach her about?
   A. how to wear her hair
   B. radio stations and other neighborhoods
   C. name chains and designer jeans
   D. Puerto Rico and Haiti

___ 9. Read the following excerpt from "Before Hip-Hop Was Hip-Hop."
   I learned how good it could feel to move with a "posse," a group of friends who had my back no matter what.

   What character trait is the author praising in the passage?
   A. generosity
   B. ambition
   C. loyalty
   D. pride

___ 10. According to the author of "Before Hip-Hop Was Hip-Hop," her seventh-grade experiences were important because they taught her which of the following?
   A. how to choose fashionable outfits
   B. words from a number of different languages
   C. valuable lessons about real life
   D. how to play a musical instrument

___ 11. The author of "Before Hip-Hop Was Hip-Hop" has an attitude toward the subject and the readers of her writing. What is this attitude called?

    A. style   B. perspective   C. tone   D. purpose

___ 12. From details in "Before Hip-Hop Was Hip-Hop," you can conclude that the author feels which of the following about present-day hip-hop?

    A. It is superior in every way to original hip-hop.

    B. It has lost the international flavor of original hip-hop.

    C. It has lost some of the spontaneous joy of original hip-hop.

    D. Unlike original hip-hop, styles today emphasize dancing over music.

___ 13. "Before Hip-Hop Was Hip-Hop" might best be described as what kind of essay?

    A. expository   B. reflective   C. persuasive   D. humorous

Essay

14. What does Rebecca Walker want readers to get out of reading "Before Hip-Hop Was Hip-Hop"? What are some of Walker's main ideas about original hip-hop and hip-hop today? Write an essay in which you discuss Rebecca Walker's message about hip-hop. Support your points with specific references to the selection.

15. In many essays, the reader gets an idea of the writer's personality through the writer's use of language. "Before Hip-Hop Was Hip-Hop" contains numerous references to pop culture, including song titles, slang, and details about clothing and music. Write an essay in which you discuss Rebecca Walker's use of distinctive language. Why do you think she uses this kind of language? What does it suggest to you about Walker's personality? Support your response with specific references to the selection.

16. **Thinking About the Big Question: Is knowledge the same as understanding?** In "Before Hip-Hop Was Hip-Hop," author Rebecca Walker uses personal knowledge to give the reader details from her own experience. She also provides information about the development of hip-hop. In an essay, discuss the greater idea and values that Walker's knowledge of hip-hop helps you understand.

"Before Hip-Hop Was Hip-Hop" by Rebecca Walker
Selection Test B

Learning About Nonfiction *Identify the letter of the choice that best completes the statement or answers the question.*

_____ 1. Which of the following is the general name for essays, articles, and speeches?
   A. persuasion
   B. short stories
   C. nonfiction
   D. exposition

_____ 2. In a nonfiction work, which of the following is the correct term for an author's attitude toward the subject and the audience?
   A. style
   B. description
   C. perspective
   D. tone

_____ 3. Which of the following identifies the particular way in which a writer uses language?
   A. tone
   B. style
   C. purpose
   D. perspective

_____ 4. What is the main difference between a speech and an article?
   A. An article is addressed to readers, while a speech is delivered to a live audience.
   B. A speech is always entertaining, but articles are mainly serious.
   C. Speeches contain more descriptive passages than articles.
   D. It is permissible to use slang in a speech, but slang should not appear in an article.

_____ 5. In nonfiction works, which of the following elements does *not* contribute to an author's style?
   A. figurative language
   B. level of formality
   C. sentence patterns
   D. accuracy of information

_____ 6. Which of the following indicates that a writer is biased?
   A. a one-sided presentation
   B. emotionally neutral language
   C. the presentation of all relevant facts
   D. an objective tone

Critical Reading

_____ 7. Which of the following best identifies the writer's form in "Before Hip-Hop Was Hip-Hop"?
   A. entertaining speech
   B. reflective essay
   C. biased essay
   D. informative article

_____ 8. In "Before Hip-Hop Was Hip-Hop," the author focuses on which of the following?
   A. present-day music videos
   B. the literary qualities of rap lyrics
   C. her seventh-grade year at school in the Bronx
   D. her early childhood in Washington, D.C.

_____ 9. According to the writer of "Before Hip-Hop Was Hip-Hop," kids today feel they know the true hip-hop neighborhoods because
   A. they have seen them in videos.
   B. they grew up in them.
   C. hip-hop is natural to them.
   D. they wear hip-hop styles.

_____ 10. In "Before Hip-Hop Was Hip-Hop," the writer includes details about her musical tastes. To which literary element do the details contribute?
   A. narration
   B. perspective
   C. persuasion
   D. purpose

_____ 11. According to Rebecca Walker, when did hip-hop first begin to develop as a musical and cultural style?
   A. the 1920s
   B. the 1960s
   C. the 1980s
   D. the 1990s

_____ 12. When Rebecca Walker first arrived at Public School 141 in the Bronx, for which of the following was she unprepared?
   A. the difficulty of her school subjects
   B. the school's high-tech computer equipment
   C. the strictness of school discipline
   D. the diversity and self-expression of the students

_____ 13. What does the use of slang in this passage contribute to Walker's style?

   A guy in a preppy, button down shirt would "sport" gold chains with pendants of every denomination: the Jewish Star of David, the Arabic lettering for Allah, and a shiny gold cross. He was everything, that was his "steelo," and everyone gave him "props" for it.

   A. symbolism
   B. figurative language not meant to be taken literally
   C. flavor and authenticity
   D. sarcasm

_____ 14. According to Rebecca Walker in "Before Hip-Hop Was Hip-Hop," which of the following is one element in breakdancing?
   A. the Brazilian martial art of Capoeira
   B. the songs of Soul Sonic Force
   C. Nike sneakers
   D. the lyrics of the Bee Gees

Unit 3 Resources: Types of Nonfiction

_____ 15. How did Rebecca Walker feel about the big street parties she attended with her friends?
  A. She was puzzled and disoriented.
  B. She strongly disapproved of the parties.
  C. She was frightened by the fights that often broke out.
  D. She was enthusiastic and exhilarated.

_____ 16. According to Rebecca Walker, which accessories did the kids desire most?
  A. broad-rimmed hats and loud T-shirts
  B. knockoff Porsche sunglasses and heavy gold chains
  C. oversize jeans and shoes
  D. fancy wallets and leather gloves

_____ 17. Which values did Rebecca Walker come to appreciate in the early years of hip-hop?
  A. pride and respect
  B. diversity and authenticity
  C. compassion and generosity
  D. fashion and self-expression

_____ 18. According to Rebecca Walker, what is one of the major differences between original hip-hop and the hip-hop of today?
  A. Original hip-hop did not come pre-packaged and was not marketed expensively.
  B. Today's breakdancing is more creative than it was in the days of original hip-hop.
  C. Hip-hop today has lost its international flavor.
  D. Original hip-hop developed slowly, but styles today change from moment to moment.

Essay

19. Write an essay in which you discuss "Before Hip-Hop Was Hip-Hop" as an example of the essay form in nonfiction. Begin by identifying the topic that Rebecca Walker has chosen for her writing. Then, discuss some examples of the way Walker uses personal viewpoints and experiences to consider hip-hop. Finally, discuss the lessons that Walker feels she learned by being part of the original days of hip-hop.

20. An author's style often reflects his or her unique personality. In an essay, analyze Rebecca Walker's style in "Before Hip-Hop Was Hip-Hop." What, if anything, does her style contribute to your interaction with the essay? Do you like her style? In your discussion, pay special attention to Walker's use of slang, her use of specific details, and her concluding paragraph, which contains a series of sentences beginning with the words "I hope . . . ."

21. **Thinking About the Big Question: Is knowledge the same as understanding?** What understanding about life and human nature or human behavior does Rebecca Walker want readers of "Before Hip-Hop Was Hip-Hop" to recognize and accept? In an essay, discuss how Walker uses details from her personal experience and from the development of hip-hop to shape and present this understanding.

Vocabulary Warm-up Word Lists

Study these words from "A Celebration of Grandfathers." Then, complete the activities that follow.

Word List A

created [kree AYT ed] *v.* made something new; came up with
  Ellen <u>created</u> a beautiful cake for the party.

image [IM ij] *n.* picture that you have in your mind
  When I looked at the clouds, an <u>image</u> of a huge rabbit appeared in my mind.

incredible [in KRED uh buhl] *adj.* amazing, very impressive
  The marathon winner was an <u>incredible</u> runner.

internal [in TER nuhl] *adj.* inner; inside something
  The driver suffered kidney damage and other <u>internal</u> injuries from the accident.

lasting [LAST ing] *adj.* continuing for a long time
  Even when football season was over, there was <u>lasting</u> bond among the teammates.

majestic [muh JES tik] *adj.* looking impressive; awe-inspiring
  The candidate's <u>majestic</u> speech brought the crowd to its feet.

respectful [ri SPEKT fuhl] *adj.* showing polite admiration or consideration
  Juan's polite behavior in school is one example of his <u>respectful</u> attitude.

source [SOHRS] *n.* origin; where something comes from
  Oil is an important <u>source</u> of energy.

Word List B

absurdity [ab SUR duh tee] *n.* silliness, something unreasonable
  The <u>absurdity</u> of his argument kept us from taking his opinion seriously.

contribution [kahn tri BYOO shuhn] *n.* something given or done to help
  His research has been a major <u>contribution</u> to medical science.

culture [KUHL chur] *n.* the shared values, beliefs, and customs of a society
  In our <u>culture</u>, it is not considered polite to lick your fingers at the table.

esteem [es TEEM] *n.* respect
  Our teacher is held in high <u>esteem</u> by all her students.

humanity [hyoo MAN uh tee] *n.* kindness, respect, and sympathy toward others
  We show our <u>humanity</u> by helping the needy.

overcome [oh ver KUHM] *v.* defeat; rise above
  He worked hard to <u>overcome</u> every problem that stood in his way.

revival [ri VY vuhl] *n.* process by which something becomes popular or active again
  When the war ended, there was a <u>revival</u> of trade between the two nations.

transformation [trans fuhr MAY shun] *n.* change of form or condition
  The story is about the ugly duckling's <u>transformation</u> into a beautiful swan.

"A Celebration of Grandfathers" by Rudolfo Anaya
Vocabulary Warm-up Exercises

Exercise A *Fill in each blank in the paragraph with an appropriate word from Word List A. Use each word only once.*

Our class trip to Washington, D.C., was an [1] _____ experience. We were all impressed by the Capitol building, with its stately columns and [2] _____ white dome. I must admit, I was not disappointed. What I saw fit the [3] _____ of this place that I had in my mind for years. The bronze statue at the top was [4] _____ by the sculptor Thomas Crawford in the 1850s. It is meant to be a symbol of freedom. The [5] _____ area of the Capitol is no less impressive than the gleaming exterior. Both the Senate and the House of Representatives, the [6] _____ of all national laws, meet in this great building. We were all very [7] _____ of the important work that is done here. Our visit left a [8] _____ impression that none of us will soon forget.

Exercise B *Decide whether each statement is true or false. Circle T or F, and explain your answer.*

1. An *absurdity* can be perfectly logical.
   T / F _____

2. If a person makes a *contribution* to society, he or she is trying to be a good citizen.
   T / F _____

3. People who live in a particular *culture* never share the same values.
   T / F _____

4. If you hold your parents in high *esteem*, you will probably not treat them very well.
   T / F _____

5. A person who volunteers to work in a hospital does not show much *humanity*.
   T / F _____

6. If you finally *overcome* a problem, you are no better off than when you began.
   T / F _____

7. If you have a *revival* of interest in a subject, you were never interested in it before.
   T / F _____

8. When something undergoes a complete *transformation*, it is greatly changed.
   T / F _____

"A Celebration of Grandfathers" by Rudolfo Anaya
Reading Warm-up A

Read the following passage. Pay special attention to the underlined words. Then, read it again, and complete the activities. Use a separate sheet of paper for your written answers.

Ben and his grandfather sat on the farmhouse porch with a bowl of peanuts between them as they watched the sun slowly set in the western sky. Neither of them spoke much. They had worked hard all day, and both of them were feeling tired. Ben had come straight home from school that afternoon and put in a solid four hours of harvesting before it started getting dark. Farm work was hard, but Ben was raised not to be afraid of hard work.

"Did you always want to be a farmer?" he asked his grandfather in the <u>respectful</u> tone he always used when addressing his elders.

His grandfather put a peanut in his mouth and chewed it carefully before replying. "My father was a farmer," he said, "and his father before him."

That does not answer my question, Ben mused, but he kept the thought to himself.

Ben gazed at the <u>majestic</u> sunset. It seemed <u>incredible</u> to him that anyone would want to spend an entire lifetime working the soil.

"Farming is hard," he said, and his grandfather nodded.

"Farming is the <u>source</u> of all life," the old man replied. "Mighty empires rise and fall, but the only <u>lasting</u> thing is the soil that feeds them."

A strange <u>image</u> then formed in Ben's mind. He pictured a great marble palace that some ancient architect <u>created</u> to satisfy the pride of a powerful king who planned to rule his land for all eternity. Then, Ben saw the centuries pass and the palace crumble to dust, and where it once stood, a man with a hoe worked the earth.

Ben felt an <u>internal</u> tightening in his stomach.

"I am not sure I want to be a farmer when I grow up," he said.

"That is what I told *my* grandfather," his grandfather said.

1. Underline the words that tell when Ben spoke in a <u>respectful</u> tone. Why do you think he spoke like this?

2. Circle the word that tells what is <u>majestic</u>. Write a sentence about something else that is *majestic*.

3. Underline the words that tell what seems <u>incredible</u> to Ben. Describe something that seems *incredible* to you.

4. Circle the word that tells what Ben's grandfather thinks is the <u>source</u> of all life. What does he mean?

5. Underline the words that tell what Ben's grandfather says is the only <u>lasting</u> thing. Write a sentence about something else that might be described as *lasting*.

6. Circle the word in the next sentence that gives a good clue to the meaning of <u>image</u>. What is an *image*?

7. Underline the words that tell what the architect <u>created</u>. Write a sentence about something that you have *created*.

8. Underline the words that tell where Ben felt an <u>internal</u> tightening. Use a word in a sentence that means the opposite of *internal*.

"A Celebration of Grandfathers" by Rudolfo Anaya
Reading Warm-up B

Read the following passage. Pay special attention to the underlined words. Then, read it again, and complete the activities. Use a separate sheet of paper for your written answers.

More than 15 million people in the United States today identify themselves as Mexican Americans. Although this is the fastest-growing ethnic group in the nation, the history and <u>culture</u> of Mexican Americans may be unknown to some.

From the time it was first settled by Europeans, much of what is now the American Southwest was claimed by Spain. After Mexico won its independence from Spain in 1821, these lands belonged to Mexico. The people who lived there were Mexicans until 1848. Then, Mexico signed a treaty giving up this territory to the United States. Those who stayed had a new national identity. The abrupt <u>transformation</u> from Mexican to Mexican American was completed with the stroke of a pen.

After 1848, Americans of European descent grew to become a majority in the lands that had once belonged to Mexico. Soon the nation began to react with concern over the large number of foreign immigrants entering the United States. Illogically, Mexican Americans came to be held in the same low <u>esteem</u> as foreign-born immigrants. The <u>absurdity</u> of this view is apparent: many Mexican Americans had lived in this country longer than the people who regarded them as outsiders.

Many Mexican Americans have <u>overcome</u> these challenges. They have made an outstanding <u>contribution</u> to many areas of society. Notable in the arts are authors Sandra Cisneros and Gary Soto. Mexican Americans in the sciences include NASA astronaut Ellen Ochoa. Senator Dennis Chávez and Congresswoman Loretta Sánchez are among the many Mexican Americans who have been elected to office.

Recently, Mexican American communities have shown a <u>revival</u> of interest in the Mexican holiday known as Day of the Dead. Many non-Mexican Americans have also come to appreciate this celebration. The holiday honors the <u>humanity</u> in all our departed loved ones. It helps us stay connected to our ancestors.

1. Circle the word that tells what is part of a people's <u>culture</u>. Write a sentence about a *culture* you consider yourself a part of.

2. Underline the words that describe the <u>transformation</u> that took place. Why was this *transformation* completed with the stroke of a pen?

3. Underline the words that tell who was held in low <u>esteem</u>. Why would this be a problem?

4. Circle the word that gives a good clue to the meaning of <u>absurdity</u>. Write a sentence about something that you consider an *absurdity*.

5. Circle two words that tell what Mexican Americans had to <u>overcome</u>. Then, explain what *overcome* means.

6. Circle two words that describe the areas to which Mexican Americans have made an outstanding <u>contribution</u>. What *contribution* to society would you be proud to make?

7. Circle the words that tell who has shown a <u>revival</u> of interest in Day of the Dead. Explain what *revival* means.

8. Explain how Day of the Dead might honor the <u>humanity</u> of departed loved ones.

"**A Celebration of Grandfathers**" by Rudolfo A. Anaya
Writing About the Big Question
Is knowledge the same as understanding?

Big Question Vocabulary

ambiguous	clarify	comprehend	concept	connection
fact	feeling	information	insight	instinct
interpret	research	senses/sensory	sources	statistics

A. *Use one or more words from the list above to complete each sentence.*

1. The narrator describes his deep _____ to his grandfather.

2. In his essay, Anaya tries to _____ his knowledge of his grandfather so that we can understand who he was.

3. Facts about people's lives can _____ our understanding of them.

4. Megan's _____ for her aunt had more to do with her understanding of her than with what she actually knew about the mysterious relative.

B. *Follow the directions in responding to each item below.*

1. List two facts you know about someone you like and care about.

   _____

   _____

2. Write two sentences telling how the facts you listed above help you understand that person. Use at least two of the Big Question vocabulary words.

   _____

   _____

C. *"A Celebration of Grandfathers" explains how the author's grandfather and people of his generation lived and what they valued. Complete the sentence below. Then, write a short paragraph in which you connect this experience to the Big Question.*

Knowing what people do and how they live can give insight into who they are because

_____

_____

_____

_____

_____

_____

"A Celebration of Grandfathers" by Rudolfo Anaya
Literary Analysis: Style

An author's **style** is his or her unique way of writing. Style includes every feature of a writer's use of language. Some elements that contribute to an author's style are

- **Diction:** the kinds of words the author uses.
- **Syntax:** the way in which the author arranges words in sentences.
- **Tone:** the author's attitude toward his or her audience or subject.

A writer's diction and syntax might be described as formal or informal, technical or ordinary, sophisticated or down-to-earth. A writer's tone might be described as serious or playful, friendly or distant, sympathetic or scathing.

DIRECTIONS: *Consider the diction and syntax in the italicized passages from "A Celebration of Grandfathers" in the left-hand column. Then write notes or a sentence in the right-hand column to describe the tone produced by these features of Anaya's style.*

Passage	Tone
1. The old ones had looked deep into *the web that connects all animate and inanimate forms of life*, and they recognized the *great design* of the creation.	1. _____ _____ _____
2. Their faith shone in their eyes; it was in the *strength of their grip*, in the *creases time wove into their faces*.	2. _____ _____ _____
3. All this they passed on to the young, *so that a new generation would know what they had known, so the string of life would not be broken*.	3. _____ _____ _____
4. After he had covered my wells with the cool mud from the irrigation ditch, my grandfather calmly said: *"Know where you stand."*	4. _____ _____ _____
5. *He was a man; he died.* Not in his valley, but nevertheless cared for by his sons and daughters and flocks of grandchildren.	5. _____ _____ _____

Name _____ Date _____

Reading: Generate Prior Questions to Identify Main Idea and Details

The **main idea** is the central message, insight, or opinion in a work of nonfiction. **Supporting details** are the pieces of evidence that a writer uses to prove the main idea. These details can include facts, statistics, quotations, or anecdotes. To **identify the main idea and supporting details** in a work, **generate questions prior to reading.** Before you read, you can ask yourself questions such as

- Why did the author choose this title?
- How might events in the author's life influence his or her attitude toward the subject?

As you read, look for details that answer those questions and point to the main idea.

A. DIRECTIONS: *Answer the following questions to guide your reading of "A Celebration of Grandfathers."*

1. Consider the connotations or associations of the word *celebration* in Rudolfo Anaya's title. What expectations does this title create in you for the content and tone of the essay?

   _____

   _____

2. In the opening paragraph, Anaya uses a greeting in Spanish: "Buenos días le de Dios, abuelo." What does this greeting lead you to expect about the way in which elders were treated in the traditional culture in which Anaya grew up?

   _____

   _____

3. Anaya, who is considered the father of Chicano literature, has called himself "an oral story-teller" who now tells his tales "on the printed page." What does this self-characterization lead you to expect about the structure and content of his essay?

   _____

   _____

B. DIRECTIONS: *In an essay celebrating grandfathers, what kind of main idea might you expect? What sorts of supporting details might you find in such an essay? Support your answer with examples from your own experience or from your reading.*

   _____

   _____

   _____

   _____

   _____

"A Celebration of Grandfathers" by Rudolfo Anaya
Vocabulary Builder

Word List

absurdity   anguish   nurturing   permeate   perplexes   revival

A. DIRECTIONS: *Revise each sentence so that the underlined vocabulary word is used logically. Be sure not to change the vocabulary word.*

1. After solving the problem brilliantly, she sadly admits how much it still <u>perplexes</u> her.

   _____

2. Because their explanation seemed so logical, we were struck by its <u>absurdity</u>.

   _____

3. The rain managed to <u>permeate</u> even the stoutest foul-weather gear, so our clothes were dry.

   _____

4. What <u>anguish</u> she felt when her doctor told her that her dog was cured.

   _____

5. They were <u>nurturing</u> the young tree and hoped to have it cut down soon.

   _____

6. Few people visited the small town after its <u>revival.</u>

   _____

B. WORD STUDY: The Latin root *-viv-* means "to live." Answer each of these questions using one of these words containing the root *-viv-*: *vivid, survive, convivial.*

1. Why might a *vivid* description help you visualize a setting?

   _____

2. Why would you rather spend time with *convivial* friends than with sad ones?

   _____

3. If you *survive* a bad case of the flu, do you begin to have more energy?

   _____

"A Celebration of Grandfathers" by Rudolfo Anaya
Enrichment: Learning From Our Elders

Rudolfo Anaya shares with readers the stories his grandfather told about nature and aging. Anaya and his peers learned valuable life lessons from people much older than they were. Interview two older adults in your family or in your community. On the lines provided, write a set of questions that you can take to your interviews. Ask your subjects about their most important life experiences, what they enjoy most about the world, and whether they have any advice to offer young people today. To find a variety of people, you might want to contact a local retirement center or your local chapter of the American Association of Retired People (AARP). Through these organizations, you might be able to arrange to spend time with local elderly people who are interested in being interviewed.

Interview Questions:

1. _____

   _____

   _____

2. _____

   _____

   _____

3. _____

   _____

   _____

4. _____

   _____

   _____

5. _____

   _____

   _____

After you have completed your interviews, share your results with a partner or small group.

"A Celebration of Grandfathers" by Rudolfoa A. Anaya
Open-Book Test

Short Answer *Write your responses to the questions in this section on the lines provided.*

1. The main idea in a work of nonfiction is the central message, insight, or opinion. Often the title of a work provides a clue to the main idea. What does the title "A Celebration of Grandfathers" reveal about this essay's main idea?

   _____

   _____

2. The tone of a literary work is the author's attitude toward the audience and the subject. What tone is suggested by the title "A Celebration of Grandfathers"?

   _____

   _____

3. In "A Celebration of Grandfathers," Anaya writes about time standing still and the awe he has felt at times. Then he quotes a passage from his first novel, *Bless Me, Ultima.* How does that passage relate to Anaya's remarks about time standing still?

   _____

   _____

   _____

4. In relating the anecdote about the anthill in "A Celebration of Grandfathers," Anaya reports that his grandfather told him, "Know where you stand." Later in the essay, in talking about adapting to change, Anaya echoes this idea when he says, "We need to know where we stand." What is the effect of this repetition?

   _____

   _____

5. Anaya describes a very dry summer and tells how his grandfather "felt connected to the cycles that brought the rain or kept it from us." Because Anaya makes this point in an essay titled "In Celebration of Grandfathers," what can readers conclude about its importance in shaping Anaya's own attitude toward nature?

   _____

   _____

   _____

6. In "A Celebration of Grandfathers," what lesson does Anaya learn from the death of the young man who was dragged by his horse?

   _____

   _____

   _____

7. In "A Celebration of Grandfathers," Anaya pauses from his musings on his grandfather to consider the way things are at the time he is writing this essay. He writes, "Today the sons and daughters are breaking with the past." Reread Anaya's essay to the end. Then, complete this chart by noting one detail that shows how Anaya supports this idea. Finally, on the line below, explain how this idea connects to Anaya's idea about respecting one's elders.

Detail:	Main Idea:
	"Today the sons and daughters are breaking with the past."

_____

_____

8. In "A Celebration of Grandfathers," Anaya suggests that old age can be a period of anguish for some people. In what way, according to Anaya, can old age be a time of anguish? Cite at least one detail from the essay, and base your answer on the definition of *anguish*.

_____

_____

_____

9. In "A Celebration of Grandfathers," the frequent use of Spanish words and phrases is an important feature of the writer's style. Why might Anaya use Spanish so often in this essay?

_____

_____

10. Consider the syntax of "A Celebration of Grandfathers"—the way in which Anaya arranges the words in his sentences. Look at the length of the sentences. Also consider the frequency with which Anaya uses sentence fragments or arranges words in an unusual order. Based on your analysis, would you describe Anaya's syntax as formal or informal? Explain your answer.

_____

_____

_____

_____

Essay

Write an extended response to the question of your choice or to the question or questions your teacher assigns you.

11. In the first paragraph of "A Celebration of Grandfathers," Rudolfo Anaya describes how respect for one's elders is "a cultural value to be passed on from generation to generation." In a brief essay, describe how Anaya supports this statement. Cite at least two details from the essay, including one of the lessons that according to Anaya, elders can teach young people.

12. Consider the title of Rudolfo Anaya's essay: "A Celebration of Grandfathers." Why might Anaya have chosen that title and not "A Celebration of Grandfather"? Does the title apply only to Anaya's own grandfather, or does the writer intend the essay to have a broader application? In an essay of your own, discuss the significance of the essay's title. Support your ideas with two or more references to Anaya's essay.

13. In "A Celebration of Grandfathers," Anaya uses anecdotes to suggest a theme or a moral related to his central idea: the need to respect and learn from one's elders. In an essay, discuss three of the anecdotes in the essay. Tell what lesson each anecdote teaches, and evaluate how effectively each anecdote contributes to the main idea of the essay.

14. **Thinking About the Big Question: Is knowledge the same as understanding?** Knowledge refers to knowing something, and understanding refers to making sense of an experience. Consider those definitions as well as what you have learned about Rudolfo Anaya from reading "A Celebration of Grandfathers." Then, in a brief essay, discuss how knowledge and understanding relate to the main idea of "A Celebration of Grandfathers." In your essay, cite one example of knowledge and one example of understanding that Anaya touches on in his essay.

Oral Response

15. Go back to question 4, 6, or 9 or to the question your teacher assigns you. Take a few moments to expand your answer and prepare an oral response. Find additional details in "A Celebration of Grandfathers" that support your points. If necessary, make notes to guide your oral response.

Name _____ Date _____

"A Celebration of Grandfathers" by Rudolfo Anaya
Selection Test A

Critical Reading *Identify the letter of the choice that best answers the question.*

_____ 1. What is the most important subject in "A Celebration of Grandfathers"?
  A. the education of the writer's grandfather
  B. the importance of respecting our elders
  C. the problems faced by poor farmers
  D. the difficulty of being a writer

_____ 2. In "A Celebration of Grandfathers," the writer describes his grandfather as "connected to the cycles that brought the rain or kept it from us." What does this description suggest about the author's personal beliefs?
  A. He thinks it is important to maintain his grandfather's village.
  B. He believes that people cannot get ahead in life if they lack a good education.
  C. He believes that people should respect and participate in the natural order.
  D. He thinks that the environment will take care of itself.

_____ 3. In "A Celebration of Grandfathers," the frequent use of Spanish words and phrases is an important feature of the writer's style. Why do you think Anaya uses Spanish so often?
  A. He wants to puzzle the reader.
  B. He wants to broaden the appeal of his essay.
  C. He wants to emphasize his respect for his heritage.
  D. He wants to compare and contrast Spanish and English.

_____ 4. How did Anaya's grandfather make his living?
  A. by farming
  B. by teaching
  C. by ranching
  D. by hunting

_____ 5. In "A Celebration of Grandfathers," Rudolfo Anaya says, "We need to know where we stand." Which one of the following best expresses the writer's meaning?
  A. We need to have an accurate sense of profit and loss.
  B. We need to recognize that times have changed.
  C. We need to uphold positive, enduring values.
  D. We need to adjust more quickly to American life.

____ 6. Which of the following best states the lesson the writer learned from the tragic death of the young man dragged by his horse?

    A. Riding a horse can be extremely dangerous.

    B. The young man's death could have been prevented.

    C. Death is part of the natural cycle of life.

    D. After the death of a loved one, people need to grieve in order to heal.

____ 7. What attitude toward the subject does the writer suggest by his choice of the title "A Celebration of Grandfathers"?

    A. dislike

    B. reluctance

    C. praise

    D. criticism

____ 8. Which of these terms means "the way a writer arranges words in sentences"?

    A. syntax

    B. diction

    C. tone

    D. predicate

____ 9. According to the author, which group dominates the images created by American media?

    A. immigrants

    B. senior citizens

    C. the beautiful and the young

    D. the rich

____ 10. In "A Celebration of Grandfathers," why does the writer return to Puerto de Luna the summer before he wrote his essay?

    A. to attend his grandfather's funeral

    B. to photograph his grandmother

    C. to attend his own wedding

    D. to celebrate the founding of the church

____ 11. According to "A Celebration of Grandfathers," how does the author believe we must live in today's society?

    A. by following simple lessons from the past

    B. by breaking with tradition

    C. by satisfying our own interests

    D. by accepting our past mistakes

Vocabulary and Grammar

___ 12. Which word below best defines *perplexes*, as it is used in this sentence?
All worked with a deep faith which perplexes the modern mind.
   A. twists
   B. involves
   C. confuses
   D. rejects

___ 13. Anaya writes that some elderly people go "withdrawing into an internal anguish few of us can know." Which of the following is most nearly opposite in meaning to *anguish*?
   A. regret
   B. guilt
   C. shame
   D. happiness

___ 14. Which word in the following sentence is the indirect object?
Grandfather gave Anaya a sense of his great strength.
   A. Grandfather
   B. Anaya
   C. sense
   D. strength

Essay

15. In "A Celebration of Grandfathers," the author writes that respect for elders is "a cultural value to be passed on from generation to generation." In a brief essay, describe how the author supports this statement. What does he say the elders can teach the young people?

16. Why do you think the author used "A Celebration of Grandfathers" as the title for his essay? Does the title refer only to Anaya's grandfather, or does it have a broader application? In an essay, discuss the meaning of the essay's title. Support your ideas with specific references to the selection.

17. **Thinking About the Big Question: Is knowledge the same as understanding?**
Knowledge refers to knowing something. Understanding refers to making sense of an experience. Consider these definitions and what you learned about author Rudolfo Anaya in "A Celebration of Grandfathers." In a brief essay, give an example of knowledge and an example of understanding that Anaya touches upon in his essay.

"A Celebration of Grandfathers" by Rudolfo Anaya
Selection Test B

Critical Reading *Identify the letter of the choice that best completes the statement or answers the question.*

_____ 1. What is the most important subject the author reflects upon in "A Celebration of Grandfathers"?
   A. his grandfather's lack of education
   B. the importance of respecting our elders
   C. the problems faced by many poor farmers
   D. the challenges facing a writer

_____ 2. Anaya's description of his grandfather as "connected to the cycles that brought the rain or kept it from us" reveals his personal belief in the importance of
   A. maintaining his grandfather's village.
   B. participating in the natural order.
   C. respecting the four seasons.
   D. obtaining a good education.

_____ 3. Anaya's frequent use of Spanish words is a stylistic device most likely intended to
   A. make his essay more challenging.
   B. illustrate the writer's knowledge of many languages.
   C. emphasize the writer's respect for his heritage.
   D. compare and contrast English and Spanish expressions.

_____ 4. In "A Celebration of Grandfathers," how did the writer's grandfather make his living?
   A. as a farmer
   B. as a rancher
   C. as a newspaper editor
   D. as a cowboy

_____ 5. In the anecdote about the anthill, the writer's grandfather tells him, "Know where you stand." Later on in the essay, the author echoes this phrase when he says, "We need to know where we stand." What is the effect of this repetition?
   A. It contradicts the underlying message of the writer's grandfather.
   B. It emphasizes that people's lives have changed.
   C. It suggests that people need to center themselves and uphold enduring values.
   D. It creates a mildly amusing resonance, reminding us of the grandfather's sense of humor.

_____ 6. Anaya probably includes the quotation from his first novel, *Bless Me, Ultima,* in order to
   A. persuade readers to buy his novel.
   B. show how Ultima contrasts in personality with his grandfather.
   C. show how Antonio resembles the writer in his awareness of the beauty of nature.
   D. illustrate the spellbinding powers of traditional medicine healers.

_____ 7. Which of the following best expresses the lesson the writer learned from the tragic death of the young man who was dragged by his horse?
   A. Unskilled riders should not attempt challenging feats of horsemanship.
   B. The young man's death could have been prevented.
   C. As part of the cycle of all nature, death is only a small transformation in life.
   D. The grieving process is a natural human reaction to death.

_____ 8. What attitude toward the subject of this essay is suggested by the title, "A Celebration of Grandfathers"?
   A. indifference
   B. hostility
   C. praise
   D. skepticism

_____ 9. What is the writer's main idea in this passage?

   One click of his tongue and the horses obeyed, stopped or turned as he wished. He never raised his whip. How unlike today when so much teaching is done with loud words and threatening hands.

   A. His grandfather had a remarkable understanding of horses.
   B. Teaching requires patience, profound understanding, and setting a good example.
   C. Today's teachers need more support in order to do their job well.
   D. Times have changed, so teaching methods also need to change.

_____ 10. What is Anaya's attitude toward the values of young people in the modern world?
   A. They have trouble discovering their authentic identity.
   B. Too often they plunge into a career without really considering their options.
   C. They don't realize the necessity for a thorough, in-depth education.
   D. They have made a harmful break with past values and traditions.

_____ 11. In "A Celebration of Grandfathers," what does the expression "the autumn of life" refer to?
   A. adolescence
   B. old age
   C. death
   D. adulthood

_____ 12. Which of the following terms is used for the way an author arranges words in sentences?
   A. syntax
   B. diction
   C. tone
   D. predicate

_____ 13. According to Anaya, which group dominates the images created by the media in America?
   A. the city dwellers
   B. the scientists and technicians
   C. the beautiful and young
   D. the college graduates and professionals

____ 14. In "A Celebration of Grandfathers," why did the writer return to Puerto de Luna the summer before he wrote the essay?
  A. to attend the wedding of a close cousin
  B. to write a magazine article on Puerto de Luna
  C. to commemorate the annniversary of his grandfather's death
  D. to attend a celebration of the founding of the church

____ 15. How does Anaya believe we must live in today's society?
  A. by following simple lessons from the past
  B. by accepting the lesson that progress is inevitable
  C. by seizing opportunities whenever fate offers them
  D. by refusing to surrender to materialism

Vocabulary and Grammar

____ 16. Which item below best defines *perplexes,* as it is used in this sentence?
  All worked with a deep faith that perplexes the modern mind.
  A. resounds   B. satisfies   C. confuses   D. heals

____ 17. Anaya writes that the old people's eyes "seem like windows that peer into a distant past and make absurdity of our contemporary world." Which of the following words is most nearly opposite to this use of *absurdity?*
  A. monstrosity   B. horror   C. hilarity   D. logic

____ 18. Which word in the following sentence is the indirect object?
  The elders can give young people the wisdom of their experiences.
  A. elders   B. people   C. wisdom   D. experiences

____ 19. In a sentence with a direct object, which of the following must also be present?
  A. a participle   C. a transitive action verb
  B. a linking verb   D. an infinitive

Essay

20. Why do you think Rudolfo Anaya chose to title his essay "A Celebration of Grandfathers" instead of "A Celebration of Grandfather"? Does Anaya's title apply only to his own grand-father, or does he intend it to have a broader application? In an essay, discuss what you take to be the significance of the essay's title. Support your ideas with specific references to the text.

21. In "A Celebration of Grandfathers," Anaya often uses brief anecdotes to suggest a theme or moral related to his central idea: the need for respecting and learning from the elders. In an essay, discuss two of these anecdotes, evaluating how effectively they contribute to the cen-tral theme of the selection as a whole.

22. **Thinking About the Big Question: Is knowledge the same as understanding?** Knowl-edge refers to knowing something, and understanding refers to making sense of an experi-ence. Consider those definitions as well as what you have learned about Rudolfo Anaya from reading "A Celebration of Grandfathers." Then, in a brief essay, discuss how knowl-edge and understanding relate to the main idea of "A Celebration of Grandfathers." In your essay, cite one example of knowledge and one example of understanding that Anaya touches on in his essay.

Vocabulary Warm-up Word Lists

Study these words from "On Summer." Then, complete the activities that follow.

Word List A

bias [BY us] *n.* an opinion about something that affects how you deal with it
Her wardrobe showed her <u>bias</u> for brightly colored clothing.

commitment [kuh MIT muhnt] *n.* promise to support or do something
I made a <u>commitment</u> to complete the project, and I will not quit now.

courageous [kuh RAY juhs] *adj.* brave when in the face of danger
The <u>courageous</u> firefighters battled the blaze.

delightfully [di LYT fuh lee] *adv.* pleasingly; enjoyably
Her sense of humor was <u>delightfully</u> original.

features [FEE chuhrz] *n.* important or interesting parts
The wireless keyboard is one of the computer's best <u>features</u>.

originally [uh RIJ uh nuh lee] *adv.* at first; in the beginning
I <u>originally</u> planned to stay late, but now I may have to leave early.

radical [RAD i kuhl] *adj.* extreme
The book proposed a <u>radical</u> way of thinking.

traditional [truh DISH uh nuhl] *adj.* customary; usual
The whole family gathered to enjoy a <u>traditional</u> Thanksgiving dinner.

Word List B

absolutely [ab suh LOOT lee] *adv.* completely; totally
Are you <u>absolutely</u> sure that you will not change your mind?

acutely [uh KYOOT lee] *adv.* very strongly; sharply
Although he looked bored, he was <u>acutely</u> aware of everything that was happening.

associate [uh SOH see ayt] *v.* connect in the mind
I <u>associate</u> that poem with my eighth-grade English teacher.

influence [IN floo uhns] *n.* one who affects someone else; role model
Her older sister was a strong <u>influence</u> on her.

invariably [in VAIR ee uh blee] *adv.* always; without change
Whenever I hear that song, I <u>invariably</u> think about the day we met.

melancholy [MEL uhn kahl ee] *n.* feeling of sadness
Everyone at the funeral was over whelmed with <u>melancholy</u>.

mellow [MEL oh] *adj.* pleasant and soothing; calm and relaxed
We all relaxed when the band switched from hard rock to <u>mellow</u> jazz.

viewpoint [VYOO point] *n.* particular way of thinking
My <u>viewpoint</u> changed when I became better informed about the subject.

"On Summer" by Lorraine Hansberry
Vocabulary Warm-up Exercises

Exercise A *Fill in each blank in the paragraph with an appropriate word from Word List A. Use each word only once.*

Although my sister [1] _____ planned on a [2] _____ wedding ceremony, things soon got out of hand. The man she was marrying had a [3] _____ against doing anything in the customary way. His most [4] _____ idea was to get married on the top of a mountain. One of the main [5] _____ of the ceremony would be the arrival of the bride and groom by helicopter. We all agreed that this idea was [6] _____ wacky, but my sister is afraid of heights and not [7] _____ enough to go up in a helicopter. She threatened to call off the wedding if she had to fly, but I knew she would never back down once she had made a [8] _____. In the end, my new brother-in-law realized an old-fashioned wedding was not so bad!

Exercise B *Write a complete sentence to answer each question. For each answer, use a word from Word List B to replace each underlined word without changing its meaning.*

1. What do you <u>always</u> do every morning, no matter what?

   _____

2. What person has had a good <u>effect</u> on you?

   _____

3. What problem in society today are you <u>very strongly</u> aware of?

   _____

4. What would you suggest to a friend who wanted to relax and be <u>calm</u>?

   _____

5. What feelings do you <u>connect</u> with autumn?

   _____

6. Do you generally feel free to express your own <u>way of thinking</u> in the classroom?

   _____

7. Would you be <u>completely</u> comfortable at a party where you did not know one person?

   _____

8. What kinds of things tend to give you <u>gloomy feelings</u>?

   _____

Name _____ Date _____

"**On Summer**" by Lorraine Hansberry
Reading Warm-up A

Read the following passage. Pay special attention to the underlined words. Then, read it again, and complete the activities. Use a separate sheet of paper for your written answers.

Long before television and video games, kids played together on the city streets. A ball, a stick, some bottle caps, and a piece of chalk were all the props they needed for an entire summer of fun.

Many games that are still played today were <u>originally</u> made up by the children of poor immigrants in the early days of the twentieth century. These immigrants represented many races and nationalities. <u>Bias</u> against foreigners was rarely a problem for their kids. If you lived in the neighborhood, you were welcome to join in the fun.

Most immigrant children felt a <u>commitment</u> to becoming real Americans. To the boys, that meant playing baseball, even though they lacked proper equipment or even a field to play on. Instead, they had to invent their own version of the national pastime. "Stickball" required only a rubber ball, a broom handle, and a bunch of kids <u>courageous</u> enough to play in the middle of city traffic. When a broom handle could not be found, there was always punchball, handball, or boxball to be played.

While the boys were playing in the street, the girls could usually be found on the sidewalk. Hopscotch and jumping rope were great favorites. Games that involved clapping and rhyming were <u>delightfully</u> simple. They required no more equipment than a good memory and a fast pair of hands. Many <u>traditional</u> games that immigrant parents had played as children were also enjoyed by the new generation.

Specific <u>features</u> of these games varied from place to place, but all of the games were easy for a newcomer to learn in a matter of minutes. No one was left out. The idea that expensive equipment or special skills might be needed to have fun was a strange and <u>radical</u> notion. Such an idea would never have occurred to the poor immigrant kids who grew up on the city streets of America!

1. Underline the words that tell when many games were <u>originally</u> made up. Then, explain what **originally** means.

2. Underline the sentence that explains why <u>bias</u> against foreigners was not a problem. What kind of **bias** are you aware of in your neighborhood?

3. Circle the words that tell what <u>commitment</u> the children felt. Write a sentence about something you feel a **commitment** to.

4. Underline the reason that kids who played stickball are described as <u>courageous</u>. Define **courageous**.

5. Underline the words that tell what kinds of activities are <u>delightfully</u> simple. What sort of games might be described as **delightfully** difficult?

6. Circle the words that tell who played <u>traditional</u> games as children. Write a sentence about a **traditional** game you know of or have played.

7. Circle the word that describes the specific <u>features</u> of the games. Why do you think this might be the case?

8. Underline the words that explain what was a <u>radical</u> notion. Write a sentence about a notion that you would consider **radical**.

Unit 3 Resources: Types of Nonfiction

"On Summer" by Lorraine Hansberry
Reading Warm-up B

Read the following passage. Pay special attention to the underlined words. Then, read it again, and complete the activities. Use a separate sheet of paper for your written answers.

Do you have a favorite season? Many people like summer the best. When school is out and the weather turns warm, most young people are delighted to leave homework behind and flock to the nearest beach, park, or playground to enjoy the long, relaxing, <u>mellow</u> days of summer.

Summer is <u>invariably</u> followed by fall, when vacation is over and everyone heads back to school. Whether this is good or bad depends on your own personal <u>viewpoint</u>. Some kids can not wait for summer vacation to be over. Kids in the North love the crisp autumn weather, and they welcome the fall as a chance for a new start. With each new school year comes the opportunity to make new friends and even learn an interesting thing or two before the term is over!

Other people love the winter best. In some parts of the country, people <u>associate</u> winter with ice-skating, skiing, and other cold-weather fun. Others <u>absolutely</u> dislike the arrival of winter. For those people, short days and freezing temperatures can bring on a kind of <u>melancholy</u> that does not end until the spring thaw.

Spring is the season of renewal. In places where winter can be brutally cold, spring is the time when trees start to bud, flowers begin to bloom, and the days grow longer and warmer. The weather can have a major <u>influence</u> on our feelings, which is why so many people experience "spring fever." Imagine a balmy afternoon in mid-April. You are sitting in the classroom and gazing out the window, much too restless to concentrate on what the teacher is saying. You are <u>acutely</u> aware of the fact that school will not be over for three more hours, but all you can do is daydream about skipping through a field of flowers. What you have is spring fever, and there is nothing you can do about it—except wait for the summer!

1. Underline the word that is a synonym for <u>mellow</u>. What do you like to do when the weather turns **mellow**?

2. Circle the word that tells what <u>invariably</u> follows summer. Explain why this is true by using a synonym for **invariably**.

3. Describe your own <u>viewpoint</u> concerning the start of a new school year.

4. Underline the words that tell what some people <u>associate</u> with winter. What kinds of things do you **associate** with winter?

5. Circle the words that tell what some people <u>absolutely</u> dislike. Give a synonym for **absolutely**.

6. Underline the words that tell what brings on a kind of <u>melancholy</u> for some people. Name two words that mean the opposite of **melancholy**.

7. Circle the word that tells what can have a major <u>influence</u> on our feelings. Write a sentence about someone or something that has an **influence** on you and why.

8. Underline the words that tell what "you" are <u>acutely</u> aware of. Write a sentence about something you are **acutely** aware of right now.

Name _____ Date _____

Writing About the Big Question

Is knowledge the same as understanding?

Big Question Vocabulary

ambiguous	clarify	comprehend	concept	connection
fact	feeling	information	insight	instinct
interpret	research	senses/sensory	sources	statistics

A. *Use one or more words from the list above to complete each sentence.*

1. To try to understand summer, Hansberry recalls _____ gathered through her _____ .

2. Her _____ with the woman in Maine added to her understanding.

3. Observing the woman's pain and laughter gave her the knowledge to partly _____ the meaning of the person's life.

4. However, she knows that a _____ about someone is only useful if we _____ it.

B. *Describe a time when you made a connection with someone. How did this connection help you understand him or her? Write three or four sentences. Use at least two of the Big Question vocabulary words.*

_____

_____

_____

_____

C. *In "On Summer," Lorraine Hansberry's growing understanding of life has changed her feelings about summer. Complete the sentence below. Then, write a short paragraph in which you connect this experience to the Big Question.*

Learning the facts of people's lives may change how we comprehend them because

_____

_____

_____

_____

_____

"On Summer" by Lorraine Hansberry
Literary Analysis: Style

An author's **style** is his or her unique way of writing. Style includes every feature of a writer's use of language. Some elements that contribute to an author's style are

- **Diction:** the kinds of words the author uses
- **Syntax:** the way in which the author arranges words in sentences
- **Tone:** the author's attitude toward his or her audience or subject

A writer's diction and syntax might be described as formal or informal, technical or ordinary, sophisticated or down-to-earth. A writer's tone might be described as serious or playful, friendly or distant, sympathetic or scathing.

DIRECTIONS: *Consider the diction and syntax in the italicized passages from "On Summer" in the left-hand column below. Then write notes or a sentence in the right-hand column to describe the tone produced by these features of Hansberry's style.*

Passage	Tone
1. The adolescence, admittedly lingering still, brought the traditional passionate commitment to melancholy autumn—*and all that.*	**1.** _____ _____ _____
2. By duration alone, for instance, a summer's day seemed *maddeningly excessive, an utter overstatement.*	**2.** _____ _____ _____
3. And it was also *cool and sweet* to be on the grass and there was usually the scent of freshly cut lemons or melons in the air.	**3.** _____ _____ _____
4. The woman that I met was *as wrinkled as a prune and could hardly hear and barely see and always seemed to be thinking of other times.*	**4.** _____ _____ _____
5. I heard later that she did live to see another summer. *And I have retained my respect for the noblest of the seasons.*	**5.** _____ _____ _____

Name _____ Date _____

"On Summer" by Lorraine Hansberry
Reading: Generate Prior Questions to Identify Main Idea and Details

The **main idea** is the central message, insight, or opinion in a work of nonfiction. **Supporting details** are the pieces of evidence that a writer uses to prove the main idea. These details can include facts, statistics, quotations, or anecdotes. To **identify the main idea and supporting details** in a work, **generate questions prior to reading.** Before you read, you can ask yourself questions such as

- Why did the author choose this title?
- How might events in the author's life influence his or her attitude toward the subject?

As you read, look for details that answer those questions and point to the main idea.

A. DIRECTIONS: *Answer the following questions to guide your reading of "On Summer."*

1. The word *on,* meaning "concerning" or "about," has been used in the titles of many essays. What expectations does Hansberry's title create in you, the reader?

   _____

   _____

2. In her first sentence, Hansberry declares, "It has taken me a good number of years to come to any measure of respect for summer." What does this opening sentence lead you to expect about the structure of Hansberry's essay?

   _____

   _____

3. A crucial fact about Hansberry's own life was her struggle against cancer and her premature death from the disease at age thirty-four. How do you think this biographical fact might affect the writer's attitude toward the seasons and the passage of time?

   _____

   _____

B. DIRECTIONS: *In an essay about summer, what kind of main idea might you expect? What sorts of supporting details might you find in such an essay? Support your answer with examples from your own experience or from your reading.*

   _____

   _____

   _____

   _____

Name _____ Date _____

"**On Summer**" by Lorraine Hansberry
Vocabulary Builder

Word List

aloofness   apex   bias   duration   melancholy   pretentious

A. DIRECTIONS: *Revise each sentence so that the underlined vocabulary word is used logically. Be sure not to change the vocabulary word.*

1. Because she mingles easily with her classmates, she has a reputation for <u>aloofness</u>.

   _____

2. The team's unexpected victory created intense feelings of <u>melancholy</u> in the stands.

   _____

3. Thoroughly <u>pretentious</u>, he always dresses casually and simply.

   _____

4. He felt that this failure was surely bound to be the <u>apex</u> of his career.

   _____

5. The chairperson acted with clear <u>bias</u> when she chose the best qualified person.

   _____

6. I knew I was out for the <u>duration</u> of the season when the doctor said my injury wasn't serious.

   _____

B. WORD STUDY: The Latin root *-dur-* means "to harden, hold out, last." Answer each of these questions using one of these words containing the root *-dur-*: *endure, durable, duress.*

1. Why is a stone sculpture more <u>durable</u> than an ice sculpture?

   _____

2. What might someone with a toothache have to <u>endure</u>?

   _____

3. Why isn't it fair to use <u>duress</u> to get someone to do something for you?

   _____

Unit 3 Resources: Types of Nonfiction
48

Name _____ Date _____

"On Summer" by Lorraine Hansberry
Enrichment: Seasonal Holidays

Throughout the world, many holidays are closely linked to the seasons. In the United States, for example, Thanksgiving Day celebrates the harvest that saved the early Massachusetts colonists from starvation in 1621. The traditional foods, decorations, and songs celebrating Thanksgiving are closely tied to the season of autumn.

DIRECTIONS: *Think of a holiday that you associate with a particular season. You may choose one of the holidays in the chart below, or you may select another holiday. On the lines below, write a description of how this holiday is celebrated, with special emphasis on how the holiday is connected with one of the four seasons.*

Spring	Summer
Easter Passover Cinco de Mayo	Independence Day Labor Day
Autumn	**Winter**
Sukkot Thanksgiving	Hanukkah Christmas

_____

_____

_____

_____

_____

_____

_____

_____

_____

_____

_____

_____

"A Celebration of Grandfathers" by Rudolfo Anaya
"On Summer" by Lorraine Hansberry
Integrated Language Skills: Grammar

Direct Objects and Indirect Objects

A **direct object** is the noun or pronoun that receives the action of a verb. You can determine whether a word is a direct object by asking *whom?* or *what?* after an action verb.

> In her essay, Hansberry praises *summer*. [praises *what?*]

> Every morning, Rudolfo greeted his *grandfather*. [greeted *whom?*]

An **indirect object** is a noun or pronoun that names the person or thing that receives the action of the verb. You can tell whether a word is the indirect object by finding the direct object and asking *to / for whom?* or *to / for what?* after the action verb. An indirect object always comes between the subject and the direct object, and it never appears in a sentence without a direct object.

> His grandfather gave *Rudolfo* some wise advice. [*gave advice to whom?*]

A. DIRECTIONS: *Identify each direct object and indirect object in the sentences below by writing the objects on the line provided. After each object, write* D.O. *for direct object and* I.O. *for* indirect object. *Note: Some sentences will have both a direct and an indirect object.*

1. In her essay "On Summer," Lorraine Hansberry tells several anecdotes.

   _____

2. Hansberry's observations offer us a subtle portrait of summer.

   _____

3. Clearly, Rudolfo Anaya greatly admired his grandfather.

   _____

4. Anaya's grandfather offered the younger generation an inspiring model.

   _____

B. Writing Application: *On the lines below, write a paragraph in which you compare and contrast Lorraine Hansberry's "On Summer" with Rudolfo Anaya's "A Celebration of Grandfathers." Use at least two direct objects and two indirect objects in your writing. Underline each direct object once and each indirect object twice.*

_____

_____

_____

_____

_____

_____

_____

"A Celebration of Grandfathers" by Rudolfo Anaya
"On Summer" by Lorraine Hansberry
Integrated Language Skills: Support for Writing Book-Jacket Copy

For your book-jacket copy, use the chart below to jot down notes under each heading.

Older Person You Admire: _____

Biographical Highlights

_____

_____

_____

_____

_____

_____

Reasons to Admire the Person

_____

_____

_____

_____

_____

_____

Now, use your notes to write copy for your book jacket. Be sure that the details you include will make readers want to know more about your subject.

"A Celebration of Grandfathers" by Rudolfo Anaya
"On Summer" by Lorraine Hansberry

Integrated Language Skills: Support for Extend Your Learning

Listening and Speaking: "A Celebration of Grandfathers"

Together with a partner, use the lines below to jot down notes for taking part in a panel discussion on the American image as it is created by the mass media.

Images of People in Media	Images of Old Age	Messages About Old Age
_____	_____	_____
_____	_____	_____
_____	_____	_____
_____	_____	_____
_____	_____	_____
_____	_____	_____
_____	_____	_____
_____	_____	_____

My Position: _____

_____

Listening and Speaking: "On Summer"

Together with a partner, use the lines below to jot down notes for taking part in a panel discussion on the seasons.

My Favorite Season: _____

Special Activities: _____

_____

_____

Reasons to Like This Season: _____

_____

_____

Reasons to Dislike This Season: _____

_____

_____

Name _____   Date _____

"On Summer" by Lorraine Hansberry
Open-Book Test

Short Answer *Write your responses to the questions in this section on the lines provided.*

1. Based on the first three paragraphs of "On Summer," do you think the author is trying to persuade readers to like summer or dislike it? Support your opinion with two details from the essay.

   _____

   _____

   _____

2. In the first paragraph of "On Summer," Hansberry writes that when she was younger, she worshipped "the cold aloofness of winter." Is aloofness a quality that is ordinarily used to describe a season? In explaining your answer, suggest why Hansberry might have described winter as having the quality of aloofness. Base your response on the definition of *aloofness*.

   _____

   _____

   _____

3. In "On Summer," Hansberry describes many summertime activities that she engaged in as a child in Chicago. There is one that she says was the best. What was that activity, and why did she enjoy it?

   _____

   _____

   _____

4. In describing her grandmother in "On Summer," Hansberry writes that her memories of slavery "didn't sound anything like *Gone with the Wind*." How would you describe Hansberry's tone in this passage? Is she being serious, childlike, or harsh? Explain your answer.

   _____

   _____

   _____

5. The author of an essay may support his or her main idea with facts, statistics, quotations, or anecdotes. What form of support does Hansberry use most frequently in "On Summer"? Cite two details to support your response.

   _____

   _____

Unit 3 Resources: Types of Nonfiction
© Pearson Education, Inc. All rights reserved.
53

6. Consider the syntax of "On Summer"—the way in which Hansberry arranges the words in her sentences. Look at the length of the sentences. Also consider the frequency with which Hansberry uses sentence fragments or arranges words in an unusual order. Based on your analysis, would you describe Hansberry's syntax as formal or informal? Explain your answer.

_____

_____

7. An author's tone may be described as his or her attitude toward his or her audience and subject. What word best describes Hansberry's tone in "On Summer"? Is she critical, sympathetic, informal, or distant? Cite one detail from the essay to support your choice.

_____

_____

_____

8. At the end of "On Summer," Hansberry describes a woman she meets in Maine. How would you describe the character of that woman? Cite one detail from the essay to support your characterization.

_____

_____

_____

9. By the end of "On Summer," how has Hansberry's attitude toward summer changed? Cite one detail to support your answer.

_____

_____

10. The title "On Summer" hints at the main idea, or central message, of the essay. Not until the end of the essay is the main idea revealed. What is main idea of "On Summer"?

_____

_____

Essay

Write an extended response to the question of your choice or to the question or questions your teacher assigns you.

11. In "On Summer," Hansberry tells how she changed her attitude toward summer. In an essay, identify the experience that convinced Hansberry that summer has value as a season. Comment as well on the broader lesson the author learned about life as a result of her experiences.

12. In "On Summer," Hansberry describes how she changed her attitude not just toward a season of the year but toward an overall approach to life. In your opinion, how difficult is it for a person to change his or her attitude toward life? What kinds of experiences could motivate such a change? In an essay, discuss your thoughts about the ability to make life-altering changes in one's outlook. Cite at least two details—from Hansberry's essay, from other reading, or from your own experience—to support your points.

13. Sensory details have to do with the five senses: sight, touch, taste, smell, and hearing. In "On Summer," Lorraine Hansberry records her sensory impressions of summer to explain both why she does not like the season and why she begins to change her mind and respect it. In an essay, cite examples of Hansberry's descriptions of summer, at least two negative ones and two positive ones. Then, tell which descriptions you find more persuasive, and explain the reasons for your preference. Use the following chart to organize your thoughts.

Negative Descriptions of Summer	Positive Descriptions of Summer

14. **Thinking About the Big Question: Is knowledge the same as understanding?** Knowledge refers to knowing something, and understanding refers to making sense of an experience. Based on those definitions and your reading of "On Summer," consider the distinction that Lorraine Hansberry might have made between knowing and understanding. Discuss this question in an essay, and support your view with at least two references to the selection.

Oral Response

15. Go back to question 1, 4, or 5 or to the question your teacher assigns you. Take a few minutes to expand your answer and prepare an oral response. Find additional details in "On Summer" that support your points. If necessary, make notes to guide your oral response.

"On Summer" by Lorraine Hansberry
Selection Test A

Critical Reading *Identify the letter of the choice that best answers the question.*

____ 1. What is Lorraine Hansberry's earliest memory of summer?
   A. waking up from a nap and feeling hot
   B. swimming in a lake
   C. eating at a cookout with neighbors
   D. eating a delicious ice cream cone

____ 2. In "On Summer," why does the author quote the poem about Mary Mack?
   A. She wants to present an exceptionally fine example of modern poetry.
   B. She wants to give an example of the street rhymes she chanted as a child.
   C. She wants to show she can memorize poems easily.
   D. She wants to show the ways in which young children pick on each other.

____ 3. How did Lorraine Hansberry's family spend steamy summer nights in Chicago?
   A. They stayed up all night.
   B. They camped out in the basement.
   C. They slept outdoors in the park.
   D. They listened to music.

____ 4. Which of the following best describes Hansberry's tone, or attitude toward her audience?
   A. critical
   B. sympathetic
   C. informal
   D. distant

____ 5. How does Lorraine Hansberry support her main idea in "On Summer"?
   A. with many facts and statistics
   B. with quotations from famous people
   C. with quotations from family members
   D. with a series of anecdotes, or brief stories

____ 6. Where did Lorraine Hansberry's mother take her one summer to visit her grandmother?
   A. Indiana
   B. Nebraska
   C. Tennessee
   D. Georgia

Unit 3 Resources: Types of Nonfiction

___ 7. Which of the following defines the term *diction?*
   A. metaphor
   B. repetition
   C. exaggeration
   D. word choice

___ 8. Hansberry would most likely agree with which of the following statements?
   A. It is better to grow up in the country than in the city.
   B. The ideas and feelings of children are not to be trusted.
   C. People care less about weather as they grow older.
   D. People should not be afraid to change their opinions.

___ 9. Which of the following best describes the character of the woman whom the author meets in Maine?
   A. forceful
   B. contented
   C. harsh
   D. timid

___ 10. What is the main idea, or central message, in Lorraine Hansberry's "On Summer"?
   A. No one wants to die in summer.
   B. Life is often unfair.
   C. Everyone should live life to the fullest.
   D. Most children have strange ideas.

___ 11. At the end of the essay, how has the author's attitude toward summer changed?
   A. from dislike to hatred
   B. from dislike to respect
   C. from hope to despair
   D. from confidence to doubt

Vocabulary and Grammar

___ 12. Hansberry writes that she associates autumn with melancholy. Which word below is most nearly opposite in meaning to *melancholy?*
   A. ugliness
   B. pushiness
   C. cheerfulness
   D. curiosity

____ 13. Hansberry calls autumn's melancholy "pretentious." Which of the following is the best synonym for *pretentious*?

    A. showy

    B. reckless

    C. unclear

    D. lazy

____ 14. Which of the following defines a direct object?

    A. a personal pronoun in the objective case

    B. a noun or pronoun that receives the action of a transitive action verb

    C. a noun or pronoun that follows a linking verb and renames the subject

    D. a noun or pronoun in apposition to the subject

____ 15. In the following sentence, which word is the indirect object?

    We sent Sue some photos of wolves we had seen in Yellowstone.

    A. We

    B. Sue

    C. photos

    D. wolves

Essay

16. In "On Summer," the writer tells how she changed her mind about summer. In an essay, identify the experience that convinced Hansberry that summer has value as a season. What broader lesson do you think the author learned about life as a result of her experiences?

17. In "On Summer," Lorraine Hansberry describes her sensory impressions of summer. She uses her descriptions to explain why she does not like the season and why she changes her mind about summer. Write an essay citing one example of her descriptions in favor of summer and one example against summer. Then, explain which description you found more persuasive.

18. **Thinking About the Big Question: Is knowledge the same as understanding?** Knowledge refers to knowing something, such as facts and events. Understanding refers to making a larger sense of an experience. Based on these definitions and your reading of "On Summer," what difference might author Lorraine Hansberry say exists between knowing and understanding? Discuss this question in an essay. Be sure to support your view with two references to the selection.

Name _____ Date _____

"On Summer" by Lorraine Hansberry
Selection Test B

Critical Reading *Identify the letter of the choice that best completes the statement or answers the question.*

_____ 1. What is the writer's earliest memory of summer?
   A. Her parents told her an entertaining folk tale on the porch of their house.
   B. She woke up from a nap and felt very hot.
   C. She recalls the smells and sounds from an outdoor barbecue.
   D. A delicious ice cream cone tasted sweet and cold.

_____ 2. Read the following excerpt from the essay.

   I came actively to associate displeasure with most of the usually celebrated natural features
   and social by-products of the season: the too-grainy texture of sand; the too-cold coldness
   of the various waters we constantly try to escape into, and the icky-perspiry feeling of bathing caps.

   Which item below best describes the writer's tone in this passage?
   A. solemn
   B. satirical
   C. scathing
   D. light

_____ 3. In "On Summer," the author most likely quotes the poem about Mary Mack in order
   to show
   A. how naive she was as a child.
   B. the street games and chants she and other children played in summer.
   C. her accurate grasp of the most important details of her childhood.
   D. the ways in which relations among children of the same age may involve conflicts.

_____ 4. How did Lorraine Hansberry's family spend steamy nights in Chicago during the summer?
   A. They slept outdoors on blankets in the park.
   B. They yearned for escape to a lakeside cottage.
   C. They stayed up all night to sing songs.
   D. They watched television and tried to forget the steamy weather.

_____ 5. When Hansberry says that her grandmother "was born in slavery and had memories of
   it and they didn't sound anything like *Gone With the Wind*," how would you describe
   the writer's tone?
   A. melancholy
   B. ironic
   C. self-mocking
   D. formal

_____ 6. Most essays have a main idea, either stated or implied. What is the author's main idea
   in "On Summer"?
   A. Summer is the cruelest time for a person to die.
   B. Life is often unpredictable; sometimes it is unfair.
   C. Since we cannot know the future, we should live life to the fullest.
   D. Women are intuitively well equipped to deal with death.

_____ 7. Which of these details from Hansberry's biography gives her essay "On Summer" an especially poignant tone?
    A. the production of her play *A Raisin in the Sun*
    B. the work of Hansberry's father in real estate
    C. the decision of Hansberry's family to live in a white neighborhood in Chicago
    D. the death of Hansberry at thirty-four from cancer

_____ 8. Which of the following best defines the term *diction?*
    A. writer's attitude
    B. word choice
    C. allusion
    D. flashback

_____ 9. Why do you think Hansberry mentions her grandparents' experiences as slaves?
    A. to surprise the reader with little-known facts
    B. to show the reader that her family is just two generations away from slavery
    C. to teach the reader some facts about slavery in American history
    D. to persuade the reader to believe what she says about summer

_____ 10. The author of "On Summer" would most likely agree with which of the following statements?
    A. Rural areas are better places than cities to raise children.
    B. The perceptions of children are inaccurate.
    C. People become less concerned about the weather as they grow older.
    D. People should not be afraid to revise their opinions.

_____ 11. Which of the following phrases best describes the character of the woman in "On Summer" whom the author meets in Maine?
    A. forceful and unyielding
    B. confident and contented
    C. harsh and cynical
    D. bitter and resigned

_____ 12. At the end of the essay, how has the author's attitude toward summer changed?
    A. from dislike to contempt
    B. from dislike to respect
    C. from respect to reverence
    D. from indifference to engagement

Vocabulary and Grammar

_____ 13. Which of the following sentences uses the word *aloofness* correctly?
    A. His *aloofness* was reflected by the fact that he had few good friends.
    B. Whenever we slept outdoors in the park, we noticed our parents' *aloofness.*
    C. *Aloofness* permitted her to accomplish nearly every task quickly and efficiently.
    D. I will never forget their *aloofness*; they talked with all the other guests at the party!

_____ 14. Hansberry says that autumn is a time of melancholy. Which word below is most nearly opposite in meaning to *melancholy*?
   A. ugliness
   B. rebelliousness
   C. cheerfulness
   D. numbness

_____ 15. She calls autumn's melancholy pretentious. Which of the following is the best synonym for *pretentious*?
   A. disguised
   B. lethargic
   C. showy
   D. contagious

_____ 16. Which of the following best defines a direct object?
   A. an abstract noun
   B. a noun or pronoun that receives the action of a transitive action verb
   C. an adjective that answers the question "which one?"
   D. a pronoun in the possessive case

_____ 17. In the following sentence, which item is the direct object?
      We sent Al and Sue some photos of the three wolves we had spotted in Yellowstone.
   A. We
   B. photos
   C. wolves
   D. Yellowstone

Essay

18. In an essay, explain the author's attitude toward summer in "On Summer." Consider what role the woman in Maine plays in changing the author's attitude and what summer represents to the author after meeting this woman.

19. In "On Summer," Hansberry describes how she changed her mind—not just about a specific season, but about an overall approach to life. How difficult do you think it is for people to change their attitudes? What kinds of experiences could motivate such a change? In an essay, discuss your thoughts and feelings about people's ability to make life-altering changes in outlook.

20. **Thinking About the Big Question: Is knowledge the same as understanding?**
   Knowledge refers to knowing something, and understanding refers to making sense of an experience. Based on those definitions and your reading of "On Summer," consider the distinction that Lorraine Hansberry might have made between knowing and understanding. Discuss this question in an essay, and support your view with at least two references to the selection.

"The News" by Neil Postman
Vocabulary Warm-up Word Lists

Study these words from "The News." Then, complete the activities that follow.

Word List A

basic [BAY sik] *adj.* forming the main or necessary part of something
Food, clothing, and shelter are all <u>basic</u> needs.

disappearance [dis uh PEER uhns] *n.* condition of no longer being seen
The family is worried about the <u>disappearance</u> of its lost pet.

dramatically [druh MA tik lee] *adv.* in a sudden or surprising way
The play began <u>dramatically</u> with a gunshot and a scream.

emphasizes [EM fuh sy zez] *v.* shows that something is important
My father <u>emphasizes</u> good grades and insists that we study hard.

journalist [JER nuh list] *n.* person whose job is to report the news
To be a newspaper <u>journalist</u>, you must be an excellent writer.

permanent [PER muh nuhnt] *adj.* existing for a long time or all time
Most countries have <u>permanent</u> borders that never change.

perspective [per SPEK tiv] *n.* way of thinking about something
My <u>perspective</u> on the problem is positive; I think it can be solved.

unthinkable [uhn THINK uh buhl] *adj.* impossible to accept or imagine
It is <u>unthinkable</u> to believe that my friend could turn against me.

Word List B

assumption [uh SUHMP shuhn] *n.* something you think is true without proof
I made the <u>assumption</u> that we would arrive in time for dinner.

chaotic [kay AH tik] *adj.* confused and without any order
With only one person to help everyone, the store was <u>chaotic</u>.

crucial [KROO shuhl] *adj.* very important
It is <u>crucial</u> to study for this test if you hope to pass.

despise [di SPYZ] *v.* to dislike very much
I <u>despise</u> cold weather and would never live anywhere where it snows.

limitation [lim i TAY shuhn] *n.* act or process of controlling or reducing
A big <u>limitation</u> on our plans is the amount of money we can spend.

sentimental [sen tuh MEN tuhl] *adj.* showing emotions like love or pity to excess
My grandmother loves <u>sentimental</u> cards that gush with feeling.

simultaneously [sy muhl TAY nee uhs lee] *adv.* done at exactly the same time
I heard two voices and knew my friends had arrived <u>simultaneously</u>.

spectator [SPEK tay tuhr] *n.* someone who watches an event
My injury kept me from playing, so I was a <u>spectator</u> at the game.

"The News" by Neil Postman
Vocabulary Warm-up Exercises

Exercise A *Fill in each blank in the paragraph with an appropriate word from Word List A. Use each word only once.*

A [1] _____ may have been kidnapped while covering the news. The strange case of his [2] _____ [3] _____ some of the dangers of reporting the news. Our [4] _____ may be that this is a new problem and that in the past it was [5] _____ that a reporter might end up in harm's way. We would be mistaken. A [6] _____ aspect of reporting is the need to go where the story is. Given that conflict has always been present and is pretty much a [7] _____ condition in the world, reporters have long been placed in threatening situations. What happens is that the danger is often overlooked until we are [8] _____ reminded that it is there.

Exercise B *Answer the questions with complete explanations.*

Example: If you had some <u>limitation</u> of movement because of an injury, what would your physical condition be?
   You would not be able to do what you normally do because <u>limitation</u> means reduction of your capabilities.

1. What would a movie with a <u>sentimental</u> ending be like?
   _____

2. Would a <u>chaotic</u> vacation be restful? Explain.
   _____

3. Would people who <u>despise</u> football willingly be <u>spectators</u> at a game? Explain.
   _____

4. What would you do before making a <u>crucial</u> decision?
   _____

5. Why are people at more risk of causing an accident when they are driving a car and <u>simultaneously</u> using a cell phone?
   _____

6. Is it wise to skip doing your homework on a night when it is snowing hard on the <u>assumption</u> that school will be closed the next day? Explain.
   _____

Name _____   Date _____

Read the following passage. Pay special attention to the underlined words. Then, read it again, and complete the activities. Use a separate sheet of paper for your written answers.

Television news has its critics, yet few have been tougher than one of the first broadcasters, Edward R. Murrow. He once said, "We cannot make good news out of bad practice." How the news is gathered and reported was very important to Murrow. He is considered the <u>journalist</u> who set the standard for television news in the 1950s.

Murrow created formats that have become a <u>permanent</u> part of how news is delivered. For instance, he developed the documentary. It continues to be used to explore news topics in-depth. His documentary program, *See It Now,* started on-location reporting with a 1952 broadcast during the Korean War. Murrow wanted to <u>dramatically</u> reveal what life was like for the common soldier. Thus, he surprised viewers by taking them to the war zone.

Another important *See It Now* offered the <u>perspective</u> of Senator Joe McCarthy. He was investigating communist activities in America. The program used McCarthy's own words to present his point of view. That is still a familiar approach because it has an impact on viewers. Back then, it awakened many people to the dangers of McCarthy's thinking.

The celebrity interview also began with Murrow. In his show *Person to Person,* he talked informally with the famous, often in their homes. An interview with a celebrity is now a <u>basic</u> feature of modern programming and an essential part of many types of broadcasts. That Murrow introduced it <u>emphasizes</u> his range as a journalist. He recognized the importance of giving viewers both hard-hitting and softer news.

Cable news appeared long after Murrow's death in 1965. We have seen the <u>disappearance</u> of one main source—the television networks—for news. It is also <u>unthinkable</u> to imagine the news limited to just a few programs daily. News is reported constantly now.

Murrow may not have conceived of 24-hour news. However, he recognized both the power of technology and its limits.

1. Circle words that are clues to <u>journalist</u>. Explain why Murrow is a famous *journalist*.

2. Underline the phrase that is a clue to <u>permanent</u>. Give an antonym for *permanent*.

3. Circle the word that is a clue to <u>dramatically</u>. Underline what Murrow wanted to show *dramatically*.

4. Underline the phrase that is a clue to <u>perspective</u>. Give a synonym for *perspective*.

5. Underline what the passage says is a <u>basic</u> of television news. Circle words that give a clue to the meaning of *basic*.

6. Underline the phrase that gives a clue to <u>emphasizes</u>. Describe something that you think television news *emphasizes*.

7. Explain what has made a <u>disappearance</u>, and explain what *disappearance* means in this sentence.

8. Circle a word and a phrase that are clues to <u>unthinkable</u>. Underline what the passage says is *unthinkable* and why.

Name _____   Date _____

"The News" by Neil Postman
Reading Warm-up B

Read the following passage. Pay special attention to the underlined words. Then, read it again, and complete the activities. Use a separate sheet of paper for your written answers.

Kit had become a celebrity. She was used to being a spectator, watching the events around her, but she was never the one in the spotlight. That had all changed since she appeared on the national news.

Over and over her story was told until Kit made the assumption that everyone in the country knew about The Rescue. She had no proof, of course, but it seemed to be true from all the cards, some of which were very sentimental and so full of feeling that they were embarrassing. It was the kind of writing Kit normally would despise, as she disliked anything too emotional. However, she understood that people meant well as they praised her actions and told her to get well. Kit had severely strained her arm muscles, and although there was still a limitation on what she could carry, she was better than right after The Rescue, when she could barely lift anything.

Actually, Kit did not know what took hold of her that day. There were many children in the theater for the new cartoon movie, which she had brought her younger sister and little cousin to see. Kit was not always a clear thinker, yet when she smelled the smoke, she had known it was crucial to stay calm and to get out fast.

Instinctively, she made a game of getting out. "Follow the leader," she said, as she crouched low and led the children toward the exit. Simultaneously, she kept the group moving and grabbed other children who were crying and afraid. Then, suddenly, they were outside and safe. It was a chaotic scene, with people screaming. It took a while in all the confusion to realize how many children she had saved: twenty, not counting her sister and cousin!

First the local news reported The Rescue, and then it became national news. She appeared on numerous interview shows and was called a hero. Kit was proud of that and delighted by the new friends who had come with fame, including, and most important, the twenty children who now called Kit their best friend!

1. Circle the word that is a clue to spectator. Describe a situation in which you might be a *spectator*.

2. Underline the sentence with the meaning of assumption. What is an *assumption* you might make about tenth grade?

3. Use clues in the passage to explain the meaning of sentimental. Can a friend be *sentimental*? Explain.

4. Underline the phrase that gives a clue to despise. Give an antonym for *despise*.

5. Explain what limitation Kit had, and why. Give a synonym for *limitation*.

6. Circle the words that give the meaning of crucial. Give a synonym for *crucial*.

7. Underline the phrase that is a clue to simultaneously. Is it wise to do your homework and watch TV *simultaneously*? Explain.

8. Underline the action that could make a scene chaotic. Circle the word that is always part of something *chaotic*.

Unit 3 Resources: Types of Nonfiction
© Pearson Education, Inc. All rights reserved.
65

Name _____ Date _____

"The News" by Neil Postman
Writing About the Big Question

Is knowledge the same as understanding?

Big Question Vocabulary

ambiguous	clarify	comprehend	concept	connection
fact	feeling	information	insight	instinct
interpret	research	senses/sensory	sources	statistics

A. *Use one or more words from the list above to complete each sentence.*

1. Every example and _____ Postman gives about TV news helps us understand how that medium works.

2. If news is _____, it cannot help us understand what is happening.

3. Adam does _____ to gain knowledge and come to an understanding.

4. He wants to gain _____ into how laws are passed.

B. *Follow the directions in responding to each item below.*

1. List three ways that you get news about current events.

   _____

   _____

2. Pick one of the methods you listed above. Tell how the information helps you understand how events in the news affect your personal life. Use at least two of the Big Question vocabulary words.

   _____

   _____

C. *In "The News," the author describes the presentation of television news. Complete the sentence below. Then, write a short paragraph in which you connect this experience to the Big Question.*

We react in different ways to the presentations of news information on television and to the presentations in other media because _____

_____

_____

_____

_____

Unit 3 Resources: Types of Nonfiction
66

"The News" by Neil Postman
Literary Analysis: Expository Essay

An **expository essay** is a short piece of nonfiction that presents information, discusses ideas, or explains a process. In a good expository essay, the writer provides evidence and examples to present an accurate and complete view of the topic. The writer may also use one or more of the following techniques to provide support, depth, and context.

- **Description:** including language that appeals to the senses
- **Comparison and contrast:** showing similarities and differences among two or more items
- **Cause and effect:** explaining the relationship between events, actions, or situations by showing how one can result in another

DIRECTIONS: *Use the lines provided to answer the questions about Neil Postman's expository essay.*

1. What is the topic that Postman discusses in his essay "The News"?

   _____

2. In paragraphs 7–10, Postman discusses the "structure" of a typical television newscast. Give three specific details that Postman includes in his description of a typical television newscast.

   _____

   _____

   _____

3. How does this description relate to Postman's main idea in the essay?

   _____

   _____

4. Postman compares and contrasts TV news and print media (newspapers and magazines). Briefly summarize three ways in which they are alike or different.

   _____

   _____

   _____

   _____

5. How does this comparison and contrast support the writer's main idea in the essay?

   _____

   _____

6. According to Postman, what underlying cause explains the fact that the national evening news has not expanded from a half-hour format to a full hour?

   _____

   _____

"**The News**" by Neil Postman
Reading: Reread to Identify Main Idea and Details

The **main idea** is the central message, insight, or opinion in a work of nonfiction. The **supporting details** in a work help to prove the writer's point. These details can include facts, statistics, quotations, or anecdotes. To help you **identify the main idea and supporting details** in a work, **reread** passages that do not seem to support the work's main idea.

- As you read, note key details to form ideas about what the main idea might be.
- If a detail does not seem to support that main idea, reread the passage to be sure you have not misinterpreted it.
- If necessary, revise your assumptions about the main idea.

DIRECTIONS: *Answer the following questions to guide your reading of "The News."*

1. Reread paragraphs three and four of the essay. Why does Postman describe moving pictures of a burning aircraft carrier as "interesting" and pictures of toppling buildings as "exciting"?

    _____

    _____

    _____

2. According to Postman, why do visual changes on TV have to be more dramatic to be interesting? (Reread the paragraph beginning, "The television screen is smaller than life.")

    _____

    _____

    _____

3. What does Postman mean when he connects television news broadcasts to the "realm of the symbolic"? (Reread the seventh and eighth paragraphs of the essay.)

    _____

    _____

    _____

4. How does the author support his claim that "it is the trivial event that is often best suited for television coverage"? (Reread the long paragraph that begins, "While the form of a news broadcast emphasizes tidiness and control. . . .")

    _____

    _____

    _____

Name _____ Date _____

"The News" by Neil Postman
Vocabulary Builder

Word List

compensation   daunting   imposition   medium   revered   temporal

A. DIRECTIONS: *Revise each sentence so that the underlined vocabulary word is used logically. Be sure not to change the vocabulary word.*

1. She settled her lawsuit for a substantial amount, refusing all <u>compensation</u> for her injuries.

   _____

2. The climb to the summit seemed <u>daunting</u>, and we thought it would be an easy hike.

   _____

3. Ray is devoted to the <u>temporal</u> realities of his job and is therefore late for work more often than not.

   _____

4. "It is because you are a <u>revered</u> expert," she said, "that we feel free to disregard your opinion."

   _____

5. No <u>medium</u> reported the interview, but it was covered in newspapers.

   _____

6. The <u>imposition</u> of a rule against leaving early gave students greater freedom.

   _____

B. WORD STUDY: The Latin root -*temp*- means "time." Answer each of these questions using one of these words containing the root -*temp*-: *temporary* (for a short time), *temporize* (to do something to gain time), *contemporary* (at the current time).

1. Why isn't President Washington a <u>contemporary</u> president?

   _____

2. When can you tell that a situation is not <u>temporary</u>?

   _____

3. Why would someone <u>temporize</u> if he were caught doing something wrong?

   _____

"The News" by Neil Postman
Enrichment: News Analysis

Critics of television news have argued that the relentless pursuit of ratings and profits has resulted in a "copy-cat" pattern in which news shows resemble each other so much as to be almost indistinguishable. According to these observers, this pattern stifles creativity and results in a tendency to "homogenize" the news.

You might test this theory by developing, along with two of your classmates, your own "news analysis." On two consecutive evenings, team members should watch the evening news broadcasts of three different stations. Each team member should use a chart like the one below to list in sequence the news story topics chosen by the producers of each broadcast. Viewers should record the time (in minutes and seconds) devoted to each story. Team members should also use the chart to note particularly striking visuals or graphics in the broadcast.

After team members have completed their charts, hold a conference to discuss results. How much overlap exists between the various networks' treatment of the news? After comparing results, teams should report their findings to the class as a whole.

Date, Time, and News Channel (Station)	News Stories in Order, with Duration of Each Story	Visual Images/Graphics

Name _____ Date _____

"The News" by Neil Postman
Open-Book Test

Short Answer *Write your responses to the questions in this section on the lines provided.*

1. In "The News," Postman examines the structure of a typical newscast. In describing the tension created at the beginning of a newscast, he refers to "the staccato beat of the teletype machines." What main idea does this detail support?

   _____

   _____

2. In "The News," Postman discusses the qualifications of television news anchors. He writes, for example, that "it would be unthinkable for the anchor to be ugly." What inference can be drawn from Postman's remarks on the role of the television news anchor?

   _____

   _____

   _____

3. In "The News," Postman compares and contrasts the image of collapsing bleachers in South America with the image of the cover of a new federal budget. What is the point of this comparison?

   _____

   _____

   _____

4. According to "The News," Walter Cronkite was "a revered" television anchorman. Does that description suggest that Postman admired Cronkite or thought poorly of him? How can you tell? Base your response on the meaning of *revered*.

   _____

   _____

5. In "The News," Postman includes a long quotation by Reuven Frank, an NBC news executive. For what reason does Postman include that quotation?

   _____

   _____

6. In "The News," Postman says that commercial television news has a need to "include everyone." Show the effect of that need by completing this diagram. Then, on the line below, name the medium that in Postman's opinion, does not need to include everyone.

Cause		**Effect**
Commercial TV news needs to "include everyone."	→	

_____

7. In "The News," Postman talks about the reasons why television news programs have not expanded to a full hour. What is the main cause of the programs' failure to expand?

_____

_____

_____

8. The evening news, Postman says in "The News," presents a world in "a permanent state of crisis." On the basis of this assertion, what inference can you make about Postman's beliefs?

_____

_____

_____

9. The tone of a literary work is the author's attitude toward the audience or the subject. Is the tone of Neil Postman's essay "The News" best described as favorable, bitter, angry, or objective? Explain your answer by citing one detail from the essay.

_____

_____

_____

10. The main idea of a work of nonfiction is the central message, insight, or opinion of the work. What is the main idea of Neil Postman's "The News"?

_____

_____

_____

Essay

Write an extended response to the question of your choice or to the question or questions your teacher assigns you.

11. In "The News," Neil Postman takes the reader behind the scenes of the television news business. According to Postman, what are the main reasons for the disadvantages and limitations of television news? In an essay, identify and discuss two of Postman's main points. Cite one detail from the essay to support each point you discuss.

12. In "The News," Neil Postman describes a number of ways in which television news differs from the news presented in the print media (newspapers and magazines). In an essay, use the information in "The News" to develop your own comparison and contrast of television news versus news in the print media. Support your main ideas with at least two details from Postman's essay. If you wish, draw on other reading and your own experience as well.

13. In "The News," Neil Postman takes a generally critical view of television news programs, arguing that they are seriously limited for a number of reasons. On the other hand, what about the strengths of television news? Assume that you disagree with Postman. In an essay, state your main idea in support of television news broadcats. Then, develop your argument by citing details from television news and the print media.

14. **Thinking About the Big Question: Is knowledge the same as understanding?** In an essay, relate knowledge (knowing something) to understanding (making sense of information). Then, relate those notions to the news. In your essay, consider these questions: How can people become better informed about current events and issues? How can they achieve a deeper and more rounded understanding of the information presented in news stories? Support your points with details from "The News," other reading, and/or your own experience.

Oral Response

15. Go back to question 1, 3, or 9 or to the question your teacher assigns you. Take a few minutes to expand your answer and prepare an oral response. Find additional details in "The News" that support your points. If necessary, make notes to support your oral response.

"The News" by Neil Postman
Selection Test A

Critical Reading *Identify the letter of the choice that best answers the question.*

____ 1. Which of the following *best* states the main idea of "The News"?
   A. TV news programs present vivid, interesting stories.
   B. TV news does a good job of covering events around the world.
   C. TV news has some serious drawbacks.
   D. TV news should expand from half an hour to a full hour.

____ 2. According to Postman, words do a much better job than visual images in communicating which of the following?
   A. size and shape
   B. color and texture
   C. past-ness and present-ness
   D. violence and destruction

____ 3. Postman states that television broadcasters prefer which kind of images?
   A. images that change
   B. static images that do not change
   C. positive images
   D. strongly contrasting images

____ 4. According to Postman, what is one effect of the small size of TV screens?
   A. Images have to be extreme and dramatic in order to be interesting on TV.
   B. Music has to accompany images on TV news.
   C. Talking heads are extremely effective on TV.
   D. TV news should be viewed on a large screen, not a small one.

____ 5. Which of the following *best* describes the overall tone of Postman's essay?
   A. favorable
   B. bitter
   C. angry
   D. objective

____ 6. In Postman's discussion of the tension created at the beginning of TV news programs, he mentions "the staccato beat of the teletype machines." Which of the following best describes this reference?
   A. symbolic detail
   B. main idea
   C. supporting detail
   D. comparison

___ 7. Which of the following is the main purpose of an expository essay?

    A. to tell a story

    B. to appeal to the senses

    C. to persuade the audience

    D. to present information

___ 8. What does Postman seem to think of anchorpersons on TV news shows?

    A. They are paid too much for the work they do.

    B. The most important thing about them is the image they project on TV.

    C. They have tried but failed to improve the quality of TV news shows.

    D. They try to be as fair as they can in reporting the news.

___ 9. According to Postman, what advice did the highly respected anchorman Walter Cronkite give to viewers of TV news?

    A. to ignore the advertisements on TV news shows

    B. to read newspapers and magazines as well as watch TV news

    C. to lobby for an expansion of TV news programs from a half hour to a full hour

    D. to lobby for an increase in the budgets for TV news programs

___ 10. Postman includes in his essay a long quotation by Reuven Frank, an NBC News executive. Frank compares news coverage in a TV news program with coverage in a newspaper. Why does Postman most likely include this quotation?

    A. It adds a note of humor to the serious essay.

    B. It gives a striking and instructive comparison of TV news and newspapers.

    C. It supports Postman's evaluation of TV news programs as thorough and complete.

    D. It illustrates the bias of TV news executives.

Vocabulary and Grammar

___ 11. An anchorperson who is *revered* inspires what sort of feeling?

    A. scorn

    B. indifference

    C. great respect

    D. amusement

____ 12. The Latin root *equi-* means "equal." If the anchorman and the sports reporter are *equidistant* from the camera, which of the following statements is true?

    A. The anchorman is closer to the camera than the sports reporter is.

    B. The sports reporter is closer to the camera than the anchorman is.

    C. Both the anchorman and the sports reporter are the same distance from the camera.

    D. Neither the anchorman nor the sports reporter is close to the camera.

____ 13. Which of the following does a predicate adjective describe?

    A. the subject

    B. the direct object

    C. the verb

    D. the indirect object

____ 14. Read the following sentence.

    For more than forty years, Neil Postman was a professor at New York University.

    Which of the following is the predicate nominative in the sentence?

    A. years

    B. Neil Postman

    C. professor

    D. New York University

Essay

15. In "The News," Neil Postman takes the reader behind the scenes of the television news business. What does Postman argue are the main reasons for the disadvantages and limitations of TV news? In an essay, identify and discuss two of Postman's main points. Give one or two specific examples to support each of these main points.

16. In his essay, Neil Postman provides a number of ways in which TV news differs from news as it is presented in the print media (newspapers and magazines). In an essay, use the information given by Postman to develop your own comparison-and-contrast discussion of TV news vs. news in the print media. Support your main ideas with specific details and examples.

17. **Thinking About the Big Question: Is knowledge the same as understanding?** In the beginning of Neil Postman's essay "The News," he points out that pictures and language are "crucial for understanding television news." What is one of Postman's examples in which not having knowledge from both words and pictures of a news event might get in the way of understanding the event?

Name _____ Date _____

"The News" by Neil Postman
Selection Test B

Critical Reading *Identify the letter of the choice that best completes the statement or answers the question.*

_____ 1. Which of the following *best* states the main idea of "The News"?
   A. TV news programs should use more violent and fast-moving graphics.
   B. TV news does a good job of covering global events.
   C. TV news is seriously flawed, despite its drama and visibility.
   D. TV news is controlled by executives with a narrow, limited view.

_____ 2. According to Postman, the "grammar of moving pictures" favors
   A. images that change.
   B. images that contain symbols.
   C. images that have exciting sounds.
   D. images related to corporations.

_____ 3. Why does Postman compare and contrast the image of a collapsing bleacher in South America with a photo of the cover of the new federal budget?
   A. to support his point that TV favors dynamic, exciting images over static ones
   B. to support his point that TV coverage is more thorough than newspaper coverage
   C. to support his statement that TV viewers prefer to watch negative news
   D. to support his idea that TV anchors exert little control over what stories are covered

_____ 4. According to Postman, what is one effect of the comparatively small size of the TV screen?
   A. TV news is better viewed on a large screen than on a small one.
   B. Images on TV news must preferably be accompanied by music.
   C. Talking heads on television are an effective way to communicate ideas.
   D. To be interesting on television, images must be extreme and dramatic.

_____ 5. Which of the following *best* describes the tone of this passage from "The News"?
   Music takes us immediately into the realm of the symbolic, a world that is not to be taken literally. After all, when events unfold in the real world, they do so without musical accompaniment. More symbolism follows.

   A. sympathetic
   B. bitter
   C. indifferent
   D. satirical

_____ 6. In Postman's discussion of the tension created at the beginning of TV newscasts, his mention of "the staccato beat of the teletype machines" is *best* described as
   A. an amusing but irrelevant detail.
   B. a symbolic evocation of symphonic music.
   C. a supporting and evocative detail.
   D. a main idea.

_____ 7. What is the primary purpose of an expository essay?
   A. to provide a historical account in chronological order
   B. to appeal to the reader's senses
   C. to persuade the audience to think or act in a certain way
   D. to present information clearly and objectively

_____ 8. From Postman's discussion of the qualifications of TV news anchors, you can conclude that
   A. their journalistic achievements are less important than the image they project on TV.
   B. anchorpeople personally select many of the stories they present in news broadcasts.
   C. qualified anchorpeople are very difficult to find.
   D. anchorpeople would also be successful in print journalism.

_____ 9. According to Postman, what did Walter Cronkite, a highly respected news anchorman, advise those who watch television news broadcast?
   A. to watch only the first five minutes of each newscast
   B. to read newspapers and magazines for more thorough news coverage
   C. to alternate between the different networks for TV news programs
   D. to pay more attention to foreign news than to domestic news

_____ 10. Postman includes an extended quotation by Reuven Frank, an NBC News executive, who discusses news coverage on TV and in newspapers. Which of the following *best* explains why Postman includes this quotation in his essay?
   A. Frank's quotation provides welcome comic relief in a serious essay.
   B. It offers an instructive comparison/contrast of news coverage on TV and in newspapers.
   C. It strengthens Postman's own credibility as a commentator on the subject.
   D. It reveals the bias and ineffectiveness of network news executives.

_____ 11. Which of the following statements from "The News" expresses a main idea, rather than an example or a supporting detail?
   A. Still, it is possible to enjoy the image of the carrier for its own sake.
   B. A narrowing of the eyes will not do.
   C. Another severe limitation on television is time.
   D. Arms control, for example, is an issue that literally concerns everyone in the world.

_____ 12. According to Postman, what cause lies behind the failure of television news programs to expand to a full hour?
   A. the tight budgets of the TV networks
   B. the low ratings of TV news programs
   C. the reluctance of local affiliate stations to reduce their profits
   D. the refusal of anchorpersons and newsroom staff to work longer hours

_____ 13. The evening news, Postman says, presents the world as a series of disasters and a permanent state of crisis. Which of the following can you reasonably infer from this assertion?
   A. Postman believes that world peace is impossible to attain.
   B. Postman thinks that TV news fundamentally distorts the impressions of the reality it offers.
   C. Postman is convinced that TV news programs must expand to a full hour in length.
   D. Postman favors an increase in the "entertainment" aspect of news.

_____ 14. According to Postman, the major effect of the need to "include everyone" in choosing stories for network TV news is that
   A. there is little or no in-depth coverage of issues and events.
   B. news stories are most often about disasters.
   C. network news shows compete for the best anchors and reporters.
   D. executives tend to select the most positive news stories.

Vocabulary and Grammar

_____ 15. Which of the following sentences uses the word *compensation* correctly?
   A. The jury awarded Jim a substantial sum in *compensation* for his work-related injury.
   B. If you skim newspaper headlines, you will acquire *compensation* with important stories.
   C. In *compensation* for the enjoyable party, they wrote the hosts a thank-you note.
   D. Can *compensation* really result from a broadcast that lasts only 22 minutes?

_____ 16. If a friend advises you that reforming TV news would be a *daunting* task, you might conclude that the project would be
   A. dangerous.   B. intimidating.   C. immense.   D. worthwhile.

_____ 17. Which of the following does a predicate adjective describe?
   A. the subject   C. the verb
   B. the direct object   D. the indirect object

_____ 18. Which kind of verb do predicate nominatives and predicate adjectives follow?
   A. action verb   B. transitive verb   C. verb phrase   D. linking verb

Essay

19. In "The News," Neil Postman takes the reader behind the scenes of the television news business in order to highlight some of the limitations of TV news. Postman presents a number of details, examples, and arguments in order to support his main idea. In an essay, clearly state what you think Postman's main idea is. Then, choose two of Postman's supporting details, examples, or arguments, and discuss how effectively you think these reinforce his overall case.

20. In "The News," Neil Postman takes a generally critical view of television news programs, arguing that they are severely limited for a number of reasons. On the other hand, what about the strengths of television news? Assume that you disagree with Postman. In an essay, clearly state your main idea opposing Postman's position. Then, use specific arguments and examples to support your view that TV news makes a valuable contribution to journalism.

21. **Thinking About the Big Question: Is knowledge the same as understanding?** In an essay, relate knowledge (knowing something) to understanding (making sense of information). Then, relate those notions to the news. In your essay, consider these questions: How can people become better informed about current events and issues? How can they achieve a deeper and more rounded understanding of the information presented in news stories? Support your points with details from "The News," other reading, and/or your own experience.

Study these words from "Single Room, Earth View." Then, complete the activities that follow.

Word List A

circular [SER kyuh luhr] *adj.* shaped like a circle
A <u>circular</u> brick walkway wound completely around the house.

continually [kuhn TIN yoo uhl lee] *adv.* with great frequency; all the time
Carly was <u>continually</u> asking her brother to stay out of her room.

drama [DRAH muh] *n.* exciting and unusual situation or event
The big fire provided a great deal of <u>drama</u> for the town.

environment [en VYE ruhn muhnt] *n.* physical surroundings; natural world
The <u>environment</u> around the marina smelled of fish.

informal [in FAWR muhl] *adj.* relaxed and casual; not official
The party is <u>informal</u>, so I am planning to wear jeans.

magnificent [mag NIF i suhnt] *adj.* very impressive because of size or beauty
The princess wore a <u>magnificent</u> gown of satin decorated with gold.

observations [ahb zer VAY shuhnz] *n.* facts learned from watching carefully
Her <u>observations</u> of animal behavior gave her ideas for a book.

sensations [sen SAY shuhnz] *n.* physical feelings received from the senses
Ty had tingling <u>sensations</u> in his legs after running the marathon.

Word List B

abrupt [uh BRUHPT] *adj.* sudden and unexpected
Margo made an <u>abrupt</u> exit from the room after the fight with Tom.

fascination [fas uh NAY shuhn] *n.* state of being very interested in something
Cal had a <u>fascination</u> with stars and loved to watch the night sky.

intriguing [in TREE ging] *adj.* very interesting because it is strange or mysterious
The popular mystery writer's life was as <u>intriguing</u> as her books.

murky [MER kee] *adj.* dark and difficult to see through
No one knew how deep the pond was because the water was so <u>murky</u>.

significantly [sig NIF uh kuhnt lee] *adv.* in a way that is noticeable or important
Her grades have improved <u>significantly</u> since she began working with a tutor.

similarly [SIM uh ler lee] *adv.* in a way that is almost but not exactly the same
Rhonda and Meg were <u>similarly</u> dressed but in different colors.

smolder [SMOHL der] *v.* to burn slowly without a flame
We let the campfire <u>smolder</u> after we toasted the marshmallows.

sophisticated [suh FIS tuh kay tid] *adj.* advanced and often complicated
The <u>sophisticated</u> computer was too difficult for Emma to use.

Name _____ Date _____

"**Single Room, Earth View**" by Sally Ride
Vocabulary Warm-up Exercises

Exercise A *Fill in each blank in the paragraph with an appropriate word from Word List A. Use each word only once.*

A visit to a [1] _____ mountain range is a chance to be awed by the natural [2] _____. Reading the [3] _____ of others is not the same as seeing the grand peaks with your own eyes. Some visitors want a guide to show them around, while others prefer an [4] _____ tour on their own. Either way, the [5] _____ of ice-capped mountains and deep-green valleys creates an unforgettable scene. For those who do more than observe, the physical challenges of climbing a mountain offer a different set of [6] _____. The sport seems to [7] _____ increase in popularity, despite the dangers. An observer may take a [8] _____ route all around a mountain, but a climber takes a more direct path: straight up, then straight down!

Exercise B *Decide whether each statement is true or false. Circle T or F, and explain your answer.*

1. A <u>murky</u> hallway might be scary to walk through.
   T / F _____

2. If two athletes performed <u>similarly</u>, one would be much better than the other.
   T / F _____

3. A <u>sophisticated</u> idea would be difficult for some people to understand.
   T / F _____

4. If rain made an <u>abrupt</u> appearance, a picnic might be over quickly.
   T / F _____

5. An <u>intriguing</u> movie probably would not hold your attention.
   T / F _____

6. You can safely assume that a mechanic has a <u>fascination</u> with cars.
   T / F _____

7. A piece of burning wood left to <u>smolder</u> is safe to touch.
   T / F _____

8. When a problem grows <u>significantly</u>, it gets easier to solve.
   T / F _____

Name _____   Date _____

"Single Room, Earth View" by Sally Ride
Reading Warm-up A

Read the following passage. Pay special attention to the underlined words. Then, read it again, and complete the activities. Use a separate sheet of paper for your written answers.

Space travel offers excitement and <u>drama</u>. It is a powerful experience for anyone who makes the voyage into outer space. Astronauts on the International Space Station offer another perspective on what it is like to live and work in space.

Astronaut Susan Helms spent 163 days on the International Space Station *Alpha*. She came to enjoy the quiet working <u>environment</u> in space. "I got very used to the peaceful life that we have up there without things like phone, mail, and cable TV and all the noise you get from daily life," she said.

The space station is a cooperative effort of the United States and other countries, including Russia, Canada, and Japan. The science facility has been inhabited <u>continually</u> since November 2000. There has been no break in crews since the first three-person team arrived.

The space station's <u>circular</u> orbit takes it around Earth sixteen times a day. Like the shuttle crews, *Alpha* astronauts study changing conditions on the planet. They make careful <u>observations</u>. To do so, they use expert data from scientific equipment. They add to it their own <u>informal</u> field notes from casual viewing. The knowledge they gain offers us information for understanding our world.

Alpha crews describe the heart-pounding <u>sensations</u> that come from getting a stars-eye look at Earth. They also worry about troubling developments. Astronaut Frank Culbertson piloted shuttle missions in the early 1990s. He took command of *ISS Alpha* in 2001. An immediate surprise was the change in what he could observe of Earth's face. Pollution now creates a far more cloudy view than in the decade before. "There is smoke and dust in wider-spread areas than we have seen before. . . ." he explained in an interview. He also recalled the <u>magnificent</u> light shows on Earth's surface at night. "It's quite amazing to see how many people actually live down there. . . ." he marveled.

1. Circle the word that is a clue to <u>drama</u>. Underline an adjective that can describe *drama* and explain why.

2. Circle the word that is a clue to <u>environment</u>. If you were concerned about the natural environment, how might you define *environment*?

3. Underline the phrase that is a clue to <u>continually</u>. Give a synonym for *continually*.

4. Underline words that are a clue to <u>circular</u>. Describe something in the classroom that is *circular*.

5. Underline two ways the passage says that astronauts make <u>observations</u>. Explain what *observations* are.

6. Circle the word that is a clue to <u>informal</u>. Explain how you would take *informal* notes.

7. Underline the clue that tells you <u>sensations</u> are something physical, and then explain why.

8. Explain why the lights on Earth are <u>magnificent</u> and what *magnificent* means here.

Name _____ Date _____

"Single Room, Earth View" by Sally Ride
Reading Warm-up B

Read the following passage. Pay special attention to the underlined words. Then, read it again, and complete the activities. Use a separate sheet of paper for your written answers.

Space travel allows the unique insight of viewing Earth from space. For thousands of years, people could only look up from Earth into the sky and stars, wondering with great interest about what was found there. Over time, that <u>fascination</u> developed into the science of astronomy.

Like modern scientists, the ancients learned a great deal from observation. One Greek philosopher and mathematician, for example, determined that the world was a sphere from his study of lunar eclipses. He noted that the <u>murky</u> shadow of Earth that darkened the moon was always round.

Today, observation is supported by <u>sophisticated</u> equipment. The equipment provides information that is far more accurate and complex than what is understood with the human eye. For the ancients, their dependence on what they could see led to a misunderstanding that <u>significantly</u> influenced their worldview. For thousands of years, they placed Earth at the center of the universe.

It was not until 1543 that a book by Nicolaus Copernicus of Poland proposed what was then a strange and <u>intriguing</u> theory: Earth circled the sun. Many found it impossible to accept this sudden, <u>abrupt</u> turnabout from a long-held belief. Earth at the center of existence also placed humans in the central role. Copernicus's theories were rejected. However, like a fire that is left to <u>smolder</u>, they were not extinguished. The fire is low but can still flame. The idea that Earth revolves around the sun would erupt again in less than a century.

By the early 1600s, a crude telescope had been invented. In Italy, Galileo Galilei refined the design to make it twenty times stronger than the human eye. Immediately, he found new stars. He located four moons revolving around Jupiter. He made other discoveries that <u>similarly</u> pointed to the same idea. The ancients did not know everything, as they believed.

1. Underline the phrase that gives a clue to <u>fascination</u>. Describe a *fascination* you have and how you can learn more about it.

2. Circle words that are clues to <u>murky</u>. Give an antonym for *murky*.

3. Underline phrases that explain the meaning of <u>sophisticated</u>. What kinds of *sophisticated* equipment might astronauts use?

4. Underline what <u>significantly</u> influenced people for thousands of years. Explain the meaning of *significantly*.

5. Circle the word that is a clue to <u>intriguing</u>. Describe something you find *intriguing*.

6. Circle the word that is a clue to <u>abrupt</u>. If a friend made an *abrupt* appearance at your home, how might you feel?

7. Underline clues to the meaning of <u>smolder</u>. Can your temper *smolder*? Explain.

8. Circle two phrases that help explain <u>similarly</u>. How might two friends behave *similarly*?

"Single Room, Earth View" by Sally Ride
Writing About the Big Question

Is knowledge the same as understanding?

Big Question Vocabulary

ambiguous	clarify	comprehend	concept	connection
fact	feeling	information	insight	instinct
interpret	research	senses/sensory	sources	statistics

A. *Use one or more words from the list above to complete each sentence.*

1. Alana didn't understand the _____ of space travel until she read Ride's essay.

2. "My _____ is that we benefit from space exploration," Mark said.

3. Ride helps _____ what it's like to actually travel in space.

4. Each _____ she gives is based on personal knowledge.

B. *Follow the directions in responding to each item below.*

1. List two things you think people gain from America's space program.

   _____

   _____

2. Choose one thing you listed and explain how Americans benefit from it. Use two Big Question vocabulary words in your answer.

   _____

   _____

C. *In "Single Room, Earth View," astronaut Sally Ride explains what it is like to see Earth from the space shuttle. Complete the sentence below. Then, write a short paragraph in which you connect this experience to the Big Question.*

Looking at Earth from space may change how we comprehend the world because

_____

_____

_____

_____

_____

_____

Name _____ Date _____

"Single Room, Earth View" by Sally Ride

Literary Analysis: Expository Essay

An **expository essay** is a short piece of nonfiction that presents information, discusses ideas, or explains a process. In a good expository essay, the writer provides evidence and examples to present an accurate and complete view of the topic. The writer may also use one or more of the following techniques to provide support, depth, and context.

- **Description:** including language that appeals to the senses
- **Comparison and contrast:** showing similarities and differences among two or more items
- **Cause and effect:** explaining the relationship between events, actions, or situations by showing how one can result in another

DIRECTIONS: *Use the lines provided to answer the questions about Sally Ride's expository essay.*

1. What is the topic that Ride discusses in her essay "Single Room, Earth View"?

   _____

2. How does Ride use comparison and contrast in the second paragraph of the essay, where she discusses airplane travel and spaceflight?

   _____

   _____

   _____

3. How does this discussion relate to Ride's main idea in the essay?

   _____

   _____

4. Give three examples of "civilization's more unfortunate effects on the environment" that Ride describes from space.

   _____

   _____

   _____

5. The space shuttle orbits the Earth once every 90 minutes. Name one effect of that 90-minute orbit.

   _____

   _____

   _____

6. In her conclusion, what does Ride say about comparing airplane travel to spaceflight?

   _____

   _____

Name _____   Date _____

"Single Room, Earth View" by Sally Ride
Reading: Reread to Identify Main Idea and Details

The **main idea** is the central message, insight, or opinion in a work of nonfiction. The **supporting details** help to prove the writer's point. These details can include facts, statistics, quotations, or anecdotes. To help you **identify the main idea and supporting details** in a work, **reread** passages that do not seem to support the work's main idea.

- As you read, note key details to form ideas about what the main idea might be.
- If a detail does not seem to support that main idea, reread the passage to be sure you have not misinterpreted it.
- If necessary, revise your assumptions about the main idea.

DIRECTIONS: *Answer the following questions to guide your reading of "Single Room, Earth View."*

1. Reread paragraph three, which begins with "While flying over the Hawaiian Islands." Explain why Ride describes the scene as "surreal" in the last sentence of the paragraph.

   _____

   _____

   _____

2. In paragraph four, why does Ride say that she found it "almost impossible to keep track of where we were at any given moment"?

   _____

   _____

3. Reread paragraph six, in which Ride mentions plate tectonics. Why does she become an instant believer in this scientific theory?

   _____

   _____

   _____

4. What does Ride mean by "the signatures of civilization" in paragraph nine? Reread the paragraph, and then explain the writer's figure of speech.

   _____

   _____

   _____

Name _____ Date _____

"**Single Room, Earth View**" by Sally Ride
Vocabulary Builder

Word List

articulate   diffused   extrapolating   muted   novice   surreal

A. DIRECTIONS: *Each of the following questions consists of a related pair of words in CAPITAL LETTERS followed by four lettered pairs of words. Choose the pair that best expresses a relationship* similar *to that expressed in the pair in capital letters.*

1. NOVICE : PROFESSIONAL ::
   A. casual : informal
   B. student : professor
   C. manager : director
   D. athlete : catcher

2. DIFFUSED : SPREAD OUT ::
   A. careful : reckless
   B. anxious : confident
   C. cautious : prudent
   D. unpopular : likable

3. EXTRAPOLATING : CONCLUSION ::
   A. summary : statistics
   B. creating : writer
   C. scientist : evidence
   D. observing : fact

4. ARTICULATE : INCOMPREHENSIBLE
   A. fierce : savage
   B. tranquil : tempestuous
   C. pretentious : ostentatious
   D. prejudiced : biased

5. SURREAL : COMMON ::
   A. historic : famous
   B. confused : puzzled
   C. idealistic : practical
   D. relieved : comforted

6. VIVID : MUTED ::
   A. loud : noisy
   B. serious : refined
   C. successful : accomplished
   D. courageous : cowardly

B. WORD STUDY: The Latin root -*nov*- means "new, recent." Words containing the root -*nov*- include *novelty, novice,* and *renovation.* Consider the meaning of these words and the root -*nov*- as you revise the following sentences so that they make sense.

1. The <u>novelty</u> of the situation comedy is that it was like so many others.

   _____

2. The <u>novice</u> mechanic had been working on cars for ten years.

   _____

3. After the <u>renovation</u>, the house was in great need of repairs.

   _____

"Single Room, Earth View" by Sally Ride
Enrichment: Plate Tectonics

Sally Ride says that she became an "instant believer in plate tectonics" while orbiting the Earth. The theory of plate tectonics proposes that the Earth's surface layer, or lithosphere, consists of a dozen large plates and several smaller ones. The Earth's continents and oceans rest on these plates, which move about on a hotter, denser layer called the asthenosphere. Plate movement causes most earthquakes, volcanic activity, and mountain building.

There are three types of plate boundaries: divergent, convergent, and transform. At *divergent plate boundaries,* plates move away from each other. Most divergent activity occurs on the ocean floor. However, divergent plate movement can also affect continents. In the Red Sea region, the Arabian Plate, including Saudi Arabia, and the African Plate, including Egypt, are moving away from each other.

At *convergent plate boundaries,* plates move toward each other, with one plate eventually moving underneath the other. This movement is responsible for many mountain-building processes. For example, over millions of years, the plate that now includes India collided with the Eurasian Plate. As the Indian-Australian Plate pushed beneath the Eurasian Plate, the Himalayas were formed.

At *transform plate boundaries,* plates slide alongside each other. Powerful earthquakes can form along these boundaries. The San Andreas Fault in California is one such example. It marks the boundary between the Pacific Plate and the North American Plate.

Although plate tectonics have dramatic results, actual plate movement happens at a relatively slow speed. On average, plates move about four inches a year. Scientists theorize that the Earth's continents used to be a single land mass called Pangaea. As plates shifted, Pangaea broke apart and formed separate continents. Scientists predict that in 50 million years, Earth's continents will have a different configuration from the current one.

DIRECTIONS: *Write your answers on the lines.*

1. In one or two sentences, summarize the theory of plate tectonics. _____
   _____
   _____

2. How does plate tectonics explain Ride's comment that "Saudi Arabia and Egypt really *are* pulling apart"? _____
   _____
   _____

3. What does Ride mean when she says, "India really *is* crashing into Asia"? _____
   _____
   _____

4. Why might Ride's view from space cause her to become "an instant believer in plate tectonics"? _____
   _____
   _____

"The News" by Neil Postman
"Single Room, Earth View" by Sally Ride
Integrated Language Skills: Grammar

A **predicate nominative** is a noun or pronoun that appears with a linking verb. (Linking verbs include *become, grow, look, seem,* and all forms of *be.*) A predicate nominative renames, identifies, or explains the subject of the sentence. In a sentence with a predicate nominative, the linking verb acts as an equal sign between the subject and the predicate nominative. They refer to the same person or thing. In the following examples, the subject is in boldface, the linking verb is in italics, and the predicate nominative is underlined.

Sally Ride *was* the first American <u>woman</u> in space.

This *is* the <u>problem</u> with television news.

A **predicate adjective** is an adjective that appears with a linking verb and describes the subject of the sentence. In the following examples, the subject is in bold type, the linking verb is in italics, and the predicate adjective is underlined.

The **aircraft carrier** *seemed* <u>enormous</u>.

Through the pollutant haze, some **colors** *looked* <u>muted</u>.

A. DIRECTIONS: *In each of the following sentences, circle the linking verb. Then, underline each predicate nominative once and each predicate adjective twice.*

1. The television screen is smaller than life.
2. In the cinema, the situation is somewhat different.
3. But they are also symbols of a dominant theme of television news.
4. Another severe limitation on television is time.
5. I also became an instant believer in plate tectonics.
6. The Great Wall of China is *not* the only man-made object visible from space.
7. In space, night is very, very black.
8. Part of the fascination with space travel is the element of the unknown.

B. Writing Application: *On the lines below, write a paragraph in which you describe either your favorite natural landscape or your favorite television show. In your paragraph, use at least two predicate nominatives and two predicate adjectives. Underline each predicate nominative once and each predicate adjective twice.*

_____

_____

_____

_____

_____

_____

Name _____ Date _____

Integrated Language Skills: Support for Writing
an Announcement Script

For your commercial or public-service announcement script, use the chart below to jot down notes under each heading. Include reasons, photos, and quotations to support your purpose.

Details That Might Persuade People to Agree	Persuasive Photos and Other Visuals	Direct Quotation and Visual

Now, use your notes to write the script for your announcement. Be sure that the words and visuals all contribute to your central purpose.

"**The News**" by Neil Postman
"**Single Room, Earth View**" by Sally Ride
Integrated Language Skills: Support for Extend Your Learning

Research and Technology: "The News"

Use the lines below to make notes for your two journal entries on how journalists prepare to write a news story. Be sure to keep track of the sources you used for your information.

Researching Information (*Who? What? When? Where? Why? How?*): _____

_____

_____

Planning the Main Idea or Focus: _____

_____

_____

Interviewing People Involved in the Story: _____

_____

_____

_____

Planning the Visuals: _____

_____

_____

_____

Sources I Used: _____

_____

_____

Research and Technology: "Single Room, Earth View"

Use the lines below to make notes for your journal entries on the training of astronauts. Be sure to keep track of the sources you used for your information.

Physical Training: _____

_____

_____

Scientific Training: _____

_____

_____

Spaceflight Simulation: _____

_____

_____

Sources I Used: _____

_____

Name _____   Date _____

"Single Room, Earth View" by Sally Ride
Open-Book Test

Short Answer *Write your responses to the questions in this section on the lines provided.*

1. In "Single Room, Earth View," Sally Ride explains that on her space flight, she easily lost track of the part of the world she was flying over. What fact explains the ease with which Ride lost track of where she was?

    _____
    _____
    _____

2. In "Single Room, Earth View," Sally Ride says that she assumed the role of a novice geologist. Is a novice geologist experienced or inexperienced? Base your answer on the definition of *novice*.

    _____
    _____

3. In "Single Room, Earth View," Sally Ride says that the view of Earth from an orbiting space shuttle is "spectacular." She points out, however, that the view of Earth from the shuttle differs from the view of Earth from the moon. Cite the main difference between the two views.

    _____
    _____
    _____

4. In "Single Room, Earth View," Sally Ride observes "some unfortunate effects on the environment" that have been caused by civilization. Cite one detail from the essay that supports this remark.

    _____
    _____
    _____

5. In "Single Room, Earth View," Sally Ride describes the appearance of the ocean from space. Why, according to Ride, would an oceanographer want to fly on the space shuttle? Cite one detail from the essay to support your answer.

    _____
    _____
    _____

6. In "Single Room, Earth View," Ride uses language that appeals to the senses. For example, she writes, "In space, night is very, very black." What feeling or feelings does that description evoke? Explain.

    _____
    _____
    _____

7. In "Single Room, Earth View," Sally Ride describes the dark side of the Earth. According to Ride, the presence or absence of the moon affects the view. Complete this chart to show how the view differs depending on the presence or absence of the moon. Then, on the line below, name the technique Ride uses in her discussion of the dark side of the planet to provide support for her essay.

View of Earth During Full Moon	View of Earth With No Moon

_____

8. Toward the end of "Single Room, Earth View," Sally Ride mentions the idea that a person can use the sensations experienced during an ordinary airline flight to get a sense of what space flight feels like. How does Ride relate this anecdote to her main idea?

_____

_____

_____

9. An author's tone is his or her attitude toward the audience and the subject. What is Sally Ride's tone in "Single Room, Earth View"? Explain.

_____

_____

_____

10. The main idea of a work of literature is its central message, insight, or opinion. What is the main idea of "Single Room, Earth View"?

_____

_____

_____

Essay

Write an extended response to the question of your choice or to the question or questions your teacher assigns you.

11. In a short expository essay, describe some of the ways in which astronauts' observations from outer space have contributed to scientists' understanding of Earth. Include two details from "Single Room, Earth View" that relate to scientists' measurements and observations. You might also include information from other reading you have done.

12. In "Single Room, Earth View" Sally Ride presents a number of details to support her main idea. In an essay, analyze the way in which Ride organizes supporting details. Begin by briefly outlining the information Ride presents. Then, identify the point at which she states her main idea. Finally, state your opinion of Ride's presentation. Did you find it difficult or easy to determine the main idea? Explain.

13. Sally Ride is both a scientist and a writer. In an essay, analyze how Ride combines her skill as a writer with her knowledge of science in "Single Room, Earth View." Cite one example of each of the following literary techniques: description, comparison and contrast, and cause and effect. Then, state what you think was Ride's purpose in writing this essay and who she intended the essay to be read by. Finally, state how well you think she achieved her purpose. Consider her use of literary techniques and her intended audience, and cite at least one detail from the essay to support your opinion.

14. **Thinking About the Big Question: Is knowledge the same as understanding?** In a brief essay, discuss how space flight contributes to both knowledge (the possession of information) and understanding (the process of making sense of information). Support your main idea with at least two examples from "Single Room, Earth View."

Oral Response

15. Go back to question 6, 8, or 9 or to the question your teacher assigns you. Take a few minutes to expand your answer and prepare an oral response. Find additional details in "Single Room, Earth View" that support your points. If necessary, make notes to guide your oral response.

"Single Room, Earth View" by Sally Ride
Selection Test A

Critical Reading *Identify the letter of the choice that best answers the question.*

_____ 1. Which of the following *best* expresses the writer's main idea in "Single Room, Earth View"?
  A. Space exploration leads to human progress.
  B. Space travel offers a unique view of Earth.
  C. Astronauts are highly trained scientists.
  D. Pollution is endangering Earth.

_____ 2. In "Single Room, Earth View," which cause explains why the author can easily lose track of her location?
  A. the high altitude of the space shuttle
  B. the blur of landforms as seen from space
  C. the sun's brightness
  D. the speed of the space shuttle

_____ 3. Which of the following does the essay's title "Single Room, Earth View" emphasize?
  A. Ride's personal observations of Earth from a small spacecraft
  B. the writer's discomfort at being in orbit for a long time
  C. the writer's fear of being confined in a small space
  D. Ride's unpleasant sense of isolation and distance from Earth

_____ 4. When you are reading an essay, what should you do if a detail seems unrelated to the author's main idea?
  A. Reread the passage to make sure you have understood the detail correctly.
  B. Continue reading in order to clarify the detail.
  C. Ignore the detail completely.
  D. Decide that the writer has deliberately included an unrelated detail.

_____ 5. Which of the following details *best* supports Sally Ride's description of "civilization's more unfortunate effects on the environment"?
  A. Astronauts can see condensation trails of airplanes flying across the Pacific Ocean.
  B. Ride can see lights twinkling along the entire east coast of the United States.
  C. A huge dust storm interferes with Ride's view of northern Africa.
  D. Oil slicks on the Persian Gulf could be seen from space.

____ 6. In Ride's essay, what feeling does the detail "Part of every orbit takes us to the dark side of the planet" help to create?

    A. anticipation and mystery

    B. fear and desperation

    C. hope and optimism

    D. regret and disappointment

____ 7. In "Single Room, Space View," which of the following details most directly supports the awe the author feels about Earth?

    A. I found Salina, Kansas.

    B. Scientists' understanding of the energy balance in the oceans has increased significantly as a result of the discoveries of circular and spiral eddies.

    C. It has carried even more sophisticated sensors in the payload bay.

    D. The drama set against the black backdrop of space and the magic of the materializing colors can't be captured.

____ 8. When your goal in reading is to identify the author's main idea, which of these strategies should you use?

    A. Use the first sentence of a selection to make a prediction.

    B. Compare the author's final sentence with the title of the selection.

    C. Reread the text to note how key details may lead to the main idea.

    D. Analyze the writer's use of figurative language such as similes and metaphors.

____ 9. Which of the following *best* states the function of the author's description of "ominous hurricane clouds expanding and rising like biscuits in the oven of the Caribbean"?

    A. It helps readers create a mental image of what the author sees from space.

    B. It creates a suspenseful mood.

    C. It supports the author's point that describing space travel is difficult.

    D. It contrasts with the writer's description of a dust storm over Africa.

Vocabulary and Grammar

____ 10. What does *diffused* mean in this sentence from "Single Room, Earth View"?
Bolts of lightning are diffused by the clouds into bursting balls of light.

    A. covered over

    B. spread out

    C. brought together

    D. made brighter

____ 11. Sally Ride says she has "to assume the role of a *novice* geologist." What kind of behavior would you expect from a *novice*?
   A. polished
   B. inexperienced
   C. scholarly
   D. greedy

____ 12. Which kind of verb do predicate nominatives and predicate adjectives regularly follow?
   A. action verb
   B. transitive verb
   C. intransitive verb
   D. linking verb

____ 13. A predicate adjective describes which of the following?
   A. verb
   B. direct object
   C. subject
   D. indirect object

Essay

14. In an essay, describe how Sally Ride organizes ideas in her expository essay, "Single Room, Earth View." Outline Ride's observations from the orbiting space shuttle. Also, tell whether the author's order of presentation helped you to identify her main points and supporting evidence. Explain why or why not.

15. In an essay, use the information from "Single Room, Earth View" to identify and describe evidence of human life that can be seen from the space shuttle. Explain what this evidence tells us about human life on Earth.

16. **Thinking About the Big Question: Is knowledge the same as understanding?** Knowledge, or information, can lead to greater scientific understanding. According to Sally Ride in "Single Room, Earth View," what two ways is information gathered during space travel? To what understanding does this knowledge lead scientists? Support your main idea in an essay, and give an example to illustrate your response.

Name _____ Date _____

"**Single Room, Earth View**" by Sally Ride
Selection Test B

Critical Reading *Identify the letter of the choice that best completes the statement or answers the question.*

_____ 1. What is the main idea in "Single Room, Earth View"?
A. Space exploration advances human progress.
B. Space travel provides a unique perspective on Earth.
C. Astronauts are highly trained scientific observers.
D. Air and water pollution are endangering Earth.

_____ 2. In "Single Room, Earth View," what cause explains why the author easily loses track of the part of Earth she is viewing?
A. The space shuttle flies at high altitudes.
B. Landforms are indistinct from space.
C. The sun's brightness blocks her view.
D. The space shuttle is moving very fast.

_____ 3. The author most likely titles her essay "Single Room, Earth View" in order to emphasize
A. the contrast between her small spacecraft and the dramatic views of Earth it affords.
B. the intense training that has prepared her for a long period of weightlessness.
C. the significant increase in applications for the astronaut program.
D. her thoughts about environmental damage to planet Earth.

_____ 4. Which of the following sentences gives the most vivid description of the author's view of land masses from space?
A. We could see smoke rising from fires that dotted the entire east coast of Africa.
B. Some cities look out of focus, and their colors muted, when viewed through a pollutant haze.
C. Spectacular as the view is from 200 miles up, Earth is not the awe-inspiring "blue marble" made famous by the photos from the moon.
D. The islands really *do* look as if that part of the world has been carpeted with a big page torn out of Rand-McNally. . . .

_____ 5. What is one effect Sally Ride mentions of the space shuttle's completing an orbit of Earth every 90 minutes?
A. It is easy to identify land masses.
B. It is easy to identify cities.
C. Half of the time Earth is in darkness.
D. It is hard to get used to the bright light.

_____ 6. In reading an essay, if you have determined that a detail does not seem to support the author's main idea, what should you do?
A. Reread the passage to be sure you have not misinterpreted the detail.
B. Ignore the detail until you reach the end of the essay.
C. Make a note of the detail and see if later details in the essay support or corroborate it.
D. Conclude that the writer made a mistake by including the detail.

_____ 7. Which of the following details *best* supports Sally Ride's observation that civilization has caused some "unfortunate effects on the environment"?
   A. Astronauts can trace thousand-mile-long condensation trails from airplanes.
   B. The author can see lights twinkling along the entire eastern coast of the United States.
   C. A huge dust storm obscures the author's view of northern Africa.
   D. Oil slicks on the Persian Gulf can be observed from space.

_____ 8. In "Single Room, Earth View," what feelings does the following detail create?
   Part of every orbit takes us to the dark side of the planet. In space, night is very, very black. . . .

   A. uncertainty and suspense
   B. terror and despair
   C. sympathy and compassion
   D. sadness and regret

_____ 9. Which of the following details helps to support the awe the author feels about spaceflight?
   A. I found Salina, Kansas (and pleased my in-laws, who live there).
   B. The drama set against the black backdrop of space and the magic of the materializing colors can't be captured in an astronomer's equations.
   C. Scientists' understanding of the energy balance in the oceans has increased significantly as a result of the discoveries of circular and spiral eddies.
   D. Not surprisingly, the effects are more noticeable now than they were a decade ago.

_____ 10. When your purpose is to identify the author's main idea, which of these strategies should you use?
   A. Make a prediction on the basis of the writer's first sentence.
   B. Consider the possible symbolic meanings of the selection's title.
   C. Note important details and consider how they may lead to the main idea.
   D. Reread aloud the portions of the text that contain figurative language.

_____ 11. Which of the following ideas does Sally Ride's discussion of photographs and observations of ocean dynamics *best* support?
   A. Future space missions should focus entirely on the ocean currents.
   B. Scientists on Earth must study what astronauts have observed from space.
   C. Space exploration has resulted in some unexpected scientific advances.
   D. Scientists' understanding improves the farther they are away from their subject.

_____ 12. The description of "ominous hurricane clouds expanding and rising like biscuits in the oven of the Caribbean"
   A. helps readers create a vivid mental image of what the author sees from space.
   B. foreshadows the development of a specific hurricane while the writer was in orbit.
   C. corroborates the author's claim that training to become an astronaut is extremely rigorous.
   D. shows the author's occasional uncertainty about what she observes from space.

_____ 13. Which of the following *best* summarizes a main idea in "Single Room, Earth View"?
    A. Certain questions about the universe are best left unanswered and unexplored.
    B. Women can make an extremely valuable contribution to the space program.
    C. Space exploration can benefit the understanding and preservation of Earth.
    D. The accomplishments of civilization are far more important than those of nature.

Vocabulary and Grammar

_____ 14. When bolts of lightning are *diffused* by the clouds "into bursting balls of light," they are
    A. disarmed.   C. gathered together.
    B. spread out.   D. unrelenting.

_____ 15. In which of the following sentences is *articulate* used correctly?
    A. *Articulate* to a fault, he served the vegetables in a large bowl.
    B. Did you understand anything at all in her *articulate* presentation?
    C. He can barely speak the language, but we expected him to present an *articulate* oration.
    D. The author presents an *articulate* series of observations in her essay.

_____ 16. Predicate nominatives and predicate adjectives typically follow which kind of verb?
    A. action verb   C. intransitive verb
    B. transitive verb   D. linking verb

_____ 17. A predicate adjective describes which of the following?
    A. the verb   C. the subject
    B. the direct object   D. the indirect object

Essay

18. In the beginning of "Single Room, Earth View," the author notes that people want to know "What did it look like?" Write an essay describing how the author uses vivid, descriptive comparisons of views of Earth from space to everyday things in order to help readers understand her observations from space.

19. Write an expository essay in which you describe some of the ways in which astronauts' observations from orbit have contributed to scientists' understanding of Earth. In your essay, mention two details Ride includes in "Single Room, Earth View" about scientists and their measurements and observations.

20. Sally Ride is both a scientist and a writer with a literary background. Write an essay analyzing how Ride's literary background affects her written observations of scientific phenomena. Provide some examples from Ride's essay to support your analysis.

21. **Thinking About the Big Question: Is knowledge the same as understanding?** In a brief essay, discuss how spaceflight contributes to both knowledge (the possession of information) and understanding (the process of making sense of information). Support your main idea with at least two examples from "Single Room, Earth View."

Vocabulary Warm-up Word Lists

Study these words from the selections. Then, complete the activities.

Word List A

baffled [BAF fuhld] *adj.* puzzled; bewildered
    I am <u>baffled</u> by these directions and do not know where to go.

betray [bi TRAY] *v.* to show feelings you are trying to hide
    Kim kept her smile bright and did not <u>betray</u> her sadness.

cunning [KUH ning] *adj.* smart in a clever or sometimes dishonest way
    <u>Cunning</u> Barbara kept everyone guessing about her new admirer.

existence [eg ZIS tuhns] *n.* the state of being alive
    No matter when they die, everyone begins their <u>existence</u> as a baby.

massive [MAS iv] *adj.* very large; solid and heavy
    It took a <u>massive</u> effort to clean up after the huge oil spill.

mirth [MERTH] *n.* happiness and laughter
    The holiday parade with its silly floats brought joy and <u>mirth</u> to the crowd.

unexpected [uhn ek SPEK tid] *adj.* surprising because not anticipated
    Rosanna is upset at the <u>unexpected</u> news that her family is moving.

unpredictable [uhn pree DIK tuh buhl] *adj.* fickle; unreliable; inconstant
    The car is old and <u>unpredictable</u> and could break down at any time.

Word List B

contrasts [KAHN trasts] *n.* differences identified through comparisons
    Among their many <u>contrasts</u>, Jack is tall and Josh is short.

demeanor [duh MEE nuhr] *n.* behavior or appearance that tells what a person is like
    Amy takes nothing seriously, and it shows in her careless <u>demeanor</u>.

favorable [FAY vuh ruh buhl] *adj.* positive and likely to make something happen
    Getting a better coach would be a <u>favorable</u> change for that team.

matchless [MACH les] *adj.* better than all others of the same kind
    She was a <u>matchless</u> student and always won the highest honors.

prematurely [pree muh CHOOR lee] *adv.* happening too early or before expected
    His hair turned <u>prematurely</u> gray when he was still a young man.

tragedy [TRAJ uh dee] *n.* very sad and shocking event
    The school bus accident was a <u>tragedy</u> for the entire town.

victorious [vik TAWR ee uhs] *adj.* successful, especially in a battle or competition
    My basketball team is <u>victorious</u> on the court and wins every game.

wavered [WAY verd] *v.* became weaker or less certain
    Paul never <u>wavered</u> in his belief that his business could succeed.

Name _____ Date _____

Vocabulary Warm-up Exercises

Exercise A *Fill in each blank in the paragraph with an appropriate word from Word List A. Use each word only once.*

Cats have long confused and [1] _____ people. Unlike a dog, a cat will [2] _____ few emotions. A dog wags its tail joyfully at the sight of its owner; if it could laugh out loud, its happiness could be called [3] _____. A cat, on the other hand, often shows only a passing interest in its owner. This may actually be a clever and [4] _____ strategy the cat has developed. By appearing not to care, the cat encourages its owner to try to win its affection with [5] _____ amounts of food and kitty treats. Then, at the most surprising and [6] _____ moments, say when its owner is hard at work on the computer, the cat will acknowledge the person's [7] _____ by jumping on top of the computer and looking eye to eye. A cat is an [8] _____ creature that keeps everyone guessing!

Exercise B *Revise each sentence so the underlined vocabulary word is used in a logical way. Be sure to keep the vocabulary word in your revision.*

Example: He gets his confident <u>demeanor</u> from a shop around the corner.
He gets his confident <u>demeanor</u> from working hard and being successful.

1. Our <u>victorious</u> team is an embarrassment for our school.
   _____

2. They were so much alike, they were a study in <u>contrasts</u>.
   _____

3. A <u>matchless</u> friend is the best person to have around to avoid a fire.
   _____

4. We received the news <u>prematurely</u> after everyone else knew.
   _____

5. It was a <u>tragedy</u> for the old couple when the storm spared their house.
   _____

6. When she finished the marathon, she <u>wavered</u> and almost dropped out.
   _____

7. A <u>favorable</u> response to my vacation request will disappoint me greatly.
   _____

from **A Lincoln Preface** by Carl Sandburg
"Arthur Ashe Remembered" by John McPhee
Reading Warm-up A

Read the following passage. Pay special attention to the underlined words. Then, read it again, and complete the activities. Use a separate sheet of paper for your written answers.

"The new kid in school." Natalie knew that that was what everyone was thinking as she entered the small lunchroom of the rural school. She had come from a large city high school, where students were constantly coming and going. Some of these kids had probably been babies together in the local hospital. Their entire <u>existence</u> had been spent with one another, whereas she was an outsider.

Natalie disliked that word, *outsider*. It was so unwelcoming. Not like *friend*—a happy word, full of <u>mirth</u>, as her grandmother would say, in her old-fashioned way.

The first day in a new school was the hardest. Natalie anticipated feeling completely <u>baffled</u> and not understanding where anything was. It usually helped if she could make a friend at lunch—and she had a plan for that.

Natalie had experience making new starts—a <u>massive</u> amount, in her view, given that she had gone to six schools in ten years.

This, her mother promised, was the last move. Before, it had always been her job that brought out the packing boxes, but this move was totally <u>unexpected</u>. Without warning, her grandmother had a stroke. Then, her mother had made a decision that Natalie never would have predicted. She quit her career and returned home to this small country town to run the family restaurant. Life is <u>unpredictable</u>, Natalie realized.

These events brought Natalie to this lunchroom. All the other times she had been in this same place had taught her a <u>cunning</u> lesson about how to make friends. She had simply learned not to <u>betray</u> her fears about whether others would like her.

"Hi, would you like to sit with us?" Natalie heard a pleasant voice asking, as two girls she remembered from homeroom that morning made room for her at their table.

"Sure, thanks!" Natalie responded, as she winked to herself inside.

1. Underline a sentence that helps explain the meaning of <u>existence</u>. Give a synonym for **existence** in this passage.

2. Circle the word that is a clue to <u>mirth</u>. Describe what someone *full of mirth* is like.

3. Underline a phrase that is a clue to <u>baffled</u>. Give a synonym for **baffled**.

4. Underline two words that are clues to <u>massive</u>. What experience does Natalie describe as **massive**, and why?

5. Circle words that are clues to <u>unexpected</u>. Underline two events that were **unexpected** for Natalie.

6. Circle a phrase that is a clue to <u>unpredictable</u>. Are **unexpected** and **unpredictable** similar words? Explain.

7. Circle a clue to <u>cunning</u>. What was **cunning** about her plan? Name another word to describe it.

8. Underline what Natalie does not <u>betray</u>. Give an antonym for **betray**. Do you agree with her logic? Explain.

from **A Lincoln Preface** by Carl Sandburg
"Arthur Ashe Remembered" by John McPhee
Reading Warm-up B

Read the following passage. Pay special attention to the underlined words. Then, read it again, and complete the activities. Use a separate sheet of paper for your written answers.

Eleanor Roosevelt, first lady and human rights champion, left a record of inspiring quotations that tell the kind of person she was and what she believed.

"No one can make you feel inferior without your consent," she said.

Young Eleanor was the plain child of a beautiful mother. She knew something about feeling that she did not measure up. Then, she lost both of her parents <u>prematurely</u>, by the time she was ten. Their early and unexpected deaths increased her insecurity.

Thanks to the influence of an extraordinary teacher, she recognized her own strengths, and her <u>demeanor</u> changed. Her willingness to help others showed that she believed in herself.

She had the courage to deal with <u>tragedy</u>, and it led to extraordinary experiences. The death of her parents was only the first sad and shocking event in her life. Her husband, Franklin, was paralyzed by polio, a disease that kept him in a wheelchair. He never <u>wavered</u> in his determination to overcome his disability.

While he was president, from 1933 to 1945, she traveled widely to investigate needs in the country. It was <u>favorable</u> for countless Americans that she did because Eleanor constantly pushed the president to develop programs that would benefit the poor. In fact, among first ladies, she is viewed as one of the very best, even <u>matchless</u>, for the respect she earned.

She said, "You must do the thing you think you cannot do."

Eleanor Roosevelt's life was a series of <u>contrasts</u>, of opportunity and difficulty. She was deeply shy as a girl, yet she grew up to be one of the most outspoken women of her time. She fought for civil rights in this country and for human rights everywhere. She never gave up the fight and, by that measure, she was <u>victorious</u>. All those who are inspired by her words and example are winners as well.

1. Circle the phrase that gives a clue to the word <u>prematurely</u>. What happened *prematurely* to Eleanor?

2. Underline the sentence that helps explain <u>demeanor</u>. How do you think Eleanor's *demeanor* changed?

3. Circle the phrase that describes a <u>tragedy</u>. Give a synonym for *tragedy*.

4. Circle a nearby word that shows the opposite of having <u>wavered</u>. Explain what Franklin Roosevelt would have done if he had *wavered*.

5. Underline the sentence that explains why it was <u>favorable</u> for Americans to have Eleanor on their side. Circle a word clue for *favorable*.

6. Circle words that are a clue to <u>matchless</u>. Describe someone whom you would call *matchless* and explain why.

7. Underline the sentence that show <u>contrasts</u> in Eleanor's life. Give a synonym and an antonym for *contrasts*.

8. Circle a word that is a clue to <u>victorious</u>. Give a synonym for *victorious* that describes Eleanor's life and explain why.

Unit 3 Resources: Types of Nonfiction

Name _____ Date _____

from **A Lincoln Preface** by Carl Sandburg
"Arthur Ashe Remembered" by John McPhee
Writing About the Big Question
Is knowledge the same as understanding?

Big Question Vocabulary

ambiguous	clarify	comprehend	concept	connection
fact	feeling	information	insight	instinct
interpret	research	senses/sensory	sources	statistics

A. *Use one or more words from the list above to complete each sentence.*

1. To _____ another person's life, we must get to know the person.

2. Brian studies _____ on Lincoln's war decisions and tries to _____ his motives.

3. What _____ and other information show how good Ashe was?

4. Lincoln's directions to his commanders could not be _____.

B. *Follow the directions in responding to each of the items below.*

1. Describe a difficult problem you had to solve.

   _____

   _____

2. When you solved the problem, did you rely on facts, information, or did you use your instincts? Explain your answer. Use at least two of the Big Question vocabulary words.

   _____

   _____

C. *Complete the sentence below. Then, write a short paragraph in which you connect this experience to the big question.*

Both of these biographers give factual descriptions and details to add both to our knowledge and our understanding of the subjects. Complete this sentence:

When a biographer presents facts fairly and truthfully, _____

_____

_____

_____.

Unit 3 Resources: Types of Nonfiction

from **A Lincoln Preface** by Carl Sandburg
"Arthur Ashe Remembered" by John McPhee
Literary Analysis: Biographical Writing

Biographical writing is a form of nonfiction in which a writer tells the life story of another person. Biographies are often written about historical figures. The best biographies do not just list the facts, events, or accomplishments in the subject's life. Although factual information is important, a good biography presents the writer's interpretation of those pieces of information. The biographer shows why an understanding of the subject's life is meaningful to readers.

In biographical writing, the details that an author chooses to describe help create our impression of the subject. Biographers often focus on one or all of the following aspects of a subject's life:

- personality
- relationships
- major life events

- upbringing
- role in important events
- influence on others

DIRECTIONS: *Write your answers to the following questions on the lines provided.*

1. In the excerpt from "A Lincoln Preface," what does the following anecdote reveal about Lincoln's personality?

   "While the war drums beat, he liked best of all the stories told of him, one of two Quakeresses heard talking in a railway car. 'I think that Jefferson will succeed.' 'Why does thee think so?' 'Because Jefferson is a praying man.' 'And so is Abraham a praying man.' 'Yes, but the Lord will think Abraham is joking.'"

   _____

   _____

   _____

2. In a sentence or two, sum up the portrait of Lincoln's personality that Carl Sandburg creates in the excerpt from *A Lincoln Preface.*

   _____

   _____

   _____

3. In "Arthur Ashe Remembered," what are two ways in which John McPhee supports his belief that "When things got tough, [Ashe] had control"?

   _____

   _____

   _____

4. In "Arthur Ashe Remembered," what writing techniques does John McPhee use to give readers a detailed portrait of Arthur Ashe?

   _____

   _____

   _____

from **A Lincoln Preface** by Carl Sandburg
"Arthur Ashe Remembered" by John McPhee
Vocabulary Builder

Word List

censure   despotic   droll   enigma   legacy   lithe

A. DIRECTIONS: *Revise each sentence so that the underlined vocabulary word is used logically. Be sure not to change the vocabulary word.*

1. Most of the people enjoy their ruler's use of <u>despotic</u> power.

   _____

2. Mary's personality is an <u>enigma</u>, so we have no difficulty discovering her true motives.

   _____

3. A successful athlete typically has no need of a <u>lithe</u> body.

   _____

4. The movie was so <u>droll</u> that we found ourselves falling asleep in our seats.

   _____

5. In our opinion, the team leader's admirable conduct deserves <u>censure</u>.

   _____

6. The brand-new temple is a <u>legacy</u> from a bygone civilization.

   _____

B. DIRECTIONS: *On the line, write the letter of the choice that is the best synonym for each numbered word.*

___ 1. despotic
   A. temporary
   B. verifiable
   C. tyrannical
   D. true

___ 2. legacy
   A. memento
   B. heirloom
   C. legal document
   D. bracelet

___ 3. lithe
   A. flexible
   B. affluent
   C. devious
   D. permanent

___ 4. enigma
   A. award
   B. joke
   C. advertisement
   D. riddle

Name _____ Date _____

from **A Lincoln Preface** by Carl Sandburg
"Arthur Ashe Remembered" by John McPhee
Writing to Compare

Use a chart like the one shown to make prewriting notes for an essay comparing your reactions to these two biographical selections.

	from *A Lincoln Preface*	"Arthur Ashe Remembered"
Importance of subject		
My response to each selection		
Main impression author wants to convey		

from **"A Lincoln Preface"** by Carl Sandburg
"Arthur Ashe Remembered" by John McPhee
Open-Book Test

Short Answer *Write your responses to the questions in this section on the lines provided.*

1. The excerpt from "A Lincoln Preface" by Carl Sandburg is biographical. What is the main reason this essay can be considered biographical?

   _____

2. In the excerpt from "A Lincoln Preface," Sandburg tells how Lincoln manipulated the admission of Nevada into the Union. What, in your opinion, is Sandburg's reason for including this account?

   _____

   _____

3. In the excerpt from "A Lincoln Preface," Abraham Lincoln declares that he "can bear censure." If a person's actions receive censure, is the person praised? Explain your answer based on the definition of *censure*.

   _____

   _____

4. In the selection from "A Lincoln Preface," Carl Sandburg's treatment of Abraham Lincoln is general and broad rather than specific and narrow. Why does Sandburg treat his subject in a general, broad way in the preface to the biography?

   _____

   _____

5. What two adjectives best describe John McPhee's tone—his attitude toward his subject—in "Arthur Ashe Remembered"?

   _____

   _____

6. A biographer has the power to shape the reader's impression of his or her subject. What is the main impression of Arthur Ashe created by John McPhee in "Arthur Ashe Remembered"?

   _____

   _____

7. The excerpt from "A Lincoln Preface" and "Arthur Ashe Remembered" have one basic and important characteristic in common. What is it?

   _____

8. In the excerpt from "A Lincoln Preface," readers learn something about Abraham Lincoln. In "Arthur Ashe Remembered," readers learn something about Arthur Ashe. On the basis of the two selections, consider the personalities of the two men. In what way does Lincoln's personality differ most strikingly from Ashe's personality?

_____

_____

9. In the excerpt from "A Lincoln Preface," Sandburg tells the story of Lincoln's meeting with the author of *Uncle Tom's Cabin*. In "Arthur Ashe Remembered," McPhee recalls a comment made by Ashe's father. Why do the biographers include such information?

_____

_____

10. At first glance it would appear that there are few similarities between Abraham Lincoln as presented in the excerpt from "A Lincoln Preface" and Arthur Ashe as presented in "Arthur Ashe Remembered." The two men did have similarities, however. Complete this chart to show two important similarities between them. Then, on the line below, tell how those similarities made the two men especially meaningful subjects for biographies.

```
            ┌─────────────────────────────────────────┐
            │   Abraham Lincoln and Arthur Ashe:        │
            │            Similarities                   │
            └─────────────────────────────────────────┘
              ↙                               ↘
┌───────────────────────────┐   ┌───────────────────────────┐
│ 1.                        │   │ 2.                        │
│                           │   │                           │
│                           │   │                           │
│                           │   │                           │
└───────────────────────────┘   └───────────────────────────┘
```

_____

Essay

Write an extended response to the question of your choice or to the question or questions your teacher assigns you.

11. One of a biographer's most useful devices is the anecdote—a brief story about an amusing, interesting, or strange event. The story is told to entertain or make a point. Identify one anecdote in the excerpt from "A Lincoln Preface" or one in "Arthur Ashe Remembered." In an essay, explain why you think the anecdote is enjoyable or thought provoking, and describe what it reveals about the subject of the biography.

12. Sandburg in the excerpt from "A Lincoln Preface" and McPhee in "Arthur Ashe Remembered" offer vivid portraits of remarkable people. In your opinion, what do Lincoln and Ashe have in common? How are they different? In an essay, briefly discuss the outstanding similarities and differences between Lincoln and Ashe as they are presented by their biographers. Cite one detail from each selection that relates to their similarities and one detail from each selection that relates to their differences.

13. Both Sandburg in the excerpt from "A Lincoln Preface" and McPhee in "Arthur Ashe Remembered" attempt to present a vivid impression of their subject's personality. However, the two biographers employ different methods to accomplish this goal. In an essay, compare and contrast the specific ways in which the two biographers present their subjects. Cite at least one detail from each selection to support your points.

14. **Thinking About the Big Question: Is knowledge the same as understanding?** In an essay, discuss how you think an experienced writer of biography might respond to the Big Question about the relationship between knowledge and understanding. Support your main ideas with details and examples from the excerpt from "A Lincoln Preface" or "Arthur Ashe Remembered."

Oral Response

15. Go back to question 4, 5, or 9 or to the question your teacher assigns you. Take a few minutes to expand your answer and prepare an oral response. Find additional details in the excerpt from "A Lincoln Preface" and/or "Arthur Ashe Remembered" to support your points. If necessary, make an outline to guide your oral response.

from **A Lincoln Preface** by Carl Sandburg
"Arthur Ashe Remembered" by John McPhee
Selection Test A

Critical Reading *Identify the letter of the choice that best answers the question.*

____ 1. What is the main focus of Carl Sandburg's biography of Lincoln in the selection from *A Lincoln Preface*?
A. Lincoln's childhood
B. the presidential election of 1860
C. the assassination of Lincoln in 1865
D. Lincoln's many-sided personality

____ 2. How does Sandburg portray Lincoln as a politician?
A. practical
B. misleading
C. dishonest
D. amateurish

____ 3. Biographical writing focuses on which of the following?
A. a writer's treatment of the life of another person
B. a person's account of his or her own life
C. a journalist's interviews with a modern-day personality
D. a historian's theories about a well-known person's possible motivations

____ 4. Establishing a purpose for reading Sandburg's description of Abraham Lincoln can help you to do which of the following?
A. focus on specific information
B. identify independent clauses
C. write an anecdote
D. evaluate the effectiveness of Lincoln's political opponents

____ 5. An anecdote is a brief story that illustrates a point. Which of the following statements about Lincoln is an example of an anecdote in Sandburg's biographical sketch?
A. "He was a chosen spokesman. . . ."
B. "He sent hundreds of telegrams. 'Suspend death sentence' or 'Suspend execution' of So-and-So, who was to be shot at sunrise."
C. "The facts and myths of his life are to be an American possession."
D. "Perhaps no human clay pot has held more laughter and tears."

_____ 6. Which of the following does Sandburg's account of the two Quaker women's conversation about Lincoln illustrate?

A. a formal speech

B. a symbol

C. a generalization

D. an anecdote

_____ 7. Which of the following best describes the biographical picture that Sandburg paints of Lincoln?

A. a warm leader who inspired northerners and southerners alike

B. a complex man who lived in a time of grave crisis

C. a president who saw the humor in every situation

D. a "one-horse lawyer" who was ill-equipped to deal with a civil war

_____ 8. In addition to his or her interpretation of factual information, what else does a good biographer need to supply about his or her subject?

A. a list of sources to check the accuracy of facts reported in the biography

B. an interpretation of the meaning of the subject's life

C. an acknowledgment of the subject's cooperation

D. a comparison of the subject with other persons living at the same time

_____ 9. According to John McPhee's biographical sketch of Arthur Ashe, what legacy did Ashe's mother pass on to her son?

A. athletic ability

B. a sense of humor

C. a controlled temper

D. the courage to take risks

_____ 10. Which of the following best describes McPhee's tone (his attitude toward his subject) in "Arthur Ashe Remembered"?

A. admiring

B. skeptical

C. critical

D. amused

___ 11. What do McPhee's "Arthur Ashe Remembered" and the excerpt from Sandburg's *A Lincoln Preface* have in common?

  A. Both selections deal with nineteenth-century Americans.

  B. Both Lincoln and Ashe overcame physical disabilities in their childhood.

  C. Lincoln and Ashe both loved books and devoted much time to educating themselves.

  D. Lincoln and Ashe were remarkable individuals of great achievement in their chosen fields.

Vocabulary

___ 12. Which of the following best describes a *droll* story?

  A. oddly funny   C. repetitive and boring

  B. bitterly sarcastic   D. humorously cheerful

___ 13. Which of the following best describes the relationship involved in a *legacy*?

  A. ancestor and descendant   C. museum official and work of art

  B. politician and voter   D. shopkeeper and client

___ 14. Which of the following best describes the feeling you might have if you face an *enigma*?

  A. rage   C. affection

  B. puzzlement   D. gratitude

Essay

15. One of a biographer's most effective devices is the anecdote—a brief story about an interesting, an amusing, or a strange event told to entertain or make a point. Identify two of your favorite anecdotes in these biographical selections. In a brief essay, explain why you think each anecdote is enjoyable or thought-provoking. Also, explain what insight each anecdote gives about the subject of the biography.

16. If you had to sum up the personalities of Abraham Lincoln and Arthur Ashe, how would you do so on the basis of these biographical sketches? In a brief essay, present a single thesis statement that concisely describes the personality of both men. Then, use details from each selection to support your main idea.

17. **Thinking About the Big Question: Is knowledge the same as understanding?** In biographical writing, you might say that knowledge refers to knowing the facts and events of a person's life. However, understanding refers to interpreting the subject's personality and achievements, as well as the significance of the person's life. In an essay, choose either biographer Carl Sandburg or John McPhee and tell whether he provides both knowledge and understanding of his subject. Support your opinion with details and examples from the excerpt from *A Lincoln Preface* or "Arthur Ashe Remembered."

from **A Lincoln Preface** by Carl Sandburg
"Arthur Ashe Remembered" by John McPhee
Selection Test B

Critical Reading *Identify the letter of the choice that best completes the statement or answers the question.*

_____ 1. Biographical writing is a form of which of the following?
A. fiction
B. nonfiction
C. oratory
D. autobiography

_____ 2. Carl Sandburg reflects on what aspect of Abraham Lincoln?
A. Lincoln's legal background
B. Lincoln's many-sided personality
C. Lincoln's simple upbringing
D. Lincoln's ease with language

_____ 3. According to Sandburg, why was Lincoln willing to stick the Constitution "in a hole"?
A. He thought the Constitution was an illegal document and should be abolished.
B. He thought the Constitution was outdated and should be revised.
C. He believed the Constitution was not valid during a civil war.
D. He believed it was necessary to violate the Constitution in order to save the Union.

_____ 4. Which of the following is an important feature of a good biography?
A. The author includes an interview with the subject.
B. The biographer selects a wealthy or powerful individual as the subject.
C. The writer restricts the biography to a list of facts and events in the subject's life.
D. The biographer shows why an understanding of the subject's life is meaningful to readers.

_____ 5. What point is Sandburg making about Lincoln when he writes the following?
In all its essential propositions the Southern Confederacy had the moral support of powerful, respectable elements throughout the North. . . .
A. Lincoln accepted the will of the people.
B. Lincoln believed in the necessity of slavery.
C. Lincoln was willing to fight for an unpopular cause.
D. Lincoln was arrogant and believed that he alone was right.

_____ 6. Which of the following passages illustrates Lincoln's sense of humor?
I. He says of a devious Senator, "He's too crooked to lie still."
II. Of the Civil War, he says, "I shan't last long after it's over."
III. He says, "I will violate the Constitution, if necessary, to save the Union."
IV. He says to the author of *Uncle Tom's Cabin,* "So you're the little woman who wrote the book that made this great war."
A. I and IV
B. II and III
C. I and III
D. III and IV

____ 7. Based on Sandburg's preface, which of the following statements is *not* true of Lincoln?
   A. He gracefully declined to support the use of elephants as a means of transportation in the United States.
   B. He abolished the right of habeas corpus.
   C. He supported plans for the transcontinental railroad.
   D. He was always good-natured with his critics.

____ 8. When Sandburg describes how Lincoln manipulated the admission of Nevada as a state in the Union, he wants to
   A. show that Lincoln used political means to gain his desired end.
   B. prove that Lincoln could make important decisions when under pressure.
   C. exaggerate Lincoln's extreme delight in wielding power.
   D. demonstrate that Lincoln was easily tricked by his enemies.

____ 9. Which of the following quotations illustrates Lincoln's humility?
   A. "He rebuked with anger a woman who got on her knees to thank him for a pardon that saved her son. . ."
   B. "I will violate the Constitution, if necessary, to save the Union."
   C. "Of men taking too fat profits out of the war, he said, 'Where the carcass is there will the eagles be gathered together.'"
   D. "I knowed he'd never come back."

____ 10. According to John McPhee, Arthur Ashe achieved international fame as a
   A. tennis player.
   B. golfer.
   C. college president.
   D. philanthropist.

____ 11. What is the most important reason why an autobiography by Ashe would be very different from McPhee's view of Ashe in "Arthur Ashe Remembered"?
   A. McPhee knows very few facts about Arthur Ashe.
   B. McPhee uses very few direct quotations in his writing.
   C. The quiet Ashe would not praise himself as much as McPhee praises him.
   D. An autobiography would focus more on Ashe's personality than on his career.

____ 12. In "Arthur Ashe Remembered," lines such as "It was maddening, sometimes, to play against him" and "at the tensest moment, he goes for the all but impossible" make the point that
   A. Ashe was unusually nervous when he played in tournaments.
   B. Ashe's self-control in difficult situations was one of his greatest qualities.
   C. Ashe faced many difficult times in his life.
   D. Ashe was a talented player and a fine human being.

____ 13. Which of the following statements best expresses an important similarity between Abraham Lincoln and Arthur Ashe as they are presented in these biographical sketches?
   A. Both Lincoln and Ashe avoided conflicts and confrontations.
   B. Lincoln and Ashe both possessed courage and determination.
   C. Both men grew up in rural surroundings.
   D. Lincoln and Ashe made many friends, but they also had powerful enemies.

_____ 14. Sandburg's story about Lincoln's meeting with Harriet Beecher Stowe, the author of *Uncle Tom's Cabin*, and McPhee's recollection of the comments by Ashe's father both illustrate which of the following devices in biographical writing?

A. simile
B. metaphor

C. flashback
D. anecdote

Vocabulary

_____ 15. Sandburg says that Lincoln "was clothed with despotic power." Which of the following is the best synonym for *despotic*?

A. preliminary
B. tyrannical

C. maniacal
D. cooperative

_____ 16. Lincoln told an officer, "I can bear censure, but not insult." Which of the following is the opposite of *censure*?

A. praise
B. blame

C. encouragement
D. repetition

_____ 17. Which of the following would most likely be *enigmatic*?

A. an advertisement
B. a love letter

C. a riddle
D. a cartoon

_____ 18. Of the following individuals, who is most likely to be described as *lithe*?

A. a dancer
B. a lawyer

C. a receptionist
D. a teacher

Essay

19. Carl Sandburg and John McPhee offer vivid portraits of two remarkable people: Abraham Lincoln and Arthur Ashe. In your opinion, what do these people have in common? How are Lincoln and Ashe different? In an essay, briefly discuss the outstanding similarities and differences between Lincoln and Ashe as they are presented by their biographers.

20. Carl Sandburg and John McPhee both attempt to give a vivid impression of their subject's personality. Yet, the two biographers employ quite different methods to accomplish their goal. Sandburg, for example, covers a wide range of personality traits by using a variety of anecdotes and quotations. McPhee, however, focuses on a single overall impression of Arthur Ashe. In an essay, compare and contrast the specific ways in which the two biographers present their subjects.

21. **Thinking About the Big Question: Is knowledge the same as understanding?** In an essay, discuss how you think an experienced writer of biography might respond to the Big Question about the relationship between knowledge and understanding. Support your main ideas with details and examples from the excerpt from *A Lincoln Preface* or "Arthur Ashe Remembered."

Name _____ Date _____

Business Communication: Business Letter

Prewriting: Choosing Your Topic

In the graphic organizer below, make a list of the products that you currently use or are interested in using, note why these products or services interest you, and decide which details matter most to you.

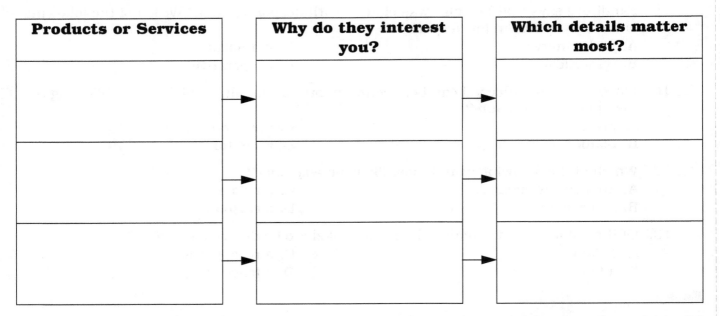

Products or Services	Why do they interest you?	Which details matter most?

Drafting: Providing Elaboration

Use the following graphic organizer to develop the body of your business letter by filling in the appropriate information on the right.

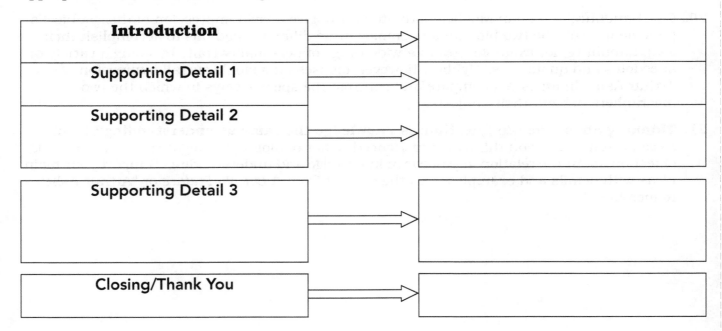

Introduction	
Supporting Detail 1	
Supporting Detail 2	
Supporting Detail 3	
Closing/Thank You	

Name _____ Date _____

Writing Workshop
Revising to Combine: Sentences with Compound Structures

Revising to Combine Sentences with Compound Structures

A series of short sentences can sound choppy and repetitious. To solve the problem, you can combine sentences by using words such as *and, but, or, either/or,* or *neither/nor* to form a compound structure.

Choppy	Compound Structure	Example
My brother Joe works hard in school. I work hard there, too.	*Combined with Compound Subject*	*My brother Joe and I work hard in school.*
I finished my homework. I studied for a math test.	*Combined with Compound Verb*	I *finished* my homework *and studied* for a math test.
I may study the textbook. I may study my class notes.	*Combined with Direct Object*	I may study *the textbook or my class notes.*
One of my favorite subjects is biology. The other is math.	*Combined with Compound Predicate Noun*	My favorite subjects are *biology and math.*
The test was long. It was not very hard.	*Combined with Compound Predicate Adjective*	The test was *long but not very hard.*

Identifying Compound Structures

A. DIRECTIONS: *On the line before each item, identify the compound structure that you would use to combine the pair of choppy sentences. The first has been done as an example.*

compound verb _____ 1. Manuel does his homework in the evening. He also watches television.

_____ 2. Sara attends a ballet class after school. Shawn attends the same ballet class.

_____ 3. Some students play basketball. Some students play softball.

_____ 4. Performing drama is enjoyable. However, it is also difficult.

Fixing Choppy Sentences by Using Compound Structures

B. DIRECTIONS: *For each item, combine the two choppy sentences into a single sentence.*

1. The swim team meets on Tuesdays. It also meets on Thursdays.

_____

2. The swim coach is strict. However, he is also fair.

_____

3. Todd belongs to the swim team. He also works as an after-school lifeguard.

_____

4. Harry may join the swim team. He may join another team.

_____

Unit 3 Resources: Types of Nonfiction

Unit 3: Types of Nonfiction
Benchmark Test 5

Literary Analysis: Style *Read the selection. Then, answer the questions that follow.*

Oh, my gosh, how can I describe what happened next? I mean, duh, if you weren't there, well, there's just no way you would understand. Okay, I'll take a deep breath and give it a try. Hold on, here it goes! The whole, what to call it, event began when the dog ran out as I opened the door. Did I mention that it was 6:30 A.M. and I was wearing pajamas?

1. Which word best describes the diction and syntax of this selection?
   A. formal   B. informal   C. subjective   D. literary

2. Which term refers to the author's attitude toward the topic?
   A. diction   B. style   C. tone   D. opinion

3. Which word best describes the tone of this selection?
   A. haunted   B. blissful   C. excited   D. angry

4. Which of the following phrases explains the term *diction*?
   A. how many words the author uses
   B. the kinds of words the author chooses
   C. how the words are arranged
   D. the definitions of the words

5. An author's style relies most on which of the following?
   A. use of diction   C. use of tone
   B. use of syntax   D. use of language

Literary Analysis: Expository Essay *Read the selection. Then, answer the questions that follow.*

The Arabian horse has a unique dished profile, huge eyes, flaring nostrils, and small muzzle. An arched neck, sloping shoulders, broad chest, and short, strong back complete the picture. Arabians come in several colors: gray, chestnut, bay, roan, and, rarely, solid black. Most Arabians stand between 14 and 15 hands high and weigh between 800 and 1,000 pounds.

6. What is the purpose of the selection?
   A. to persuade readers that Arabian horses are the best breed
   B. to entertain readers by creating a word picture of the Arabian horse
   C. to present the author's opinion of Arabian horses
   D. to describe the Arabian horse in detail

7. In addition to description and comparison-and-contrast writing, expository writing includes which of the following techniques?

    A. annotation   C. argument

    B. cause and effect   D. opinion

8. What is the tone of most expository writing?

    A. critical   C. sentimental

    B. objective   D. all-knowing

Literary Analysis: Biography

9. On which aspect of a subject's life would a biography most likely focus?

    A. the personality of the subject's parents

    B. the subject's grades in school

    C. the subject's career

    D. the subject's children

10. Which of these statements about biography is correct?

    A. Biography is the true story of a person's life told by that person.

    B. Biography is a form of fiction about a person's life.

    C. Biography rarely requires research.

    D. Biography interprets information about the subject's life.

11. Which of the following are characteristics of fiction?

    A. characters and plot   C. plot and facts

    B. narrator and facts   D. narrator and plot

Reading Skill: Main Idea and Supporting Details

12. Which of the following questions would help you determine the main idea of a reading selection?

    A. What conclusion does the author reach?

    B. What is the author's tone?

    C. How many details does the author include?

    D. What syntax does the author use?

13. Which of the following strategies would you use to determine the main topic of a selection?

    A. outlining

    B. rereading

    C. paraphrasing

    D. graphing

Name _____ Date _____

Read the selection. Then, answer the questions that follow.

[1] Butterflies are a wonderful addition to any garden if you can attract them, and they are absolutely free. [2] Who doesn't love butterflies? [3] The first element to consider is color. [4] Butterflies love red, yellow, and pink flowers. [5] They also go for white and purple. [6] Pay attention to bloom times. [7] Make sure at least one kind of flower is blooming in the garden all summer so the butterflies stay in your garden. [8] The plants you choose should provide nectar and a comfortable perch for your butterfly guests, too. [9] Here are a few plants that butterflies love: rock cress, sweet William, candytuft, lavender, primrose, lilac, and, of course, butterfly bush.

14. Which sentence states the main idea?
    A. 1
    B. 5
    C. 7
    D. 8

15. Which sentence contains a detail that does not support the main idea?
    A. 1
    B. 2
    C. 3
    D. 4

16. Which sentence gives the most specific details?
    A. 1
    B. 3
    C. 5
    D. 9

17. Which of the following titles would be the best one for this selection?
    A. Butterflies
    B. Colorful Gardens All Season Long
    C. Butterfly Gardens
    D. Who Doesn't Love Butterflies?

18. Which of the following details would help you grow a successful butterfly garden?
    A. what time of day butterflies like to eat
    B. what kind of butterflies live in your area
    C. when the plants mentioned in the selection bloom
    D. how much the various kinds of plants cost

Reading Skill: Generate Relevant Questions

19. When might generating relevant questions be most helpful?
    A. when you read a novel
    B. when you read a short story
    C. when you read a journal entry
    D. when you read a technical document

20. Which element in a technical document is most likely to provide the information you need?
    A. a diagram
    B. the author's name
    C. the main idea sentence
    D. the title

21. If you were reading about how to build a fire in the woods, which question would be most relevant?
    A. What temperature is a blue flame?
    B. What is the difference between a grease fire and an electrical fire?
    C. What can you use to get your fire started?
    D. What can you cook over an open flame?

Grammar

22. Which sentence uses *ball* as a direct object?
    A. The red ball flew into the neighbor's yard.
    B. I gave the little boy a red ball.
    C. The size of the ball made it hard to throw.
    D. The most popular toy was a large ball.

23. Which word in the following sentence is an indirect object?

    Shawn gave his best friend his locker combination.

    A. friend
    B. locker
    C. Shawn
    D. combination

24. What is the direct object in the following sentence?

    Juan bought a new car for his mother.

    A. Juan
    B. car
    C. mother
    D. new

25. Which of the following sentences contains a predicate nominative?
    A. Susan told Ms. Anderson that she had forgotten her homework.
    B. Ms. Anderson lectured the class for half an hour.
    C. Ms. Anderson was my ninth-grade biology teacher.
    D. Ms. Anderson is extremely patient and understanding.

26. Which sentence uses *beautiful* as a predicate adjective?
    A. The day was so beautiful that we had class outside.
    B. All the girls were envious of Lilly's beautiful natural blond hair.
    C. The most beautiful painting was not for sale.
    D. The book was dedicated "to my beautiful daughter."

27. Which part of speech was combined to join the following two choppy sentences?
    The latest model is sleek. It is fast.
    The latest model is sleek and fast.
    A. compound predicative adjective
    B. compound verb
    C. compound object
    D. compound predicative nominative

28. Which part of speech was combined to join the following two choppy sentences?
    Sheila bought orange towels. She bought orange curtains.
    Sheila bought orange towels and curtains.
    A. compound verb
    B. compound object
    C. compound predicative nominative
    D. compound predicative adjective

29. Which part of speech was combined to join the following two choppy sentences?
    Randall huffed when he climbed stairs. He panted when he ran.
    Randall huffed when he climbed stairs and panted when he ran.
    A. compound verb
    B. compound object
    C. compound predicative nominative
    D. compound predicative adjective

30. Which part of speech was combined to join the following three choppy sentences?
    My little sister is a pest. She is also a sneak. She is also a whiner.
    My little sister is a pest, a sneak, and a whiner.
    A. compound verb
    B. compound object
    C. compound predicative nominative
    D. compound predicative adjective

Vocabulary: Word Roots

31. In the following sentence, what is the meaning of the word *revived*?
    Rising fuel costs and concerns about pollution have revived public interest in alternate energy sources.
    A. overshadowed
    B. renewed
    C. upstaged
    D. insisted

32. In which of the following sentences is the word *duration* used correctly?
   A. Forests and fields are often cleared through the process of duration.
   B. The duration of funds is determined by the numeric value printed on them.
   C. Most bears hibernate for the duration of winter, but may come out to feed if the weather is mild.
   D. There was much controversy over the duration of the old stadium – the fans were disappointed to hear it was to be destroyed.

33. In the following sentence, what does the word *endurance* mean?

Physical endurance, skill, and commitment are all necessary to be a professional athlete.

   A. ability   C. agility
   B. speed   D. strength

34. The words *temporal*, *temporary*, and *tempo* contain the root word *temp*. What is the meaning of the root *temp*?
   A. distance   C. climate
   B. time   D. mood

35. In the following sentence, what is the meaning of the word *temperate*?

San Diego and Tahiti both have temperate climates which greatly reduces the need for heat and air conditioning in homes and businesses.

   A. moderate   C. excessive
   B. enjoyable   D. variable

36. In which of the following sentences is the word *diffusion* used correctly?
   A. The students were asked to join a serious diffusion concerning where their prom would be held.
   B. The bomb squad was called in to handle the diffusion of the bomb.
   C. The distribution of dandelion seeds by wind is a good example of diffusion.
   D. The densely compressed particles of metals best explain the process of diffusion.

ESSAY

37. Write the script for a radio advertisement for your favorite brand of jeans. Make your main point very clear and provide sufficient detail to support it.

38. Someone you look up to has just written his or her autobiography. He or she has asked you to write the book jacket copy for the book. Write a brief paragraph that includes why you admire the person and why a reader should want to read the autobiography.

39. The super-fashionable and super-expensive gym shoes you bought last week have started to fall apart. The laces are unraveling, too. Write a business letter to the manufacturer of the shoes. Present your complaint in a calm, businesslike manner, yet forcefully enough to convince the company to send you a new pair of shoes or a refund. Remember to use business letter format and include all the parts of a business letter.

Name _____

Unit 3: Types of Nonfiction Skills Concept Map—2
Is knowledge the same as understanding?

Literary Analysis:
Types of Nonfiction

Words you can use
to discuss the Big
Question

Reading Skills and Strategies:
Persuasive Techniques

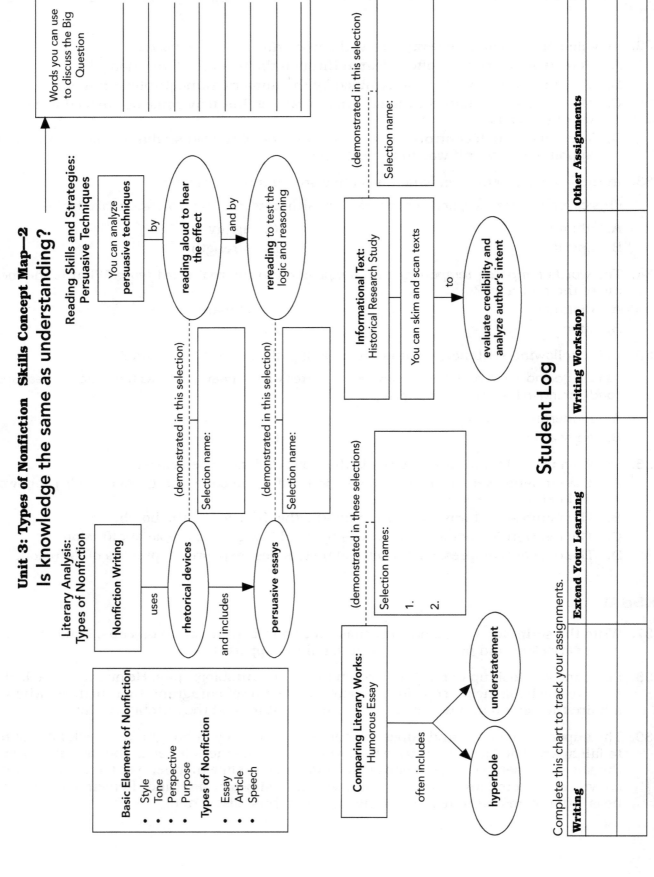

You can analyze
persuasive techniques

by

**reading aloud to hear
the effect**

and by

rereading to test the
logic and reasoning

(demonstrated in this selection)

Selection name:

Nonfiction Writing

uses

rhetorical devices

and includes

persuasive essays

(demonstrated in this selection)

Selection name:

(demonstrated in this selection)

Selection name:

Basic Elements of Nonfiction

- Style
- Tone
- Perspective
- Purpose

Types of Nonfiction

- Essay
- Article
- Speech

Comparing Literary Works:
Humorous Essay

often includes

understatement

hyperbole

(demonstrated in these selections)

Selection names:

1.
2.

Informational Text:
Historical Research Study

You can skim and scan texts

to

**evaluate credibility and
analyze author's intent**

(demonstrated in this selection)

Selection name:

Student Log

Complete this chart to track your assignments.

Writing	Extend Your Learning	Writing Workshop	Other Assignments

"Carry Your Own Skis" by Lian Dolan
Vocabulary Warm-up Word Lists

Study these words from "Carry Your Own Skis." Then, complete the activities.

Word List A

applying [uh PLY ing] *n.* act of making a formal request
   Applying to college often requires writing an essay.

assignment [uh SYN muhnt] *n.* task that is given to someone
   I had to do research to complete the homework assignment.

attitude [A ti tood] *n.* feelings or opinions you have about something or someone
   A positive attitude can help you get through hard times.

concept [KAHN sept] *n.* idea
   The director had an interesting concept for her new movie.

involves [in VAHLVZ] *v.* includes, entails, requires
   My new job involves greeting visitors and answering the telephone.

occasional [uh KAY zhuh nuhl] *adj.* happening sometimes, but not often
   Despite an occasional disagreement, the brothers usually get along very well.

painful [PAYN fuhl] *adj.* hurting, upsetting
   I still have painful memories of the day I got lost in the woods.

typical [TI pi kuhl] *adj.* having the usual qualities of something
   On a typical weekend, I spend several hours playing with my friends.

Word List B

adulthood [uh DUHLT hood] *n.* time when you are a fully grown person
   Most teenagers look forward to reaching adulthood.

cleanup [KLEEN up] *n.* act of making things clean or orderly
   We did a thorough cleanup of our campsite before heading home.

commit [kuh MIT] *v.* to say you will do something
   If you commit to doing the job, you have to finish it.

deadline [DED lyn] *n.* time by which something must be finished
   She finished the project just in time to meet the deadline.

option [AHP shuhn] *n.* choice
   Staying out past midnight is an option that my parents will not discuss.

participate [par TIS uh payt] *v.* take part in something
   They were eager to participate in the new after-school program.

paycheck [PAY chek] *n.* check given to a worker as payment for work done
   My mother deposits her paycheck at the bank on her way home from work.

pursuit [pur SOOT] *n.* act of going after something
   They went to the discount store in pursuit of a bargain.

"Carry Your Own Skis" by Lian Dolan
Vocabulary Warm-up Exercises

Excercise A *Fill in each blank in the paragraph with an appropriate word from Word List A. Use each word only once.*

On a [1] _____ school day, I have math first thing in the morning. Last night, however, I had trouble completing the math homework [2] _____. I considered [3] _____ for the special tutoring program but that [4] _____ staying late after school several times a week. The mere thought of missing soccer practice to study math is [5] _____ to me! Fortunately, I understood the homework problems better the next morning when the teacher explained the fundamental [6] _____ that the problems were based on. I asked the teacher if I could pay her an [7] _____ visit for help instead of going for daily tutoring. She said that my request for help showed that I had an excellent [8] _____ and she said to stop by any time.

Exercise B *Answer the questions with complete explanations.*

1. How will you know when you have achieved *adulthood*?

   _____

2. After a barbecue, what is the worst part of *cleanup*?

   _____

3. What happens if you *commit* to serving on a committee and then change your mind?

   _____

4. If you have a *deadline* for completing a report, can you start working on it whenever you want?

   _____

5. If you have the *option* of attending a club meeting, do you have to go?

   _____

6. Why would someone *participate* in planning the school yearbook?

   _____

7. Does a person need a job in order to receive a *paycheck*?

   _____

8. Can you be in *pursuit* of something you already have?

   _____

Name _____ Date _____

"Carry Your Own Skis" by Lian Dolan
Reading Warm-up A

Read the following passage. Pay special attention to the underlined words. Then, read it again, and complete the activities. Use a separate sheet of paper for your written answers.

Skiing began back in the Stone Age. It was a means of transportation for people who lived in snow-covered regions of the world. Rock carvings show that skis were also used thousands of years ago by hunters looking for game. The first skis were probably made of large animal bones.

Most likely, the concept of skiing as a sport arose first in Norway. It became an event in the Winter Olympics of 1924. The Olympic competition now involves such events as downhill racing, ski jumping, and cross-country racing. Anyone interested in trying out for the Olympic ski team should be prepared to train long and hard in order to qualify.

Before the 1920s, the typical skier was a brave and hardy soul who risked life and limb to ski in the European Alps. Millions of people now enjoy downhill and cross-country skiing. Better equipment and new techniques have made skiing safer and more enjoyable. Learning to ski no longer has to be a painful experience. It can be a lot of fun if you approach it with the proper attitude. Of course, beginners still have to expect an occasional fall while they are learning. Even the experts tumble once in a while. That is why it is a good idea to learn the basics on level ground and not on top of a mountain!

Be sure to take a few lessons from a licensed instructor before you ski for the first time. A beginner's first assignment will be to learn how to balance. Try lifting one ski a few inches off the ground to see how your body adjusts its balance. The next task that you will need to take on is learning how to stop. Slow down by pressing the front tips of your skis together. Keep practicing and try not to get discouraged. Before long, you will be ready to hit the slopes! If you become an expert, you may just decide that applying for a job as a ski instructor is the best route to go.

1. Circle the word that tells where the concept of skiing as a sport probably began. Write a sentence using the word **concept**.

2. Circle three events that the Olympic competition now involves. Explain what **involves** means.

3. Circle two adjectives that describe a typical skier before the 1920s. Describe a **typical** ninth-grader.

4. Circle the words that tell what no longer had to be a painful experience. Describe a **painful** experience.

5. Circle the words that tell what learning to ski can be if you have the proper attitude. What do you think the proper **attitude** toward learning to ski would be?

6. Circle the words in the next sentence that give a hint to the meaning of occasional. Write about an **occasional** event in your life.

7. Underline the word in the paragraph that could be a synonym for assignment. What **assignment** have you enjoyed recently?

8. Underline the words that tell what an expert might be applying for. Write a sentence about **applying** for something.

"**Carry Your Own Skis**" by Lian Dolan
Reading Warm-up B

Read the following passage. Pay special attention to the underlined words. Then, read it again, and complete the activities. Use a separate sheet of paper for your written answers.

Randy had always been a lazy kid. His homework was never ready when it was supposed to be. No matter how far off the <u>deadline</u> was, Randy had an excuse for missing the due date. If you asked him to <u>commit</u> to any kind of project, he always had a reason not to do it. When it was time to take responsibility for his mistakes, Randy always blamed someone else for whatever had gone wrong.

Randy was constantly in <u>pursuit</u> of a good time. His ability to avoid hard work was well known. Randy loved to eat, but he was never around when it was time to shop, cook, or help with the <u>cleanup</u> after a meal. Given the <u>option</u> to work or play, Randy chose play every time. If you invited him to a party, Randy was never too busy to attend, but if you asked him to <u>participate</u> in a carwash, he always had something else to do.

Somehow, Randy managed to get through high school and even to complete a few years of college. Unfortunately, <u>adulthood</u> proved to be a much greater challenge than childhood had ever been. Randy was shocked to learn that his employers actually expected him to do a day's work for a day's pay. He soon realized that they were not as forgiving as his teachers had been when he offered them his lame excuses for not getting the job done. Randy quickly discovered that he was going to have to take his responsibilities a lot more seriously if he wanted to earn his weekly <u>paycheck</u>.

Unfortunately, taking responsibility was not a skill that Randy had ever been very good at.

Randy was hired and fired many times before he started figuring out that his old tricks just were not working anymore. One day, he looked at himself in a mirror and realized that the time had come to change his ways.

"I can do it," he told himself. "I can take charge of my own life."

That was the day Randy finally understood that growing up meant more than just growing older.

1. Underline the sentence that gives an example of missing a <u>deadline</u>. Write about a *deadline* you have had to meet.

2. Underline the words that tell to what Randy was unwilling to <u>commit</u>. Write about something you have been asked to *commit* to.

3. Circle the words that tell what Randy was in <u>pursuit</u> of. Explain what *pursuit* means.

4. Circle the words that tell when the <u>cleanup</u> took place. Why do you think Randy was never around for the *cleanup*?

5. Circle the word that tells which <u>option</u> Randy always chose. Describe an *option* that you have been given. What did you do?

6. Circle the words that tell what someone might ask Randy to <u>participate</u> in. What sort of activities do you like to *participate* in?

7. Circle the word that means the opposite of <u>adulthood</u>. What event in a person's life might represent the beginning of *adulthood*?

8. Circle the word that tells how often Randy received his <u>paycheck</u>. Write a sentence using *paycheck*.

Name _____ Date _____

Writing About the Big Question

Is knowledge the same as understanding?

Big Question Vocabulary

ambiguous	clarify	comprehend	concept	connection
fact	feeling	information	insight	instinct
interpret	research	senses/sensory	sources	statistics

A. *Use one or more words from the list above to complete each sentence.*

1. Emily understands the _____ of carrying her own skis.

2. Her _____ is that people who don't know how to take care of themselves won't be successful.

3. Dolan uses an example to help people _____ her meaning.

4. Albert will try to _____ his understanding by asking for facts.

B. *Follow the directions in responding to each item below.*

1. Describe an experience you have found meaningful.

   _____

   _____

2. How did the experience you describe above teach you a lesson about life? Use at least two Big Question vocabulary words in your answer.

   _____

   _____

C. *In "Carry Your Own Skis," the author draws an analogy between carrying your own skis and taking responsibility for yourself. Complete the sentence below. Then, write a short paragraph in which you connect this experience to the Big Question.*

Personal responsibility is a concept that many people do not understand because

_____

_____

_____

_____

_____

_____

_____

131

"Carry Your Own Skis" by Lian Dolan
Literary Analysis: Persuasive Essay

A **persuasive essay** is a short nonfiction work that tries to persuade a reader to think or act in a particular way. Persuasive essays usually include one or both of the following:

- **Appeals to reason:** logical arguments based on verifiable evidence, such as facts, statistics, or expert testimony
- **Appeals to emotion:** statements intended to affect listeners' feelings about a subject. These statements often include charged language—words with strong positive or negative associations.

DIRECTIONS: *Use the lines provided to answer the questions about Lian Dolan's persuasive essay.*

1. What opinion or course of action is summed up in the title of the essay, "Carry Your Own Skis"? State the writer's position in your own words.

   _____

   _____

2. In paragraph 2, Dolan mentions luxuries that were not available in the mid-1960s when she learned to ski—for example, valet parking, condos, clothing that keeps you warm and dry. How do these details about what skiing was like in the 1960s support Dolan's main idea?

   _____

   _____

   _____

3. Reread the following excerpt from the essay:

   The real world is riddled with people who have never learned to carry their own skis—the blame-shifters, the no-RSVPers, the coworkers who never participate in those painful group birthdays except if it's their own. I admit it: I don't really get these people.

   In this passage, what are two words or phrases with strong emotional associations? Are these emotional associations positive or negative? Explain your answer.

   _____

   _____

   _____

4. Does Dolan's use of repetition in the essay appeal primarily to reason or to emotion? Write a brief paragraph analyzing the writer's use of repetition. Support your main idea with specific references to the text.

   _____

   _____

   _____

   _____

   _____

"Carry Your Own Skis" by Lian Dolan
Reading: Reread to Analyze and Evaluate Persuasive Appeals

Persuasive appeals in an essay are the arguments the author makes to persuade readers or listeners to think or act in a particular way. To **analyze and evaluate persuasive appeals,** identify passages in which the author makes an argument in support of his or her position. Then, **reread** those passages to test the logic and reasoning of the author's arguments. Ask yourself these questions:

- Is the author's argument supported by evidence, or is it based on faulty assumptions?
- Does the author demonstrate clear connections between ideas, or does the author make leaps in logic?

A. DIRECTIONS: *Answer the following questions about Lian Dolan's use of persuasive appeals in "Carry Your Own Skis."*

1. Reread the first three paragraphs of the essay. Why do you think Dolan chose to begin her essay about the importance of responsibility with a description of how and why her mother and aunt took up skiing?

_____

_____

_____

2. According to Dolan, what are two of the consequences of *not* taking responsibility for yourself and your stuff? How does she support her argument?

_____

_____

_____

3. Reread the next-to-last paragraph in the essay, beginning, "Now I have a life that includes a husband, two children, a dog, a house." What analogy (comparison) does Dolan draw in this paragraph? Does this analogy support her case effectively, in your view? Why or why not?

_____

_____

_____

B. DIRECTIONS: *Think of two more persuasive appeals that Dolan might have included to support her main idea in this persuasive essay. The persuasive appeals might be appeals to reason or appeals to emotion. In the space below, list and comment on two persuasive appeals that you think might effectively support Dolan's main idea.*

_____

_____

_____

_____

Name _____ Date _____

"**Carry Your Own Skis**" by Lian Dolan
Vocabulary Builder

Word List

collective   entailed   forgo   inevitability   potential   riddled

A. DIRECTIONS: *On the line, write the letter of the choice that is the best synonym for each word.*

___ 1. riddled
   A. exposed
   B. permeated
   C. tainted
   D. polished

___ 2. inevitability
   A. certainty
   B. credibility
   C. ambiguity
   D. complexity

___ 3. potential
   A. possibility
   B. desire
   C. probability
   D. withdrawal

___ 4. entailed
   A. required
   B. endured
   C. profited
   D. released

___ 5. collective
   A. individual
   B. supportive
   C. collaborative
   D. substitute

___ 6. forgo
   A. reveal
   B. complain
   C. indulge
   D. abstain

B. WORD STUDY: The Latin root -*potens*- means "able" or "having the essence of." Answer each of the following questions using one of these words containing -*potens*-: *potency, omnipotence, potential.*

1. How can you determine the <u>potency</u> of a medicine?

_____

2. Why might a king believe he has <u>omnipotence</u>?

_____

3. What would you do if a talent scout claimed you had the <u>potential</u> to become a big star?

_____

Name _____ Date _____

Enrichment: Decisive Experiences

In "Carry Your Own Skis," Lian Dolan discusses a decisive experience in her own life: the training in responsibility that her mother gave to her and her siblings. Assume that you are about to write an autobiographical sketch. What are some of the decisive events and experiences that have shaped your attitudes, interests, and goals? Use the chart below to describe three experiences from your own life and to explain their long-term significance. (If you would prefer, you may describe events for a biographical sketch of someone you know or of someone you have learned about in your reading.)

Experience/Event	Significance

Name _____ Date _____

"**Carry Your Own Skis**" by Lian Dolan
Open-Book Test

Short Answer *Write your responses to the questions in this section on the lines provided.*

1. In "Carry Your Own Skis," Lian Dolan says that in the mid-1960s, when her mother learned to ski, "skiing was work." What does she mean by that remark?

   _____

   _____

   _____

2. An author's tone is his or her attitude toward the audience or subject. Tone can be stated in one or two words—for example, friendly, serious, playful, mocking, critical, and/or harsh. What is the tone in this sentence from "Carry Your Own Skis": "At the end of the day, there were no hot toddies by a roaring fire in furry boots or drinks in the hot tub of a slopeside condo"? Explain your response.

   _____

   _____

3. When Lian Dolan's mother and aunt finished their ski runs in "Carry Your Own Skis," they "faced the inevitability of a station wagon with a dead battery and the long, dark drive back home in wet clothes." What is Dolan saying about her mother's return home from her ski trips? Base your answer on the definition of *inevitability.*

   _____

   _____

4. Although "Carry Your Own Skis" is not meant to be a portrait of the writer's mother, a reader can make inferences about Lian Dolan's mother based on the essay. For example, the essay appears to reflect the values that Dolan's mother stressed when she was raising her children. Based on the essay, what value do you think the mother stressed more than most others? Explain.

   _____

   _____

   _____

5. In "Carry Your Own Skis," Lian Dolan declares, "The 'carry your own skis mentality' filtered into almost every area of our life as we were growing up." What does Dolan mean by the "carry your own skis mentality"?

   _____

   _____

6. In "Carry Your Own Skis," Lian Dolan says, "The real world is riddled with people who have never learned to carry their own skis." Does she mean that there are many such people, few of them, or an unknown number? Explain her meaning based on the definition of *riddled*.

_____

_____

7. In "Carry Your Own Skis," Lian Dolan attempts to persuade readers of something. In the process, she makes several claims. Evaluate the claim quoted below by completing this diagram.

Claim: "The real world is riddled with people who have never learned to carry their own skis."	→	**Evidence:**

Evaluation:

8. In "Carry Your Own Skis," Lian Dolan calls some people "blame-shifters" and "no-RSVPers." She says, "I don't really get these people." In that passage, is Dolan appealing to reason or emotion? Cite a detail from the passage to support your answer.

_____

_____

9. Not only is "Carry Your Own Skis" the title of Lian Dolan's essay but the phrase is repeated throughout the essay. By repeating the phrase, is Dolan appealing to reason or emotion? Explain.

_____

_____

10. "Carry Your Own Skis" is a persuasive essay. What is Dolan trying to persuade readers to do or think?

_____

_____

Essay

Write an extended response to the question of your choice or to the question or questions your teacher assigns you.

11. In "Carry Your Own Skis," Lian Dolan uses repetition as a persuasive technique. In an essay, discuss Dolan's use of repetition. Cite at least one example from the essay, and explain how Dolan's use of repetition works as an appeal to reason or emotion. Then, state your opinion of the effectiveness of this technique. Support your opinion with at least one reason.

12. How does the title of Lian Dolan's essay relate to its central message, or main idea? In an essay, identify the main idea of "Carry Your Own Skis." Then discuss the ways in which the author supports her point of view. Does she use appeals to reason, appeals to emotion, or both? Support your points with details from the text.

13. Persuasive essays most often focus on controversial topics: topics on which people have strong differences of opinion. In "Carry Your Own Skis," however, Lian Dolan promotes a message with which few people would disagree: the importance of personal responsibility. In an essay, discuss how Dolan attempts to make her message appealing, believable, and persuasive. Then, state your opinion of whether Dolan succeeds in making her writing fresh and forceful. Provide valid reasons to support your opinion.

14. **Thinking About the Big Question: Is knowledge the same as understanding?** In "Carry Your Own Skis," Lian Dolan shows that she has both knowledge and understanding. In a brief essay, explain how Dolan gained the knowledge involved in the concept of carrying her own skis. Did she understand the concept before she gained the knowledge, or did she gain the knowledge first and then come to understand it? Support your points with a reference to the text.

Oral Response

15. Go back to question 2, 7, or 10 or to the question your teacher assigns you. Take a few minutes to expand your answer and prepare an oral response. Find additional details in "Carry Your Own Skis" that support your points. If necessary, make notes to guide your oral response.

Name _____ Date _____

Critical Reading *Identify the letter of the choice that best answers the question.*

____ 1. In "Carry Your Own Skis," when did the author's mother start skiing?
  A. when she was a very young child
  B. when she was a teenager
  C. when she was forty years old
  D. when she became a grandmother

____ 2. What does Lian Dolan mean in "Carrying Your Own Skis" when she says that "skiing was work"?
  A. Skiing was not at all enjoyable.
  B. Skiers then did not have the conveniences they have now.
  C. Skiing was a very expensive sport, and you had to work hard to pay for it.
  D. Many young people had jobs working in ski lodges and on ski slopes.

____ 3. Which of the following best describes the author's tone, or attitude, in this passage from "Carry Your Own Skis"?

  At the end of the day, there were no hot toddies by a roaring fire in furry boots or drinks in the hot tub of a slopeside condo.

  A. respectful
  B. romantic
  C. slightly mocking
  D. factual

____ 4. According to Dolan, why did her mother and her aunt learn to ski?
  A. They wanted to enjoy free time together.
  B. They wanted to escape their chores at home.
  C. They wanted to get some exercise outdoors.
  D. They wanted to teach their children to ski.

____ 5. From Lian Dolan's description, which of the following do you think her mother stressed most with her children?
  A. being responsible
  B. improving one's athletic ability
  C. safety on the ski slopes
  D. fun on the ski slopes

____ 6. Which of the following does a persuasive essay usually contain?
   A. appeals to reason and emotion
   B. direct address of the reader
   C. chronological order
   D. sensory language

____ 7. What does "'carry your own skis' mentality" mean in this passage from Dolan's essay?

   The "carry your own skis" mentality filtered into almost every area of our life as we were growing up.

   A. Work hard and you will be rewarded.
   B. Be responsible for yourself.
   C. Live every day one day at a time.
   D. Be cautious about taking risks.

____ 8. What is the writer's purpose in a persuasive essay, such as "Carry Your Own Skis"?
   A. to inform the audience of specific facts
   B. to express the writer's feelings
   C. to entertain readers with an exciting narrative
   D. to persuade readers to think or act in a certain way

____ 9. In "Carry Your Own Skis," the writer uses the words "blame-shifters" and "no-RSVPers." What tone, or attitude, do these words convey?
   A. positive
   B. negative
   C. neutral
   D. puzzled

____ 10. How can you best evaluate the persuasive appeals in any persuasive essay?
   A. Look for references in the text to other authors who agree with the writer.
   B. Keep an open mind till you reach the end of the essay.
   C. Test the logic and reasoning of the author's arguments.
   D. Compare and contrast the appeals to reason and the appeals to emotion.

____ 11. Which of the following quotations best states the main idea of "Carry Your Own Skis"?
   A. "Be responsible for yourself and your stuff or you miss out."
   B. "As a result, I was invited to go on a lot of camping trips."
   C. "I can still feel the damp long underwear and the wet wool during the endless ride home."
   D. "But whether I liked to ski or not didn't really matter."

Vocabulary and Grammar

___ 12. How would you feel about an <u>inevitability</u>?
    A. doubtful
    B. hesitant
    C. very certain
    D. amused

___ 13. If your tennis coach tells you that you have <u>potential</u>, what will your reaction be?
    A. fear
    B. pleasure
    C. disgust
    D. disappointment

___ 14. Which of the following do adjectives describe?
    A. adverbs and verbs
    B. conjunctions
    C. prepositions
    D. nouns and pronouns

___ 15. Which words are adjectives in this sentence from "Carry Your Own Skis"?
    I can still feel the damp long underwear and the wet wool during the endless ride home.
    A. damp, wool, home
    B. damp, long, wet, endless
    C. feel, wet, during, home
    D. damp, long, ride, home

Essay

16. In "Carry Your Own Skis," Lian Dolan uses repetition as a persuasive appeal. In an essay, discuss the writer's use of repetition, mentioning specific examples from the text. In your essay, explain why you think Dolan's use of repetition appeals to reason, to emotion, or to a mixture of both.

17. The first part of Dolan's essay "Carry Your Own Skis" deals with skiing. The second part of her essay deals with many other experiences in her life. In an essay, explain how Dolan makes use of her mother's rule—"carry your own skis"—in the second part of her essay. Give two specific examples of how she applied the rule off the ski slopes in her teenage and adult life. Then, tell what her persuasive essay aims to persuade her readers to believe or do.

18. **Thinking About the Big Question: Is knowledge the same as understanding?** In "Carry Your Own Skis," Lian Dolan writes that she recognized that some people did not show personal responsibility. In a brief essay, explain how Dolan gained the knowledge that she should carry her own skis. Then, explain how this lesson helped her to understand the idea of personal responsibility. Support your points with information from her persuasive essay.

Name _____ Date _____

"**Carry Your Own Skis**" by Lian Dolan
Selection Test B

Critical Reading *Identify the letter of the choice that best completes the statement or answers the question.*

_____ 1. When she asserts that in the mid-sixties "skiing was work," Dolan evidently means
A. that skiing was an extremely disagreeable and arduous sport.
B. that skiers then lacked many of the conveniences we now take for granted.
C. that skiing was costly and few people could afford the equipment and fees.
D. that skiers came largely from the working class.

_____ 2. Which of the following best describes the writer's tone in this passage from "Carry Your Own Skis"?

Forgo that last run of the day in near darkness, cold and alone and crying because your siblings have skied on ahead without you? Who'd want to miss all that fun?

A. nostalgic
B. ironic
C. enthusiastic
D. factual

_____ 3. Dolan says that the reason her mother and her aunt learned to ski was to
A. enjoy their leisure time together at Powder Hill.
B. escape the responsibilities of their daily routines.
C. get some strenuous outdoor exercise.
D. take their collective children skiing.

_____ 4. From Lian Dolan's description of how she learned to ski, you can infer that her mother emphasized which of the following with her children?
A. responsibility
B. proficiency
C. safety
D. dependence

_____ 5. To support her statement that "No one wanted to get left in the lodge," Dolan uses a series of parallel passages, like the following:

Miss the lunches of soggy tuna fish sandwiches and mini chocolate bars? No way!

This passage is an example of
A. an extended metaphor.
B. a series of symbols.
C. a humorous rhetorical question.
D. foreshadowing.

_____ 6. Which of the following does a persuasive essay usually include?
A. both strong and weak arguments
B. appeals to reason and emotion
C. figurative language and symbols
D. a chronological survey of the topic

_____ 7. Which of the following best expresses what Lian Dolan means by "'carry your own skis' mentality"?
   A. Don't be afraid of hard work as you strive to reach your goals.
   B. Be responsible for yourself and don't expect others to take care of you.
   C. Analyze every challenge and solve a problem one step at a time.
   D. Before you plunge into a new enterprise, explore what you need to know.

_____ 8. Read the following excerpt from "Carry Your Own Skis."

> But me? I would sign up to make the PB&Js and to clean up the mess. I'd load the canoes onto the truck and take 'em off again. And the tent? I'd put it up and I'd take it down. I didn't know any different. As a result, I was invited to go on a lot of camping trips. The lodge and back, baby—that was my attitude.

Which of the following best describes the author's style in this passage?
   A. elevated and serious
   B. emotionally charged
   C. colloquial and breezy
   D. formal and solemn

_____ 9. Which of the following does a persuasive essay typically have as its goal?
   A. to inform the audience about a specific topic
   B. to express the feelings of the writer about a specific topic
   C. to entertain the audience with a suspenseful or amusing narrative
   D. to persuade readers to believe something or to act in a particular way

_____ 10. In "Carry Your Own Skis," the author says that she really doesn't "get" people like the "blame-shifters" and the "no-RSVPers." Which of the following best describes the language she uses?
   A. positively charged
   B. negatively charged
   C. ambiguous
   D. neutral

_____ 11. One helpful way to evaluate the persuasive appeals in a persuasive essay is to
   A. see if the author quotes other writers who agree with the writer's position.
   B. refrain from making up your mind until you finish reading the essay.
   C. evaluate the logic and reasoning of the author's arguments.
   D. compare and contrast the writer's appeals to reason and to emotion.

_____ 12. In her essay, Lian Dolan most likely repeats variations of the phrase "carry your own skis" in order to
   A. reinforce the persuasive emotional appeal of her central metaphor.
   B. emphasize how much she appreciated learning how to ski as a child.
   C. highlight the importance of doing activities together as a family.
   D. stress how irresponsibly her siblings behaved sometimes.

____ 13. In "Carry Your Own Skis," how does Lian Dolan support her main idea?
   A. with facts and statistics
   B. with examples from her own life
   C. with examples from other people's lives
   D. with quotations from experts

Vocabulary and Grammar

____ 14. If your theory is *riddled* with flaws, how might it be described?
   A. slightly inconsistent
   B. realistic
   C. logically inadequate
   D. only partially valid

____ 15. What are the adjectives in this sentence from "Carry Your Own Skis"?

   My mother had the responsibility for her gear, the giant lunch, the car, and the occasional trip to the ER for broken legs.

   A. responsibility, lunch
   B. gear, occasional, legs
   C. my, her, giant, occasional, broken
   D. giant, trip, legs

____ 16. Read the following sentence.

   Ticket buyers were expected to side step up and down slopes and herringbone the lift lines.

   Which words in the sentence are nouns used as adjectives?
   A. *buyers* and *slopes*
   B. *ticket* and *lines*
   C. *ticket* and *lift*
   D. *side step* and *herringbone*

Essay

17. How does the title of Lian Dolan's "Carry Your Own Skis" relate to the writer's central message? In an essay, identify the theme of this selection and then discuss the ways in which the author supports her point of view. Does she use appeals to reason, appeals to emotion, or a mixture of both? Support your main ideas with specific references to the text.

18. Persuasive essays most often focus on controversial topics on which people can have legitimate differences of opinion. In "Carry Your Own Skis," however, Lian Dolan promotes a message with which few people would disagree: the necessity for individual responsibility. What specific details does Dolan select in order to give her essay audience appeal, credibility, and persuasive power? In an essay, discuss how Dolan manages to make her writing fresh and forceful.

19. **Thinking About the Big Question: Is knowledge the same as understanding?** In "Carry Your Own Skis," Lian Dolan shows that she had both knowledge and understanding. In a brief essay, explain how Dolan gained the knowledge involved in the concept of carrying her own skis. Did she understand the concept before she gained the knowledge, or did she gain the knowledge first and then come to understand it? Support your points with a reference to the text.

"Libraries Face Sad Chapters" by Pete Hamill
Vocabulary Warm-up Word Lists

Study these words from "Libraries Face Sad Chapters." Then, complete the activities that follow.

Word List A

civilization [siv i luh ZAY shuhn] *n.* society that is well organized and developed
  Computer technology and the Internet are just two contributions to <u>civilization</u>.

combined [kuhm BYND] *adj.* two or more things joined together
  Their <u>combined</u> income was not enough to afford the new car.

illustrations [il uh STRAY shuhnz] *n.* pictures in a book
  The <u>illustrations</u> in the new edition of this book are all in color.

powerful [POW er fuhl] *adj.* strong; effective
  He felt a <u>powerful</u> urge to get up and leave.

presumed [pri ZOOMD] *v.* accepted as true until proven otherwise
  We <u>presumed</u> that the meeting would end on time.

recited [ri SYT id] *v.* read aloud in public or spoke aloud
  Our teacher <u>recited</u> the poem from memory.

reduced [ri DOOST] *v.* decreased in number
  The size of our class was <u>reduced</u> when two students moved away.

volumes [VOL yoomz] *n.* books or issues of a magazine
  This one leather <u>volume</u> had ten copies of our favorite magazine in it.

Word List B

aura [AW ruh] *n.* quality or feeling that seems to come from a person or place
  He had an <u>aura</u> of mystery about him.

circulating [SUHR kyoo layt ing] *adj.* moving from person to person or place to place
  The <u>circulating</u> documents were passed from desk to desk.

establishment [i STAB lish muhnt] *n.* act of setting up or starting something
  We raised enough money for the <u>establishment</u> of a community center.

imaginative [i MAJ uh nuh tiv] *adj.* containing new and interesting ideas
  Everyone enjoyed her <u>imaginative</u> story.

moral [MAWR uhl] *adj.* having to do with right and wrong
  His conscience bothered him when he made the wrong <u>moral</u> decision.

pledge [PLEJ] *n.* promise
  We made a <u>pledge</u> to get more exercise this year.

teeming [TEEM ing] *adj.* packed, crowded
  The playground, <u>teeming</u> with children, was the noisiest spot in the park.

voluntary [VAHL uhn ter ee] *adj.* done willingly, without being forced
  Attendance was <u>voluntary</u>, but we decided to go anyway.

Name _____ Date _____

Exercise A *Fill in each blank in the paragraph with an appropriate word from Word List A.*
Use each word only once.

My father often said that the love of literature is the mark of [1] _____.
He always [2] _____ that his children would grow up loving to read. He
[3] _____ poetry to us from the time we were babies. Long before we
could read, we enjoyed looking at the charming [4] _____ that enlivened
the pages of many [5] _____ that lined our bookshelves at home. Our
mother also had a [6] _____ effect on our love of literature. She wrote
many of the poems that my father read, and their [7] _____ influence on
us was truly remarkable. I considered many careers when I was growing up, but my
choices were eventually [8] _____ to just one. To no one's surprise, I
became a writer.

Exercise B *Decide whether each statement is true or false. Circle* T *or* F, *and explain your*
answers.

1. If there is an *aura* of excitement in the room, everyone is bored.
   T / F _____

2. When books are *circulating,* only one person gets to see them.
   T / F _____

3. Congress is responsible for the *establishment* of new laws.
   T / F _____

4. An interesting writer is likely to be an *imaginative* person.
   T / F _____

5. It is a bad idea to live a *moral* life.
   T / F _____

6. You should think carefully before making a *pledge.*
   T / F _____

7. The oceans are *teeming* with fish.
   T / F _____

8. If club dues are *voluntary,* everyone has to pay.
   T / F _____

"Libraries Face Sad Chapters" by Pete Hamill
Reading Warm-up A

Read the following passage. Pay special attention to the underlined words. Then, read it again, and complete the activities. Use a separate sheet of paper for your written answers.

Paul found himself lying on the floor in the science fiction section of the public library.

He stood up slowly and glanced at the many volumes that lined the library shelves. Paul had read a huge number of these books, and some of them had had a powerful influence on the way he thought about things.

Paul presumed that he was in the middle of a dream. He figured it was probably the combined effect of eating a pepperoni pizza and staying up much too late to finish the new fantasy novel he had borrowed the week before.

He really did not mind this dream, though. Paul loved the library, and he loved science fiction. He gazed at the books that surrounded him and carefully recited their titles out loud, feeling as if he were among old friends.

Then, he picked up a graphic novel he had never seen before. The color illustrations were dazzling, but it was the story that attracted him. It took place in a world whose people believed that they had reached the very highest level of civilization. War and crime were nonexistent. Robots did all the work, while people passed the time sitting around and listening to music. Strangest of all, there were no libraries in this world. The people did not think they needed books. All of their knowledge and wisdom had been reduced to a single sentence that was engraved on a marble column in the center of their capital city. Paul quickly flipped to the last page of the book, and his heart began to pound as he prepared to read the words on the marble column.

Then, he heard a familiar ringing. He struggled to ignore his alarm clock long enough to read the words on the column, but the page before him had already begun to fade. "*Wait!*" he thought, but waiting was impossible. Paul opened his eyes and shut off the alarm. He thought about the strange dream, took a deep breath, and shook his head in wonder.

"A world without libraries," he thought. "What a nightmare!"

1. Underline the words that tell what the volumes did. Where else might *volumes* be found?

2. Underline the words that tell what the books had a powerful influence on. Tell about a book that had a *powerful* influence on you.

3. Underline the words that tell what Paul presumed. Write a sentence using *presumed*.

4. Underline the words that tell of what things Paul thought he was feeling the combined effects. What does *combined* mean?

5. Circle the word that tells what Paul recited. Tell about something you have *recited*.

6. Circle two words that describe the illustrations. Write about *illustrations* that you have enjoyed.

7. Circle two words that would be part of a civilization. Describe a society that had truly reached the very highest level of *civilization*.

8. Underline the words that tell what had been reduced to a single sentence. Write a single sentence that you would have *reduced* this to.

Name _____ Date _____

"Libraries Face Sad Chapters" by Pete Hamill
Reading Warm-up B

Read the following passage. Pay special attention to the underlined words. Then, read it again, and complete the activities. Use a separate sheet of paper for your written answers.

No one knows exactly when the first library was founded. People began writing down information and ideas thousands of years ago. The earliest records were kept on clay tablets and scrolls of papyrus, an ancestor of paper. Almost 2,000 years ago, the rulers of ancient Egypt borrowed papyrus scrolls from distant lands and made copies of them. The <u>establishment</u> of the Alexandrian Library made Alexandria, Egypt, a great center of culture and learning. The library, <u>teeming</u> with information, contained more than 700,000 scrolls.

Unlike the <u>circulating</u> books you borrow from your school or public library, these scrolls never left the building. Scholars came from far and wide to study the scrolls. An <u>aura</u> of wonder hung over this very special place where educated people could gather to study and to teach. Here they could discover new facts. They also could learn about the <u>moral</u> teachings of philosophers and religious leaders from distant lands.

Over the centuries, <u>imaginative</u> people around the world have come up with new and better ways to preserve and share the written word. The invention of paper in China around 100 B.C. made books easier and less costly to produce. In the 1400s, a German printer named Gutenberg figured out how to print books with movable type. As books became available and more people learned to read, libraries began sprouting up around the world.

The oldest library in the United States was started at Harvard University in 1638. A century later, Benjamin Franklin founded the first subscription library in the country. For a small fee, subscribers could borrow books in exchange for their solemn <u>pledge</u> to return the books to the library when they had finished reading them. Other libraries supported themselves with <u>voluntary</u> donations from the people who used them. The first tax-supported free libraries in the United States appeared in the early 1800s. Today, public libraries can be found in almost every community in the nation.

1. Underline the words that tell what the <u>establishment</u> of the Alexandrian Library did. Rewrite the sentence using a synonym for **establishment**.

2. Underline the words that tell what was <u>teeming</u> in the library. Describe something you know that is **teeming** with something.

3. Underline the words that tell how these scrolls were different from <u>circulating</u> books. Write a sentence about something else that might be described as **circulating**.

4. Circle the word that identifies the library's <u>aura</u>. What is an **aura**?

5. Underline the words that tell whose <u>moral</u> teachings could be learned. How are **moral** teachings different from facts?

6. Underline the words that tell what <u>imaginative</u> people came up with. Why might these people be described as **imaginative**?

7. Underline the words that identify the subscribers' <u>pledge</u>. What **pledge** have you taken?

8. Underline the words that tell who made <u>voluntary</u> donations. Write a word that means the opposite of **voluntary**.

Name _____ Date _____

Writing About the Big Question

Is knowledge the same as understanding?

Big Question Vocabulary

ambiguous	clarify	comprehend	concept	connection
fact	feeling	information	insight	instinct
interpret	research	senses/sensory	sources	statistics

A. *Use one or more words from the list above to complete each sentence.*

1. _____ alone only tell us facts; they do not help us understand.

2. Libraries are _____ of _____ that leads us toward knowledge and understanding.

3. John went to the library to do _____ on the Carnegie libraries.

4. He wanted to gain _____ into Carnegie's motive for donating so much money.

B. *Follow the directions in responding to each item below.*

1. Describe two recent occasions when you used the library to do research.

   _____

   _____

2. How could you make better use of your time in the library? Give one example. Use at least two of the Big Question vocabulary words.

   _____

   _____

C. *In "Libraries Face Sad Chapter," the author urges readers to contribute to a fund to support public libraries, a source of knowledge. Complete the sentence below. Then, write a short paragraph in which you connect this experience to the Big Question.*

Libraries, as a source of information and a place for research, are still important because _____

_____

_____

_____

_____

_____

_____

Name _____ Date _____

Literary Analysis: Persuasive Essay

A **persuasive essay** is a short nonfiction work that tries to persuade a reader to think or act in a particular way. Persuasive essays usually include one or both of the following:

- **Appeals to reason:** logical arguments based on verifiable evidence, such as facts, statistics, or expert testimony
- **Appeals to emotion:** statements intended to affect listeners' feelings about a subject. These statements often include charged language—words with strong positive or negative associations.

DIRECTIONS: *Answer these questions about Pete Hamill's persuasive essay.*

1. What is Pete Hamill's opinion and suggested course of action in his essay "Libraries Face Sad Chapter"? State the writer's position in your own words.

   _____

   _____

2. Identify two logical arguments Hamill uses to support his case for the importance of libraries and freely circulating books.

   _____

   _____

   _____

   _____

3. Reread the following excerpt from the essay:

   No teacher sent us to those leathery cliffs of books. Reading wasn't an assignment; it was a pleasure. We read for the combined thrills of villainy and heroism, along with the knowledge of the vast world beyond the parish. Living in those other worlds, we could become other people

   In this passage, what are two words or phrases with strong emotional associations? Are these emotional associations positive or negative? Explain your answer.

   _____

   _____

   _____

   _____

4. At the end of his essay on libraries, Hamill stresses a "debt" that must be honored. On the lines below, explain how Hamill conceives of this "debt" and why it does (or does not) constitute an effective conclusion for his persuasive essay.

   _____

   _____

   _____

   _____

"**Libraries Face Sad Chapter**" by Pete Hamill
Reading: Reread to Analyze and Evaluate Persuasive Appeals

Persuasive appeals in an essay are the arguments the author makes to persuade readers or listeners to think or act in a particular way. To **analyze and evaluate persuasive appeals,** identify passages in which the author makes an argument in support of his or her position. Then, **reread** those passages to test the logic and reasoning of the author's arguments. Ask yourself these questions:

- Is the author's argument supported by evidence, or is it based on faulty assumptions?
- Does the author demonstrate clear connections between ideas, or does the author make leaps in logic?

A. DIRECTIONS: *Answer the following questions about Pete Hamill's use of persuasive appeals in "Libraries Face Sad Chapter."*

1. Reread the first section of the essay. Why do you think Hamill chose to open this essay with a reminiscence of how he and his friends used libraries in their childhood?

   _____

   _____

   _____

   _____

2. According to Hamill, why are libraries more important than ever in hard times? In the section "Built by Carnegie," what arguments does Hamill use to support this opinion?

   _____

   _____

   _____

   _____

3. Reread the section entitled "Immigrants' Appreciation." In your opinion, does Hamill appeal primarily to reason or to emotion in this section? Use specific references to the text to explain your answer.

   _____

   _____

   _____

   _____

B. DIRECTIONS: *On the lines below, explain how Hamill uses a mixture of idealism and realism to appeal to his audience. Is this combination effective, in your opinion? Why or why not?*

   _____

   _____

   _____

Name _____ Date _____

Vocabulary Builder

Word List

    curtailed   duration   emulate   medium   presumed   volumes

A. DIRECTIONS: *Revise each sentence so that the underlined vocabulary word is used logically. Be sure not to change the vocabulary word.*

1. We were extremely upset to find out that the <u>duration</u> of the exam was only half an hour.

   _____

2. The championship tennis match was <u>curtailed</u> by rain, leaving the spectators certain about the outcome.

   _____

3. Since e-mail is a rapid and cheap <u>medium</u>, its popularity today is hard to explain.

   _____

4. If the author wrote so many books, why are so many <u>volumes</u> of his work in the library?

   _____

5. We <u>presumed</u> he was going with us, so we left before he met us.

   _____

6. Alexandra likes to <u>emulate</u> her sister, so she never wears the same kind of clothes.

   _____

B. WORD STUDY: The Latin root -*sum*- means "to take." Answer each of the following questions using one of these words containing -*sum*-: *consumer, assumption,* and *resume.*

1. How does a <u>consumer</u> usually get what he or she wants?

   _____

   _____

2. What happened as a result of Columbus's <u>assumption</u> that the world is round?

   _____

   _____

3. When do TV programs <u>resume</u> when commercials interrupt the broadcast?

   _____

   _____

Name _____ Date _____

"Libraries Face Sad Chapter" by Pete Hamill
Enrichment: The Role of Libraries

Comparing libraries to "treasure houses," Pete Hamill focuses on the importance of freely circulating books in our society. Today, however, libraries are far more than collections of books. In numerous communities, libraries are playing a greatly expanded role.

For example, ever since the explosive popularity of the Internet in the 1990s, libraries have become critical links for those who lack the hardware or the technical savvy to go on-line. For some people, their local library serves as an invaluable resource for surfing the Web and sending and receiving e-mail. Most libraries provide this service at no charge, although many libraries have time restrictions. Some libraries offer instruction in Internet literacy: for example, in how to use a search engine.

Libraries have also begun to function as community centers in a variety of ways. For example, they host activities such as weekly card games and bag lunches for seniors; they have developed storytelling hours and puppetry workshops for children; and they organize lectures, slide presentations, charity events, and musical performances for the community at large, utilizing volunteer talent and local resources.

DIRECTIONS: *Research the programs and resources offered by your local library. Conduct your research by making a personal visit, interviewing library employees and members of the public, or browsing the library's Web site. On the lines below, report the results of your research.*

_____
_____
_____
_____
_____
_____
_____
_____
_____
_____
_____
_____
_____
_____

Name _____ Date _____

"**Carry Your Own Skis**" by Lian Dolan
"**Libraries Face Sad Chapter**" by Pete Hamill
Integrated Language Skills: Grammar

Adjectives

An **adjective** is a word used to describe a noun or pronoun or to give a noun or pronoun a more specific meaning. Adjectives modify nouns and pronouns by telling *what kind, which one, how many,* or *how much.* Sometimes a noun, pronoun, or verb may serve as an adjective.

Adjective:	the *typical* lodge (modifies *lodge*)
Noun as Adjective:	a *rope* tow (noun *rope* modifies *tow*)
Pronoun as Adjective:	carried *her* skis (pronoun *her* modifies *skis*)
Verb as Adjective:	children *left* in the lodge (past participle *left* modifies *children*)

A prepositional phrase may function as an adjective: for example, "rows *of picnic tables.*"

A. DIRECTIONS: *Read the following sentences from "Carry Your Own Skis" and "Libraries Face Sad Chapter." Write all the adjectives in each sentence. You can omit the adjectives a, an, and the, but do not forget to list any nouns, pronouns, and verbs used as adjectives.*

1. Getting across the icy parking lot and back seemed a small price to pay for the potential of great fun.

   _____

2. Most days, skiing for me was about freezing rain and constantly trying to catch up to my older, faster, more talented siblings.

   _____

3. We passed into that library between two mock-Corinthian columns that gave the building a majestic aura.

   _____

4. Since those ancient nights around prehistoric campfires, we have needed myth. And heroes. And moral tales.

   _____

B. Writing Application: *Write a brief paragraph describing your school or local library. Include specific details. Use at least five adjectives in your writing and underline each one.*

_____

_____

_____

_____

_____

_____

"Carry Your Own Skis" by Lian Dolan
"Libraries Face Sad Chapter" by Pete Hamill
Integrated Language Skills: Support for Writing an Abstract

For your abstract, use the chart below to jot down notes under each heading.

Topic: _____
_____

Main Idea: _____
_____

Supporting Details:

1. _____
_____
_____

2. _____
_____
_____

3. _____
_____
_____

4. _____
_____
_____

Now, use your notes to write your abstract. Give enough information so that someone who has not yet read the essay can get a clear understanding of what the essay is about.

Name _____ Date _____

"Carry Your Own Skis" by Lian Dolan
"Libraries Face Sad Chapter" by Pete Hamill

Integrated Language Skills: Support for Extend Your Learning

Research and Technology: "Carry Your Own Skis"

Use a format such as the one below for your comparative chart on sports.

Sport	Participation	Audience
1. _____	_____	_____
2. _____	_____	_____
3. _____	_____	_____
4. _____	_____	_____
5. _____	_____	_____

My Source of Information: _____

Summarizing Statement: _____

_____

_____

_____

_____

Research and Technology: "Libraries Face Sad Chapter"

Use the chart below to gather information for your comparative chart on library services.

Library Services	Average Numbers Using Service
1. _____	_____
2. _____	_____
3. _____	_____
4. _____	_____
5. _____	_____

My Source of Information: _____

Summarizing Statement: _____

_____

_____

_____

_____

"Libraries Face Sad Chapter" by Pete Hamill
Open-Book Test

Short Answer *Write your responses to the questions in this section on the lines provided.*

1. In the first seven paragraphs of "Libraries Face Sad Chapter," Pete Hamill lays out the background for his appeal. In that section of the essay, what is the main source of the information the author provides?

   _____

2. In "Libraries Face Sad Chapter," Hamill writes that the services provided by libraries and the hours of operation might be curtailed. Does Hamill see this as a good thing or a bad thing? Explain your answer based on the definition of *curtailed*.

   _____

3. In "Libraries Face Sad Chapter," Pete Hamill uses various claims to try to persuade his readers of something. Analyze the claim quoted below. First, reread the paragraph in which the claim appears (the second paragraph under the heading "Built by Carnegie"). Then, complete the diagram. You may fill in only one box or both boxes. Then, on the line below, state whether the claim is an appeal to reason, an appeal to emotion, or both.

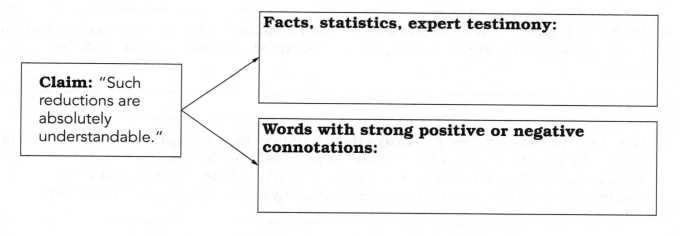

4. What evidence does Pete Hamill offer in "Libraries Face Sad Chapter" to support the idea that young readers might make up a large audience?

   _____

5. Reread the paragraph toward the end of "Libraries Face Sad Chapter" that begins "Today, the libraries of this city are still doing that work." Does Hamill support this argument with evidence or with faulty assumptions? Cite two details to support your answer.

_____

_____

_____

_____

6. In "Libraries Face Sad Chapter," Hamill says that Andrew Carnegie "used his wealth to create more than 1,600 public libraries." What can readers infer about Carnegie based on that information?

_____

7. By bringing up the example of Andrew Carnegie in "Libraries Face Sad Chapter," Pete Hamill makes a point about public libraries in the United States. How does that point relate to Hamill's argument?

_____

_____

8. In the final paragraph of "Libraries Face Sad Chapter," what argument does Hamill use to support his proposal that private citizens should help public libraries survive?

_____

_____

9. Writers of persuasive essays always have a motive for writing their essays. In other words, they have a reason for wanting to persuade readers to think or do something. In "Libraries Face Sad Chapter," what is Pete Hamill's motive for wanting readers to support the public library system during a budget crisis?

_____

_____

10. An author's tone is his or her attitude toward the audience or subject. Tone can be stated in one or two words—for example, friendly, respectful, playful, mocking, critical, and/or harsh. What is Pete Hamill's attitude toward his subject in "Libraries Face Sad Chapter"? Cite one detail from the essay to support your answer.

_____

_____

_____

Essay

Write an extended response to the question of your choice or to the question or questions your teacher assigns you.

11. In "Libraries Face Sad Chapter," Pete Hamill is trying to persuade his readers to do something. In an essay, analyze Hamill's argument. First, state his main idea—the action he wants readers to take. Then, summarize two reasons Hamill gives to try to persuade his readers to take that action. Explain whether each reason is an appeal to reason or an appeal to emotion, and evaluate its effectiveness.

12. In "Libraries Face Sad Chapter," Pete Hamill refers twice to libraries and the imaginative world of books as "treasure houses." Do you think his argument justifies the use of this metaphor? In an essay of your own, explain how Hamill paints a picture of the "treasures" that books can offer their readers. Support your points with references to the text.

13. In "Libraries Face Sad Chapter," Hamill proposes a "voluntary tax" to finance the public libraries for the duration of a budget crisis. What do you think of that proposal? Is the suggestion practical? Does it strengthen Hamill's other arguments in his essay? If so, why? In an essay, discuss your views on these questions. Offer reasons and evidence to support your opinion.

14. **Thinking About the Big Question: Is knowledge the same as understanding?** In a brief essay about "Libraries Face Sad Chapter," identify what Pete Hamill might be saying about knowledge. Consider in particular his childhood experiences in the library and his use of the term "treasure house of the imagination." Then, relate the word *understanding* to what Hamill says about the role of libraries in the lives of immigrants and poor people.

Oral Response

15. Go back to question 5, 6, or 9 or to the question your teacher assigns you. Take a few minutes to develop an expanded answer and prepare an oral response. Find additional details in "Libraries Face Sad Chapter." If necessary, make notes to guide your oral response.

"Libraries Face Sad Chapter" by Pete Hamill
Selection Test A

Critical Reading *Identify the letter of the choice that best answers the question.*

____ 1. In "Libraries Face Sad Chapter," how does Pete Hamill describe his childhood visits to the library?
   A. He visited the library only to do his school assignments.
   B. He went to the library because it was a pleasure.
   C. His parents forced him to go to the library.
   D. He didn't go to the library very often.

____ 2. Which one of the following arguments does Hamill *not* mention in his argument against cutting back on libraries' hours and staff?
   A. the human need for myth and heroes
   B. the need to learn about the world
   C. the need to make books available to the poor
   D. the need for computers and access to the Internet

____ 3. Which of the following would you *not* expect to find in persuasive appeals to reason?
   A. evidence that can be checked
   B. highly charged language
   C. expert testimony
   D. statistics

____ 4. How can you analyze an author's persuasive appeals in a persuasive essay, such as Hamill's "Libraries Face Sad Chapter"?
   A. Look for examples of chronological order in the text.
   B. Reread the text to test the logic and reasoning of the author's arguments.
   C. Ask yourself what most of the people you know would think about the arguments.
   D. Compare the author's style with that of other writers on the same topic.

____ 5. What evidence does Hamill offer to support the idea that young readers are a large audience?
   A. the popularity of books about pirates
   B. the success of the Harry Potter books
   C. the fact that many books are published for children each year
   D. a petition to the mayor signed by young readers

_____ 6. According to Hamill, which of the following groups especially need public libraries?
  A. professors
  B. the elderly
  C. immigrants
  D. public officials

_____ 7. In "Libraries Face Sad Chapter," what source does Hamill use for most of his emotional appeals?
  A. a speech by the mayor
  B. quotations from immigrants
  C. the experiences of friends
  D. the author's own experiences

_____ 8. Which of the following best defines persuasive appeals?
  A. arguments intended to persuade readers to think or act in a particular way
  B. words and phrases with strong negative or positive associations
  C. an expert's opinion on a particular subject
  D. leaps in logic made by a persuasive writer

_____ 9. Toward the end of "Libraries Face Sad Chapter," what proposal does Hamill make to solve the problem facing New York's public libraries?
  A. Shorten the hours, cut the services, and reduce the staff at most libraries.
  B. Pass a new city sales tax to raise funds specifically for the libraries.
  C. Ask people to contribute to a private fund to maintain the libraries at full strength.
  D. Appeal for help only to extremely rich New Yorkers.

_____ 10. In the last paragraph, which argument does Hamill make to support his proposal to help libraries survive?
  A. Support of libraries would be a fitting gesture to recognize people who supported them in the past.
  B. Middle-class people have to take the place of wealthy patrons like Andrew Carnegie.
  C. If immigrants do not have access to libraries, they will not learn to be good citizens.
  D. Public support of libraries will send a message to politicians that they need to contribute more funds.

Vocabulary and Grammar

___ 11. What would be the result if your workday was <u>curtailed</u>?
   A. You would have to work later.
   B. You would have to focus on a single project.
   C. You would have more free time.
   D. You would have an argument with your employer.

___ 12. What does the word *medium* mean in this sentence from Hamill's essay?
   "Human beings need what books give them better than any other medium."
   A. environment
   B. a middle state or degree
   C. means of communication
   D. liquid mixed with pigments in painting

___ 13. Which of the following phrases does *not* contain an adjective?
   A. bright moonbeams
   B. four children
   C. an honest opinion
   D. looked sharply

Essay

14. In "Libraries Face Sad Chapter," what is Pete Hamill trying to persuade his readers to do? What reasons does he give to convince them? In an essay, analyze Hamill's use of appeals to reason in his essay. First, state Hamill's main idea—the action he wants readers to take. Then, summarize and evaluate two reasons Hamill gives to persuade his readers to take that action.

15. What do you think should be done to improve your school or local library? In a persuasive essay, tell what you think readers should do to improve the library. Begin your essay with a clear statement of your opinion. Then, support your opinion with appeals to reason and to emotion that will persuade your readers that your opinion is right. As part of your argument, you may describe your experiences with libraries, using Pete Hamill's account as a model.

16. **Thinking About the Big Question: Is knowledge the same as understanding?** Knowledge refers to knowing something specific. Understanding refers to making larger sense of the world or of an experience. Reread author Pete Hamill's childhood experiences in the first section of "Libraries Face Sad Chapter." Next, in an essay, tell what specific knowledge he gained from library books. Then, explain the greater understanding he gained from those books.

"Libraries Face Sad Chapter" by Pete Hamill
Selection Test B

Critical Reading *Identify the letter of the choice that best completes the statement or answers the question.*

_____ 1. According to Pete Hamill, how did he and the other children go to the library when they were about ten or eleven years old?
   A. once a week
   B. voluntarily
   C. unwillingly
   D. seldom

_____ 2. In his essay, Hamill argues against cutting back on libraries' services, hours, and staff. To support his opinion, he uses all of the following arguments *except*
   A. the human need for myth, heroes, and moral tales.
   B. the need to learn about the world beyond one's neighborhood.
   C. the especial need for freely circulating books in hard economic times.
   D. the need for public access to the Internet.

_____ 3. In a persuasive essay, all of the following are appeals to reason *except*
   A. verifiable evidence.
   B. emotionally charged language.
   C. expert testimony and quotations.
   D. facts and statistics.

_____ 4. To analyze and evaluate the persuasive appeals in any persuasive essay, it is best to
   A. examine the text for the use of figurative language and analogy.
   B. discover whether the majority of your peers would agree with the writer's opinion.
   C. reread the text to test the logic and reasoning of the author's arguments.
   D. compare the clarity of the author's style with that of other writers on the same topic.

_____ 5. What evidence does Hamill give to prove his point that there is a potentially immense audience of young readers?
   A. the popularity of books about pirates and explorers
   B. the success of the Harry Potter books
   C. the crowded children's sections of public libraries
   D. a petition to the mayor signed by young readers

_____ 6. In "Libraries Face Sad Chapter," for his emotional appeals Hamill chiefly relies on
   A. quotations from immigrants and their children who are using public libraries.
   B. statistics showing that library use has increased over the years.
   C. a moving speech about libraries by the mayor of New York City.
   D. his own experiences in the public library as a child.

_____ 7. According to Hamill, why is it important that libraries be available to older immigrants?
   A. They need to read many books to learn to speak English well.
   B. They need to do research to find better jobs and information about becoming citizens.
   C. They need to help their children with their homework and research assignments.
   D. They need to send e-mail messages to relatives in their native countries.

____ 8. Persuasive appeals in an essay are best defined as
   A. the arguments a writer uses to make readers believe or act in a specific way.
   B. the conclusions, opinions, and anecdotes that an author conveys to readers.
   C. the expert testimony to which an author refers.
   D. the emotionally charged language that an author uses.

____ 9. Toward the end of "Libraries Face Sad Chapter," what concrete proposal does Hamill suggest to maintain the public libraries of New York?
   A. Curtail hours of operation, cut some services, and let some staff members go.
   B. Pass a mandatory new city tax to finance the library's budget needs.
   C. Establish a voluntary private fund to raise money for the libraries.
   D. Sell some of the libraries' holdings to make up for the budget shortfall.

____ 10. In the final paragraph of his essay, which of the following arguments does Hamill use to support his proposal that people should help libraries survive?
   A. Support would be a means of honoring the sacrifices of people in the past whose taxes helped finance the library system.
   B. Support by the middle class must take the place of the generous donations of wealthy philanthropists like Andrew Carnegie.
   C. If recent immigrants do not have access to libraries, they will not become well-informed citizens.
   D. Support will send a message to politicians that the city has exaggerated the extent of the budget crisis.

____ 11. Which of the following best describes Hamill's writing style in this persuasive essay?
   A. formal   C. eloquent
   B. ironic   D. factual

____ 12. Reread the closing sentences in "Libraries Face Sad Chapter."
   "We who dreamed of Ebbets Field and the Chateau d'If on the same American nights owe debts to New York that we can never pay. This is one that must be honored."

   Which of the following best describes the author's emphasis in this conclusion?
   A. the life of the mind   C. civic responsibility
   B. romantic escapism   D. admiration for philanthropy

____ 13. From details in "Libraries Face Sad Chapter," we can infer that Andrew Carnegie
   A. amassed a great deal of wealth but was miserly.
   B. urged immigrants to learn about the Constitution and the Bill of Rights.
   C. urged librarians to completely overhaul their system for classifying books.
   D. believed that public libraries were important civic institutions.

____ 14. Hamill's essay can be classified as a persuasive essay because it
   A. states a problem and offers several solutions.
   B. tries to persuade readers to take a specific action.
   C. compares and contrasts the past and present.
   D. recounts the writer's thoughts and feelings about a particular subject.

Vocabulary and Grammar

____ 15. If your workday is <u>curtailed</u>, which of the following would most likely result?
A. You would have to work longer hours.
B. Your workday would be occupied by a single project.
C. You would have more time for leisure activities.
D. You would experience a serious conflict with your employer.

____ 16. If you wish to <u>emulate</u> someone else, how do you probably feel about that person?
A. skeptical
B. admiring
C. contemptuous
D. indifferent

____ 17. Which of the following phrases from Hamill's essay does *not* contain an adjective?
A. "a majestic aura"
B. "do it ourselves"
C. "leathery cliffs of books"
D. "more expensive than ever"

____ 18. Identify all of the adjectives in the following sentence from Hamill's essay:
"The older people want information about this new world, and how to get better jobs and green cards and citizenship."

A. *older, information, better, jobs*
B. *older, green, cards, citizenship*
C. *older, this, new, better, green*
D. *older, information, new, better, green*

Essay

19. In "Libraries Face Sad Chapter," why do you think Pete Hamill devotes so much space to personal recollections of his childhood? Does this autobiographical element in the essay enhance or lessen the effectiveness of Hamill's persuasive appeals? In an essay, evaluate and discuss Hamill's use of his childhood recollections in his persuasive essay. Give specific examples from the essay.

20. Hamill refers several times to libraries and the imaginative world of books as "treasure houses." Do you think his essay justifies this metaphor? In an essay of your own, explain how Hamill paints a picture of the "treasures" that books can offer their readers. Support your points with specific references to the text.

21. What do you think of the suggestion of a "voluntary tax" to finance libraries that Hamill advances toward the end of his essay? Is this suggestion practical, in your opinion? How appealing do you think it would be to Hamill's audience? Does the suggestion lend more credibility to the arguments in the essay, and if so, why? In an essay, discuss your views on these questions. Offer specific reasons and evidence to support your opinion.

22. **Thinking About the Big Question: Is knowledge the same as understanding?** In a brief essay about "Libraries Face Sad Chapter," identify what Pete Hamill might be saying about knowledge. Consider in particular his childhood experiences in the library and his use of the term "treasure house of the imagination." Then, relate the word *understanding* to what Hamill says about the role of libraries in the lives of immigrants and poor people.

"I Have a Dream" by Martin Luther King, Jr.
Vocabulary Warm-up Word Lists

Study these words from "I Have a Dream." Then, complete the activities.

Word List A

character [KAR ik tuhr] *n.* good qualities, such as honesty, that people admire
   He was admired for his good <u>character</u> and good deeds.

difficulties [DI fi kuhl teez] *n.* problems or things that cause trouble
   She overcame many <u>difficulties</u> before achieving success.

faith [FAYTH] *n.* strong feeling of trust
   We have <u>faith</u> in your ability to get the job done.

glory [GLOHR ee] *n.* splendor; outstanding worth
   We marveled at the <u>glory</u> of the sunset.

liberty [LIB uhr tee] *n.* freedom to act without asking permission from people in power
   They fought the tyrant to win their <u>liberty</u>.

mighty [MY tee] *adj.* powerful and strong
   A <u>mighty</u> tornado swept across the plain.

peaks [PEEKS] *n.* pointed tops of mountains
   The mountain climbers set out to scale the highest <u>peaks</u>.

situation [si chuh WAY shuhn] *n.* combination of circumstances
   Our parents helped us figure out the complicated <u>situation</u>.

Word List B

discords [DIS kohrdz] *n.* quarreling or disagreements between people
   The judge was asked to resolve their <u>discords</u>.

equal [EE kwuhl] *adj.* having the same rights and chances as everyone else
   Laws exist in the United States giving all people <u>equal</u> rights to jobs and education.

former [FOHR mer] *adj.* having been in the past
   The <u>former</u> mayor decided to run for governor.

hamlet [HAM lit] *n.* very small village
   The <u>hamlet</u> we live in is too small to appear on the state map.

injustice [in JUHS tuhs] *n.* unfair treatment and violation of rights
   The abolitionists spoke out against the <u>injustice</u> of slavery.

oppression [uh PRE shuhn] *n.* act of treating people in an unfair and cruel way
   The peasants struggled to put an end to their miserable <u>oppression</u>.

symphony [SIM fuh nee] *n.* something that is harmonious or blends well together
   The meal was a <u>symphony</u> of exquisite flavors.

transform [trans FOHRM] *v.* change completely in form or appearance
   I hope that going to kindergarten will <u>transform</u> my little sister into a child who enjoys sharing.

Name _____ Date _____

Exercise A *Fill in each blank in the following paragraph with an appropriate word from Word List A. Use each word only once.*

My Uncle David has traveled all over the United States. He has climbed the

highest [1] _____ of the Rocky Mountains and sailed down the

[2] _____ Mississippi River. Last year, he camped out at Yellowstone

National Park and marveled at the [3] _____ of the American wilderness.

Despite the [4] _____ he encountered in his travels, he always had

[5] _____ in his ability to handle any [6] _____

that might arise. Uncle David, courageous and honest, is a man of strong

[7] _____ and personal integrity. If he has one fault, it is his

refusal to give up even the smallest bit of freedom. Uncle David values his

[8] _____ above all.

Exercise B *Revise each sentence so that the underlined vocabulary word is used in a logical way. Be sure to keep the vocabulary word in your revision.*

Example: The painting was a <u>symphony</u> of colors that disturbed everyone who viewed it.
The painting was a <u>symphony</u> of colors that pleased everyone who viewed it.

1. <u>Discords</u> between Marco and Beth eventually resulted in the beginning of their friendship.

   _____

2. Tim and Carla were <u>equal</u> partners in the business, so Tim received less than half of the profits.

   _____

3. The <u>former</u> president of our club was elected today for the first time.

   _____

4. The <u>hamlet</u> we live in is one of the largest villages in the United States.

   _____

5. The governor vowed to support <u>injustice</u> wherever she found it.

   _____

6. The <u>oppression</u> of the people began when the evil tyrant was overthrown.

   _____

7. The tadpole is going to <u>transform</u> itself into a snake.

   _____

"I Have a Dream" by Martin Luther King, Jr.
Reading Warm-up A

Read the following passage. Pay special attention to the underlined words. Then, read it again, and complete the activities. Use a separate sheet of paper for your written answers.

On July 4, 1776, representatives of the thirteen colonies in North America came together to declare their independence from Britain. The <u>difficulties</u> between the colonists and Britain had begun long before. Many people still had <u>faith</u> that the problems could somehow be worked out. Others believed that the <u>situation</u> would only get worse as time went on. The colonists chose men of the highest <u>character</u> to represent them at a Continental Congress. After much debate, the members of Congress agreed to do whatever was necessary to win their precious <u>liberty</u>. Thomas Jefferson of Virginia was given the task of drafting a document to declare colonial independence.

The <u>glory</u> of the Declaration of Independence lies in both its noble ideas and its beautiful language. Jefferson worded his argument clearly and concisely. He wrote that all men are born with the same rights. He believed that these rights could not be taken away by the government. Governments exist to serve the people, not the other way around. Furthermore, people have the right and duty to throw off an unjust government.

Such ideas were truly radical in the eighteenth century! Still, many people were inspired by Jefferson's bold statements. They agreed that the king of Britain should no longer rule the colonies that lay far across the Atlantic. From the Massachusetts Bay to the southernmost <u>peaks</u> of the Blue Ridge Mountains, the people of the thirteen colonies were ready to speak together with one voice. For the first time, the colonists saw themselves as more than just New Yorkers or Virginians or Georgians. The Declaration of Independence made them all Americans.

Of course, the king of Britain was not about to give up the North American colonies without a fight. Could the ragtag Americans possibly hope to defeat the <u>mighty</u> British army in a war for independence? The answer to that question would cost both the Americans and British many lives. It would also change the fate of the colonies forever.

1. Underline the word in the next sentence that gives a hint to the meaning of <u>difficulties</u>. Write about *difficulties* that you have experienced.

2. Underline the words that tell what many people had <u>faith</u> in. Describe something that you have *faith* in.

3. Circle the word that tells what some people believed the <u>situation</u> would become. Write a sentence using *situation*.

4. Underline the word that tells what kind of <u>character</u> the men had. What personal qualities would you expect people with *character* to have?

5. Circle the words that tell what the members of Congress agreed to do to win their <u>liberty</u>. Why would people want to win their *liberty*?

6. Underline the words that tell where the <u>glory</u> of the Declaration of Independence can be found. Give a synonym for *glory*.

7. Circle the word that means the same as <u>peaks</u>. What *peaks* are located in or near your state?

8. Circle the words that tell who was <u>mighty</u>. Write a sentence using *mighty*.

"I Have a Dream" by Martin Luther King, Jr.
Reading Warm-up B

Read the following passage. Pay special attention to the underlined words. Then, read it again, and complete the activities. Use a separate sheet of paper for your written answers.

Coretta Scott King was married to the great civil rights leader Dr. Martin Luther King, Jr. After his murder in 1968 in Tennessee, she carried on his unfinished work.

Coretta Scott grew up on a farm in a small <u>hamlet</u> near Marion, Alabama. She graduated at the top of her high school class. She enrolled at Antioch College as a major in music and education. Unfortunately, the local public schools refused to accept any African American student teachers. Coretta Scott protested this <u>injustice</u>, but her protests fell on deaf ears.

She then decided to become a professional singer. The talented young woman was accepted by the New England Conservatory of Music. It was there in Boston that she met a theology student named Martin Luther King, Jr. They soon married and moved to Montgomery, Alabama, where Dr. King began his work as a minister.

Together, Martin Luther King, Jr. and Coretta Scott King helped lead the struggle to gain <u>equal</u> rights for all Americans, regardless of their color. They gave many speeches and led many marches. Tirelessly, they protested the <u>oppression</u> of African Americans.

A <u>former</u> music student, Coretta Scott King used her talent to give vocal concerts in support of the civil rights movement. Inspired by the Kings, a <u>symphony</u> of voices rose up as one against racial discrimination.

Just four days after her husband's death, Coretta Scott King led 50,000 people in a march through the streets of Memphis, Tennessee. She then traveled to India, Italy, and England to speak out about the <u>discords</u> that were tearing apart American society.

Before the year ended, she founded the King Center in Atlanta, Georgia, to educate people about Dr. King's work and beliefs. The Center's records of the civil rights movement are a tribute to the women and men whose courageous struggle helped <u>transform</u> the United States into a more just nation.

1. Circle the word that tells what kind of place a <u>hamlet</u> is. Name a place in your state that would definitely not be described as a *hamlet*. Explain.

2. Underline the words that tell what <u>injustice</u> Coretta Scott protested. Describe an *injustice* that exists today.

3. Underline the words that tell for whom the Kings hoped to gain <u>equal</u> rights. Explain what *equal* means in the sentence.

4. Underline the words that tell whose <u>oppression</u> the Kings protested against. Explain what *oppression* means.

5. Circle the words that tell who was a <u>former</u> music student. Write a word that means the opposite of *former*.

6. Explain what "a <u>symphony</u> of voices" means.

7. Underline the words that tell what the <u>discords</u> were doing. What *discords* are you familiar with? How do you think they can be resolved?

8. Underline the words that tell who helped to <u>transform</u> the United States. Write a sentence about something that you can help to *transform*.

"**I Have a Dream**" by Martin Luther King, Jr.
Writing About the Big Question

Is knowledge the same as understanding?

Big Question Vocabulary

ambiguous	clarify	comprehend	concept	connection
fact	feeling	information	insight	instinct
interpret	research	senses/sensory	sources	statistics

A. *Use one or more words from the list above to complete each sentence.*

1. The _____ helped Jill understand the civil rights movement.

2. King spoke with great _____ that helped people understand his message.

3. He made a powerful _____ with his audience as he gave them information on the injustices suffered by many people.

4. Andrew better understood King's appeal when he read _____ about all the people who went to hear King speak.

B. *Follow the directions in responding to each item below.*

1. When have you heard a good speaker? Describe the occasion.

_____

_____

2. How did the speaker help you understand the topic? What techniques or methods did the speaker use? Use at least two of the Big Question vocabulary words.

_____

_____

C. In "I Have a Dream," Martin Luther King makes a logical and emotional speech to help listeners understand his dream of freedom and equality. Complete the sentence below. Then, write a short paragraph in which you connect this experience to the Big Question.

The concept of equality might be ambiguous to some people because _____

_____

_____

_____

_____

_____

Name _____ Date _____

"I Have a Dream" by Martin Luther King, Jr.
Literary Analysis: Persuasive Speech

A **persuasive speech** is a speech that tries to convince listeners to think or act in a certain way. Persuasive speeches may appeal to reason or emotion or both. In order to engage the audience, speakers often include **rhetorical devices,** special patterns of words and ideas that create emphasis and stir emotion in the audience. Common rhetorical devices include the following:

- **Parallelism:** repeating a grammatical structure or arrangement of words to create a sense of rhythm and momentum
- **Restatement:** expressing the same idea in different words to clarify and stress key points
- **Repetition:** expressing different ideas using the same words or images in order to reinforce concepts and unify the speech

DIRECTIONS: *Read each of the following passages from King's "I Have a Dream" speech. On the lines provided, identify the rhetorical device or devices in each passage. (You may find more than one rhetorical device.) Then briefly explain your answer by citing the words and phrases that exemplify the device.*

1. But one hundred years later, the Negro still is not free. One hundred years later, the life of the Negro is still sadly crippled by the manacles of segregation and the chains of discrimination. One hundred years later, the Negro lives on a lonely island of poverty in the midst of a vast ocean of material prosperity.

   Rhetorical Device(s): _____

   Explanation: _____

   _____

   _____

2. When the architects of our republic wrote the magnificent words of the Constitution and the Declaration of Independence, they were signing a promissory note to which every American was to fall heir. This note was a promise that all men . . . would be guaranteed the unalienable rights of life, liberty, and the pursuit of happiness.

   Rhetorical Device(s): _____

   Explanation: _____

   _____

   _____

3. It is obvious today that America has defaulted on this promissory note insofar as her citizens of color are concerned. Instead of honoring this sacred obligation, America has given the Negro people a bad check; a check which has come back marked "insufficient funds."

   Rhetorical Device(s): _____

   Explanation: _____

   _____

   _____

Name _____ Date _____

"**I Have a Dream**" by Martin Luther King, Jr.
Reading: Analyze Persuasive Techniques

Persuasive techniques are devices used to influence the audience in favor of the author's argument. In addition to presenting evidence in a persuasive speech, a speaker may use the following:

- emotionally charged language
- rhetorical devices, such as parallelism, restatement, and repetition

To analyze and evaluate persuasive techniques, **read aloud** to hear the effect. Notice the emotional impact of the sounds of certain words, as well as the rhythm and momentum created by the word patterns that the author uses. Consider both the purpose and effect of these persuasive techniques and evaluate the author's success in using them to make a convincing argument.

DIRECTIONS: *Read the following excerpts from "I Have a Dream." Then, on the lines provided, answer the questions that follow.*

1. Five score years ago, a great American, in whose symbolic shadow we stand today, signed the Emancipation Proclamation.

   A. To which "great American" does King allude in this sentence? _____

   B. What place does King refer to in saying "in whose symbolic shadow we stand"?

   _____

   C. What well-known speech in American history does King echo in saying "five score years ago"? _____

2. Now is the time to make real the promises of Democracy.
   Now is the time to rise from the dark and desolate valley of segregation to the sunlit path of racial justice.

   A. How does this passage illustrate parallelism? _____

   _____

   B. What emotionally charged words or phrases does King use in this passage? _____

   _____

3. This sweltering summer of the Negro's legitimate discontent will not pass until there is an invigorating autumn of freedom and equality.

   A. What image dominates this passage? _____

   _____

   B. How does the passage illustrate parallelism? _____

   _____

"I Have a Dream" by Dr. Martin Luther King, Jr.
Vocabulary Builder

Word List

creed   defaulted   degenerate   hallowed   momentous   oppression

A. DIRECTIONS: *In each item, think about the meaning of the underlined word and then answer the question.*

1. If you think that a certain place is <u>hallowed</u> ground, would you consider it with respect or indifference? Explain.

   _____

2. Why is a <u>creed</u> something that most people take seriously?

   _____

3. If the condition of your house were to <u>degenerate</u> over the next few years, what might you do?

   _____

4. Why do people often take photographs during <u>momentous</u> occasions in their lives?

   _____

5. How would you feel if you loaned a friend some money and he <u>defaulted</u> on his promise to pay it back?

   _____

6. Why do you think many people dislike living under <u>oppression</u>?

   _____

B. WORD STUDY: The Latin root *-cred-* means "to trust, to believe." Answer each of the following questions using one of these words containing *-cred-*: *credence* ("the act of believing"), *credible* ("believable"), *credulous* ("ready to believe").

1. Why isn't it wise to give <u>credence</u> to everything you hear on commercials?

   _____

2. Why do lawyers want <u>credible</u> witnesses to support their case?

   _____

3. What kind of trouble might someone who is too <u>credulous</u> get into?

   _____

Name _____ Date _____

"**I Have a Dream**" by Martin Luther King, Jr.
Enrichment: Timeline of an Era

Under the leadership of inspiring figures such as Dr. Martin Luther King, Jr., the civil rights movement reached a peak during the 1950s and 1960s.

Using Internet and library resources, create an annotated timeline of this era in the struggle for racial justice and economic opportunity. On your timeline, locate and briefly explain events such as the following: the Supreme Court decision of *Brown* v. *Board of Education*; the Montgomery bus boycott; the founding of the Southern Christian Leadership Conference; the lunch-counter sit-ins in such cities as Greensboro, North Carolina; King's "Letter from Birmingham City Jail"; the march on Washington; the Civil Rights Act; the Voting Rights Act; the march on Selma; and King's assassination.

You may use the space below or a separate sheet of paper for your timeline.

1950 _____

_____

_____

_____

1955 _____

_____

_____

_____

1960 _____

_____

_____

_____

1965 _____

_____

_____

_____

1970 _____

_____

"'I Have a Dream'" by Martin Luther King, Jr.
Open-Book Test

Short Answer *Write your responses to the questions in this section on the lines provided.*

1. In the first sentence of "I Have a Dream," Martin Luther King, Jr., refers to "a great American, in whose symbolic shadow we stand today." Whom is King referring to?

   _____

   _____

2. Parallelism is the repetition of a grammatical structure. It is used to emphasize a point and heighten dramatic effect. What is one example of parallelism in the second paragraph of "I Have a Dream"?

   _____

   _____

   _____

3. In the third paragraph of "I Have a Dream," Martin Luther King, Jr., refers to the Constitution and the Declaration of Independence. What is the effect of referring to those important documents?

   _____

   _____

   _____

4. Reread the fourth paragraph of "I Have a Dream," in which King talks about a promissory note. In that paragraph, what idea does King emphasize using the rhetorical device of restatement? Describe the idea in your own words.

   _____

   _____

   _____

   _____

5. In "I Have a Dream," King describes the place where he is delivering his speech as a "hallowed spot." Why does he consider the place hallowed? Base your answer on the definition of *hallowed*.

   _____

   _____

   _____

   _____

6. Read aloud or to yourself the following lines from "I Have a Dream." Underline the parallel expressions, and circle the words that you think were meant to be emphasized. Then, on the line below, describe the effect of the persuasive techniques King used here.

> We can never be satisfied as long as the Negro is the victim of the unspeakable horrors of police
> brutality. We can never be satisfied as long as our bodies . . . cannot gain lodging in . . .
> motels . . . and . . . hotels . . . . We cannot be satisfied as long as the Negro's basic mobility
> is from a small ghetto to a larger one . . . . No, no, we are not satisfied, and we will not be
> satisfied until justice rolls down like waters and righteousness like a mighty stream.

_____

7. Midway through "I Have a Dream," Martin Luther King, Jr., tells his audience, "Let us not wallow in the valley of despair." With that remark, King recognizes that a "valley of despair" exists and pleads with his listeners not to "wallow" in it. In your own words, explain King's message in this sentence.

_____

_____

_____

8. In "I Have a Dream," King refers to the creed of the United States. The word *creed* often appears in references to discrimination: A person may not be discriminated against on the basis of his or her creed. Use the definition of *creed* to explain the meaning of that idea.

_____

_____

9. In "I Have a Dream," Martin Luther King, Jr., quotes a verse from the song "My Country 'Tis of Thee." What is the effect of including words from this song?

_____

_____

_____

10. In the last seven paragraphs of "I Have a Dream," King uses a line from "My Country 'Tis of Thee" to create parallelism. What line from the song does he use?

_____

_____

Essay

Write an extended response to the question of your choice or to the question or questions your teacher assigns you.

11. Martin Luther King, Jr., was a gifted speaker, in part because he used rhetorical devices effectively. In a brief essay, identify and analyze two rhetorical devices (such as parallelism, repetition, restatement, and analogy) that King uses in "I Have a Dream." Cite one example of each technique, and explain how it adds to the persuasive effect of King's speech.

12. In "I Have a Dream," Martin Luther King, Jr., says that his dream is "deeply rooted in the American dream." In an essay, define the American dream. Then, compare King's dream to your definition of the American dream. Describe the ways in which they are the same and the ways in which they are different.

13. In "I Have a Dream," Martin Luther King, Jr., attempts to persuade his audience to feel optimistic. Was King's task difficult, or was his audience already optimistic? In an essay, evaluate the difficulty of King's task. Consider that King was talking not just to the people in his audience on the day of his speech but to people—including the nation's leaders—who would read it in the newspaper in the following days. Cite at least two places in the speech where King implies that his listeners might feel other than optimistic. Finally, state your opinion of the difficulty of King's task. Be sure you support your opinion with evidence and/or a well-reasoned argument.

14. **Thinking About the Big Question: Is knowledge the same as understanding?** In "I Have a Dream," how well does Martin Luther King, Jr., fuse knowledge with understanding? Consider these questions: How much does King know about his subject? How well does he use his knowledge? Does he understand how best to persuade blacks and whites of the wisdom of his dream? Does he understand how to deal with the white Americans who want to keep black Americans from achieving that dream? Cite details from the speech or from other reading to support your points.

Oral Response

15. Go back to question 1, 7, or 9 or to the question your teacher assigns you. Take a few minutes to expand your answer and prepare an oral response. Find additional details in "I Have a Dream" that support your points. If necessary, make notes to guide your oral response.

"**I Have a Dream**" by Dr. Martin Luther King, Jr.
Selection Test A

Critical Reading *Identify the letter of the choice that best answers the question.*

____ 1. In front of which building in Washington, D.C., did Dr. Martin Luther King, Jr., deliver his "I Have a Dream" speech in August 1963?
A. the Lincoln Memorial
B. Union Station
C. the White House
D. the National Cathedral

____ 2. Which of the following best defines *parallelism?*
A. the use of symbols and figures of speech
B. the repetition of a grammatical structure or arrangement of words
C. the use of words or phrases with emotional associations
D. the expression of the same idea in different words

____ 3. Why do you think Dr. King refers to the Constitution and the Declaration of Independence in his speech?
A. He wants to remind his audience that America became independent.
B. He believes that every listener should carefully reread both of these documents.
C. He wants to stress that all Americans are guaranteed certain rights.
D. He believes that the Constitution and the Declaration of Independence are in conflict.

____ 4. In his speech, which does Dr. King state as a reminder to his own people?
A. They must never be satisfied.
B. They must register to vote.
C. They must conduct their struggle with discipline and dignity.
D. They should regard all white people with suspicion.

____ 5. Read this excerpt from "I Have a Dream":
Go back to Mississippi, go back to Alabama, go back to South Carolina, go back to Georgia, go back to Louisiana, go back to the slums and ghettos of our northern cities, knowing that somehow this situation can and will be changed.

Which of the following words or phrases in this passage illustrate parallelism?
A. slums and ghettos
B. go back to
C. knowing that somehow
D. will be changed

_____ 6. When Dr. King tells his audience, "Let us not wallow in the valley of despair," what is he urging them to do?

A. He wants them to move to communities where they will be welcome.

B. He wants them to feel hope that the present situation will change.

C. He wants them to help each other get over feelings of depression.

D. He wants them to resist physical force with all their might.

_____ 7. What does Dr. King mean when he says that one day "the rough places will be made plains, and the crooked places will be made straight"?

A. Americans will enjoy a more efficient highway system.

B. National, state, and local elections will be fairer.

C. Judges will be chosen on the basis of their merits.

D. Racial discrimination and injustice will end.

_____ 8. Which of the following best describes the underlined words in this sentence from "I Have a Dream"?

We can never be satisfied as long as the Negro is the victim of the unspeakable horrors of police brutality.

A. symbolism

B. metaphor

C. repetition

D. emotionally charged language

_____ 9. Which of the following best states Dr. King's persuasive purpose in "I Have a Dream"?

A. He wants everyone in his audience to register to vote.

B. He wants Americans to appreciate their heritage more.

C. He wants to challenge his audience to improve the civil rights of all Americans.

D. He wants America to apologize for the evils of slavery.

_____ 10. Which of the following best identifies the "dream" Dr. King expresses in his speech?

A. more wealth and prosperity for all Americans

B. power for the disadvantaged and nonvoters

C. liberty and justice for all Americans

D. election of more public officials from minority ranks

_____ 11. The ending of Dr. King's "I Have a Dream" speech evokes a strong feeling of which of the following?

A. hope and optimism

B. fear and isolation

C. joy and doubt

D. anger and disappointment

Vocabulary and Grammar

___ 12. Which of the following verbs is closely related to the meaning of the noun *creed*?
  A. gamble
  B. reflect
  C. doubt
  D. believe

___ 13. Which of the following would best describe a discussion that begins to *degenerate*?
  A. The discussion is growing more lively.
  B. The discussion is growing unpleasant.
  C. People are contributing intelligent comments.
  D. People are asking intelligent questions.

___ 14. Which of the following suffixes is often used to turn an adjective into an adverb?
  A. *-ness*
  B. *-able*
  C. *-ly*
  D. *-ior*

Essay

15. Dr. Martin Luther King, Jr., was widely respected as a gifted speaker. In a brief essay, identify and analyze two persuasive techniques (such as parallelism, repetition, and emotionally charged language) that Dr. King uses in "I Have a Dream." Give specific examples from the text, and tell how each example adds to the persuasive effect of Dr. King's speech.

16. The tone of a work is the author's attitude toward his or her subject matter or audience. How would you describe Dr. King's tone in "I Have a Dream"? Does the tone remain the same throughout the speech, or does it change? If it changes, how does it change? In an essay, describe the tone of the speaker and relate this tone to the way you think Dr. King's speech affected his listeners, both logically and emotionally.

17. **Thinking About the Big Question: Is knowledge the same as understanding?** In his speech entitled "I Have a Dream," Dr. Martin Luther King, Jr., uses knowledge to lead to understanding. He cites his knowledge of history, the Constitution, and current events to make his point about the injustices African Americans were facing in the early 1960s. How does this knowledge help his listeners understand his dream for Americans? Cite details from the speech to respond to this question.

"I Have a Dream" by Dr. Martin Luther King, Jr.

Selection Test B

Critical Reading *Identify the letter of the choice that best completes the statement or answers the question.*

_____ 1. In August 1963, in which of the following cities did Dr. Martin Luther King, Jr., deliver his "I Have a Dream" speech?
  A. New York, New York
  B. Atlanta, Georgia
  C. Chicago, Illinois
  D. Washington, D.C.

_____ 2. In the opening sentence of "I Have a Dream," to whom is Dr. King referring?
  > Five score years ago, a great American, in whose symbolic shadow we stand, signed the Emancipation Proclamation.

  A. George Washington
  B. Thomas Jefferson
  C. Abraham Lincoln
  D. Woodrow Wilson

_____ 3. In the second paragraph of "I Have a Dream," which of these phrases exemplifies the speaker's use of parallelism?
  A. we must face
  B. one hundred years later
  C. a lonely island of poverty
  D. the corners of American society

_____ 4. In the third paragraph of his speech, Dr. King refers to the Constitution and the Declaration of Independence in order to
  A. remind his listeners that they should reread these documents.
  B. show his critics that he is well educated.
  C. inform elected officials that they have violated the law.
  D. stress that certain rights are guaranteed to all Americans.

_____ 5. Read the following excerpt from "I Have a Dream."
  > It is obvious today that America has defaulted on this promissory note insofar as her citizens of color are concerned. Instead of honoring this sacred obligation, America has given the Negro people a bad check; a check which has come back marked "insufficient funds."

  Which of the following rhetorical devices does this passage illustrate?
  A. parallelism
  B. emotionally charged language
  C. repetition and restatement
  D. simile and personification

_____ 6. In his speech, which of the following courses does Dr. King recommend to his own people?
  A. to overlook the urgency of the moment
  B. to meet physical force with soul force
  C. to allow the end to justify the means
  D. to turn out in large numbers to vote

____ 7. What does Dr. King mean when he says that one day "every hill and mountain shall be made low"?
   A. The United States will become the same everywhere.
   B. Prejudice will exist everywhere in the United States.
   C. The need to struggle for basic rights will no longer exist.
   D. Travel between states will become easier when discrimination ends.

____ 8. Read the following excerpt from "I Have a Dream":
   We can never be satisfied as long as the Negro is the victim of the unspeakable horrors of police brutality.

   The words *victim, unspeakable, horrors,* and *brutality* exemplify which of the following?
   A. extended metaphor
   B. symbolism
   C. emotionally charged language
   D. historical allusion

____ 9. Dr. King quotes from the song "My Country, 'Tis of Thee" in order to illustrate that
   A. minorities may need to use violence in order to achieve their goals.
   B. the United States was founded by people fighting for their freedom.
   C. Americans are extremely proud of their ethnic backgrounds.
   D. this country has many people who are unhappy with their lives.

____ 10. Dr. King's use of persuasive techniques in "I Have a Dream" is to achieve which of the following purposes?
   A. to chastise Americans for their failures
   B. to deepen people's appreciation of their physical and social environment
   C. to challenge people to improve the civil rights of all Americans
   D. to urge a united front in the war against poverty

____ 11. The persuasive speech "I Have a Dream" reveals Dr. King as a
   A. speaker who prefers to speak extemporaneously—with no prior preparations.
   B. leader who is deeply concerned about the future of African Americans.
   C. politician who knows how to manipulate an audience to accept his viewpoint.
   D. minister who is unprepared to fight for civil rights.

____ 12. Which of the following most accurately states the dream that Dr. King reveals in his speech?
   A. increased economic opportunity for all Americans
   B. liberty and justice for all Americans
   C. empowerment for women
   D. an official apology for the evils of slavery

____ 13. In the last part of "I Have a Dream," which of the following does Dr. King use to create parallelism?
   A. "if America is to become a great nation"
   B. "Let freedom ring"
   C. "we will be able to speed up that day"
   D. "sing in the words of the old Negro spiritual"

Vocabulary and Grammar

____ **14.** Which of the following is the best synonym for *degenerate*?
  A. grow worse
  B. grow old
  C. improve slowly
  D. grow depressed

____ **15.** Which of the following is most nearly the opposite of *hallowed*?
  A. consecrated
  B. duplicated
  C. shouted
  D. cursed

____ **16.** In the following sentence, which word is an adverb?
  One hundred years later, the life of the Negro is still sadly crippled by the manacles of seg-regation and the chains of discrimination.
  A. hundred
  B. sadly
  C. crippled
  D. manacles

____ **17.** In the following sentence, which of the following is an adverb?
  "We must forever conduct our struggle on the high plane of dignity and discipline."
  A. We
  B. forever
  C. conduct
  D. high

Essay

18. In the speech, Dr. Martin Luther King, Jr., describes his dream for all Americans. What is his dream? How is this dream "deeply rooted in the American dream"? Compare his dream to *your* dream, both for yourself and for all Americans. Use powerful, persuasive language in an essay that describes your dream.

19. The ending of "I Have a Dream" evokes a strong feeling of potential and optimism. Reread the last part of Dr. King's speech (following the "I have a dream" list). In an open-book essay, cite details from the speech's conclusion that support this interpretation, as well as details from earlier in the speech that help lead up to Dr. King's inspirational close.

20. Thinking About the Big Question: Is knowledge the same as understanding? In "I Have a Dream," how well does Dr. Martin Luther King, Jr., fuse knowledge with understanding? Consider these questions: How much does Dr. King know about his subject? How well does he use his knowledge? Does he understand how best to persuade blacks and whites of the wisdom of his dream? Does he understand how to deal with the white Americans who want to keep black Americans from achieving that dream? Cite details from the speech or from other reading to support your points.

"First Inaugural Address" by Franklin Delano Roosevelt
Vocabulary Warm-up Word Lists

Study these words from the "First Inaugural Address" by Franklin Delano Roosevelt. Then, complete the activities that follow.

Word List A

boldly [BOHLD lee] *adv.* with confidence and with a willingness to take risks
 The search party <u>boldly</u> entered the jungle to find the plane that crashed.

critical [KRIT ik uhl] *adj.* very important
 It is <u>critical</u> to carry plenty of water when we cross the desert.

destiny [DES ti nee] *n.* fate; what is meant to happen
 The child's early success as a dancer foretold her <u>destiny</u> as a ballerina.

effective [e FEK tiv] *adj.* producing the result that was wanted
 Her speech was so <u>effective</u> that many signed up immediately to help out.

leadership [LEE der ship] *n.* quality or position of leading something
 Thanks to her strong <u>leadership</u>, the club now has more active members.

primarily [pry MAIR i lee] *adv.* mainly
 Our family likes to vacation <u>primarily</u> at the beach.

recognition [rek uhg NI shuhn] *n.* act of understanding something is true
 There is a growing <u>recognition</u> of the need to exercise for good health.

stricken [STRIK uhn] *adj.* very badly affected by trouble, illness, sadness
 The boy was <u>stricken</u> with grief after the death of his lifelong pet.

Word List B

confront [kuhn FRUHNT] *v.* to meet or face
 The hospital will have to <u>confront</u> the shortage of blood donors very soon.

courageously [kuhr AY juhs lee] *adv.* bravely
 Margo <u>courageously</u> jumped into the water to rescue the child.

extraordinary [ek STROHR duhn nair ee] *adj.* very unusual, special, or surprising
 His skill in football, tennis, and track make him an <u>extraordinary</u> athlete.

humbly [HUHM blee] *adv.* modestly; not in a showy way
 The captain gave credit to the crew when he <u>humbly</u> accepted the award.

obligation [ah bli GAY shuhn] *n.* duty to do something
 Every member has an <u>obligation</u> to work hard for the team.

policy [PAH li see] *n.* official way of doing things
 Our school <u>policy</u> requires students to wear uniforms.

strife [STRYF] *n.* trouble or disagreement between people or groups
 Conflict over use of the athletic field is causing <u>strife</u> between the teams.

vigorous [VIG uh ruhs] *adj.* requiring a lot of energy or strength
 I do a <u>vigorous</u> workout that includes running and lifting weights.

Name _____ Date _____

"First Inaugural Address" by Franklin Delano Roosevelt
Vocabulary Warm-up Exercises

Exercise A *Fill in each blank in the paragraph below with an appropriate word from Word List A. Use each word only once.*

Fate did not mean for us to be the basketball champions, even though our players won that [1] _____ game against our biggest rival. Our team played [2] _____ that night, taking risks to score again and again. The teamwork was the most [3] _____ ever, with all players cooperating to achieve a well-earned victory. Naturally, we have stars who take charge and provide the [4] _____ for the team. In the end, we lost the championship [5] _____ because we lost two of those stars. Our fastest players shared a meal that was bad, and both were [6] _____ with food poisoning. We tried hard to rally; however, as the other team racked up the points, there was a gradual [7] _____ of our fate. Apparently, it was not our [8] _____ to win.

Exercise B *Answer the questions with complete explanations.*

Example: Could the winner of a contest who acts <u>humbly</u> be called boastful?
   No, because if you are acting <u>humbly</u>, you are downplaying your talents and success.

1. If poor grades are a problem that will <u>confront</u> you this semester, what should you do?

   _____

2. Would a friendship filled with <u>strife</u> be enjoyable? Explain.

   _____

3. If you are acting <u>courageously</u>, what is <u>extraordinary</u> about your behavior?

   _____

4. If you break a school <u>policy</u>, what may happen next?

   _____

5. Might your heart rate increase with <u>vigorous</u> exercise?

   _____

6. If you have an <u>obligation</u> to go with a friend to the library, would you feel free to cancel?

   _____

"First Inaugural Address" by Franklin Delano Roosevelt
Reading Warm-up A

Read the following passage. Pay special attention to the underlined words. Then, read it again, and complete the activities. Use a separate sheet of paper for your written answers.

In 1933, when Franklin Delano Roosevelt became president, the United States was beginning the fourth year of the Great Depression. What had happened to the country that made this a <u>critical</u> time and this president an important one for the future of America?

The crisis began in October 1929 when the price of stock in companies all over America fell dramatically. Many individuals' savings were wiped out. Companies cut back or closed, and people lost their jobs. The country was <u>stricken</u> with fear of financial catastrophe.

President Herbert Hoover was in office then. Unfortunately, he lacked a deep understanding and clear <u>recognition</u> of what had happened. He believed the country's problems were caused <u>primarily</u> by the normal ups and downs of business.

As a result, President Hoover did little to change things. He did not work to develop <u>effective</u> programs that would strengthen companies and create jobs. One month after the crash, he <u>boldly</u> stated, "Any lack of confidence in the economic future or the basic strength of business in the United States is foolish." This was a risky statement. The economy was not strong.

In 1929, the unemployment rate was under 5 percent. Just five months after the crash, some 1.5 million people had lost their jobs. By Roosevelt's inauguration, 25 percent of able workers were unemployed. Banks failed, too. In December 1931, the Bank of the United States went broke, losing $200 million in depositors' savings. As conditions got worse, people became more desperate. Food riots broke out, such as one in Minneapolis that took one hundred policemen to stop. People wondered about America's <u>destiny</u> and whether its future was in jeopardy.

By 1932, many Americans had lost faith in Herbert Hoover's <u>leadership</u> and wanted a take-charge president. They got one when they elected Franklin Delano Roosevelt, soon known by all as "FDR."

1. Underline the crisis that made this a <u>critical</u> time. Circle the synonym for **critical** in the same sentence.

2. Circle what the country was <u>stricken</u> with, and underline what it was that people were afraid of.

3. Circle the synonym for <u>recognition</u>. Do you think **recognition** of a problem is the first step to solving it?

4. Underline the words that tell what President Hoover thought <u>primarily</u> caused America's problems. Circle a phrase meaning **primarily** in the next sentence.

5. Underline the words that tell what <u>effective</u> programs would do. Give a synonym for **effective**.

6. Circle the word Hoover used that shows he spoke <u>boldly</u> about people's lack of confidence in the future. Was he right to speak **boldly**?

7. Circle the word that is a synonym for <u>destiny</u>. Use your knowledge of United States history to explain America's **destiny**.

8. Underline the phrase that describes the <u>leadership</u> people wanted. Then, explain why.

Name _____ Date _____

"**First Inaugural Address**" by Franklin Delano Roosevelt
Reading Warm-up B

Read the following passage. Pay special attention to the underlined words. Then, read it again, and complete the activities. Use a separate sheet of paper for your written answers.

In 1932, Franklin D. Roosevelt (FDR) accepted the Democratic nomination with a stirring speech. He said, "I pledge you, I pledge myself, to a new deal for the American people." When FDR took office, he made good on that pledge with his New Deal administration.

Roosevelt believed it was the <u>obligation</u> of the federal government and the duty of the president to take action. The beliefs of the previous president, Herbert Hoover, had caused great <u>strife</u>. By 1933, people were troubled and angry with the government.

FDR understood the country's desperate needs. His economic <u>policy</u> was designed to strengthen banks and businesses. His official positions and government-sponsored programs were aimed at getting people back to work.

FDR realized it was unemployment that was causing <u>extraordinary</u> hardships for many Americans. The extreme levels of suffering were physical and emotional.

FDR's New Deal plans were developed to <u>confront</u> these problems and meet them head-on. Government programs created jobs and hope. Americans with the energy and will took on <u>vigorous</u> new projects. The Civil Works Administration (CWA) provided a boost for more than 4 million workers who built or repaired roads and airports. Some 2.5 million joined the Civilian Conservation Corps (CCC) to restore forests, parks, and beaches. The Works Progress Administration (WPA) hired 8 million Americans to construct or repair schools and hospitals.

Men in the CCC crews worked for $1 a day, plus free board and job training. Millions <u>humbly</u> accepted these jobs. They never dreamed of insisting that they deserved more pay.

With a New Deal in hand, Americans <u>courageously</u> fought the worst economic period in our country's history. They bravely overcame the dark days of the 1930s. They even overcame, as FDR famously said, "fear itself."

1. Circle a synonym for <u>obligation</u>. Describe an *obligation* you have to your parents or teachers.

2. Underline the phrase that describes how Americans experienced <u>strife</u>. Give a synonym for *strife*.

3. Underline the phrase that means about the same thing as <u>policy</u>. Give an example of a school *policy* that you agree with.

4. Circle a synonym for <u>extraordinary</u>. Describe something that is *extraordinary* about you, and support the statement.

5. Underline a phrase that helps explain the meaning of <u>confront</u>. What did FDR do to *confront* the Great Depression that Hoover did not?

6. Circle a word that helps explain the meaning of <u>vigorous.</u> Why did New Deal jobs need *vigorous* workers?

7. Underline the sentence that helps explain the meaning of <u>humbly</u>. Is *arrogantly* a synonym for *humbly*? Explain.

8. Circle a synonym for <u>courageously</u>. Briefly describe someone you know or someone in history who behaved *courageously*.

"**First Inaugural Address**" by Franklin Delano Roosevelt
Writing About the Big Question

Is knowledge the same as understanding?

Big Question Vocabulary

ambiguous	clarify	comprehend	concept	connection
fact	feeling	information	insight	instinct
interpret	research	senses/sensory	sources	statistics

A. *Use one or more words from the list above to complete each sentence.*

1. When a person acts out of a natural _____, is that person relying on knowledge or understanding?

2. Roosevelt gave _____ and _____ so Americans would understand what needed to be done.

3. Roosevelt tried to _____ the causes of the Great Depression.

4. By reading Roosevelt's speech, Maya got a new _____ into his presidency.

B. *Follow the directions in responding to each item below.*

1. Why should our presidents explain their understanding of national events?

   _____

   _____

2. How did Roosevelt help you understand the Great Depression? Use two of the Big Question vocabulary words.

   _____

   _____

C. *In "First Inaugural Address," President Roosevelt acknowledges the cold realities of the Great Depression and he promises to do whatever is necessary to help the nation recover. Complete the sentence below. Then, write a short paragraph in which you connect this experience to the Big Question.*

For leaders to inspire confidence, they must comprehend _____

because _____

_____

_____

_____

_____

"First Inaugural Address" by Franklin Delano Roosevelt
Literary Analysis: Persuasive Speech

A **persuasive speech** is a speech that tries to convince listeners to think or act in a certain way. Persuasive speeches may appeal to reason or emotion or both. In order to engage the audience, speakers often include **rhetorical devices,** special patterns of words and ideas that create emphasis and stir emotion in the audience. Common rhetorical devices include the following:

- **Restatement:** expressing the same idea in different words to clarify and stress key points
- **Repetition:** expressing different ideas using the same words or images in order to reinforce concepts and unify the speech
- **Analogy:** drawing a comparison that shows a similarity between unlike things
- **Parallelism:** repeating a grammatical structure or arrangement of words to create a sense of rhythm and momentum

DIRECTIONS: *Read each of the following passages from Roosevelt's "First Inaugural Address." On the lines provided, identify the rhetorical device or devices in each passage. (You may find more than one rhetorical device.) Then briefly explain your answer by citing the words and phrases that exemplify the device.*

1. Values have shrunken to fantastic levels; taxes have risen; our ability to pay has fallen

   Rhetorical Device(s): _____

   Explanation: _____

   _____

2. Nature still offers her bounty and human efforts have multiplied it. Plenty is at our doorstep, but a generous use of it languishes in the very sight of the supply.

   Rhetorical Device(s): _____

   Explanation: _____

   _____

3. The money changers have fled from their high seats in the temple of our civilization. We may now restore that temple to the ancient truths.

   Rhetorical Device(s): _____

   Explanation: _____

   _____

4. In the field of world policy I would dedicate this nation to the policy of the good neighbor— the neighbor who resolutely respects himself and . . . the rights of others.

   Rhetorical Device(s): _____

   Explanation: _____

   _____

"**First Inaugural Address**" by Franklin Delano Roosevelt
Reading: Analyze Persuasive Techniques

Persuasive techniques are devices used to influence the audience in favor of the author's argument. In addition to presenting evidence in a persuasive speech, a speaker may use the following:

- emotionally charged language
- rhetorical devices, such as parallelism, restatement, and repetition

To analyze and evaluate persuasive techniques, **read aloud** to hear the effect. Notice the emotional impact of the sounds of certain words, as well as the rhythm and momentum created by the word patterns that the author uses. Consider both the purpose and effect of these persuasive techniques and evaluate the author's success in using them to make a convincing argument.

DIRECTIONS: *Read the following excerpts from Roosevelt's "First Inaugural Address." Then, on the lines provided, answer the questions that follow.*

1. Primarily, this is because the rulers of the exchange of mankind's goods have failed through their own stubbornness and their own incompetence, have admitted that failure and abdicated. Practices of the unscrupulous money changers stand indicted in the court of public opinion, rejected by the hearts and minds of men.

    A. How does the passage illustrate parallelism? _____

    _____

    B. What are three examples of emotionally charged language in the passage? Are the emotional associations positive or negative? _____

    _____

2. Small wonder that confidence languishes, for it thrives only on honesty, on honor, on the sacredness of obligations, on faithful protection, on unselfish performance. Without them it cannot live.

    A. How does this passage exemplify parallelism? _____

    _____

    B. How does Roosevelt use restatement in the passage? _____

    _____

3. We face the arduous days that lie before us in the warm courage of national unity; with the clear consciousness of seeking old and precious moral values; with the clean satisfaction that comes from the stern performance of duty by old and young alike.

    A. What are the emotional associations of the adjectives *warm, clear, precious,* and *clean*?

    _____

    B. How would you describe the rhythm of this passage? _____

    _____

Name _____ Date _____

"**First Inaugural Address**" by Franklin Delano Roosevelt
Vocabulary Builder

Word List

abdicated   arduous   candor   discipline   feasible   induction

A. DIRECTIONS: *Revise each sentence so that the underlined vocabulary word is used logically. Be sure not to change the vocabulary word.*

1. Because the task was so <u>arduous</u>, we completed it with little effort.

   _____

   _____

2. The people hoped that the queen's rule would last a lifetime, so it came as a welcome surprise that she <u>abdicated</u> the throne in the second year of her reign.

   _____

   _____

3. On my cousin's <u>induction</u> into the army, our family gathered to welcome him home.

   _____

   _____

4. Because she always spoke with <u>candor</u>, no one ever believed her.

   _____

   _____

5. The child didn't need any <u>discipline</u> because she was so frightfully disobedient.

   _____

   _____

6. If you are a good student, it is quite <u>feasible</u> that you'll never do well in college.

   _____

   _____

B. WORD STUDY: The Latin root *-duct/duc-* means "to lead" or "bring." Answer each of the following questions using one of these words containing *-duct/duc-: conduct, reduction, deduct.*

1. Why would anyone want to <u>conduct</u> an orchestra?

   _____

2. How would a price <u>reduction</u> help you buy more music CDs?

   _____

3. Why should you <u>deduct</u> what something costs from how much money you have before making a purchase?

   _____

Name _____ Date _____

"First Inaugural Address" by Franklin Delano Roosevelt
Enrichment: The New Deal

As he had promised, Franklin D. Roosevelt set out in the opening days of his first term to put the nation on the path of economic recovery from the Great Depression. The government's efforts to accomplish this goal lasted for the remainder of the 1930s and involved numerous initiatives and new agencies. Collectively, these programs defined the New Deal, the term by which this period in American history is known. Many of Roosevelt's programs and agencies are still referred to by an "alphabet soup" of abbreviations: for example, TVA for Tennessee Valley Authority and NLRB for National Labor Relations Board.

Using Internet or library resources, compile a brief dictionary of New Deal agencies and initiatives. Each dictionary entry should begin with the abbreviated title of a bill, program, or agency, followed by its full name, the year it was established, and its purpose. Put your dictionary entries in alphabetical order. You may use the lines below or a separate piece of paper for your New Deal dictionary.

_____

_____

_____

_____

_____

_____

_____

_____

_____

_____

_____

_____

_____

_____

_____

_____

_____

_____

_____

"I Have a Dream" by Dr. Martin Luther King, Jr.
"First Inaugural Address" by Franklin Delano Roosevelt
Integrated Language Skills: Grammar

Adverbs

An **adverb** is a word that modifies a verb, an adjective, or another adverb. Adverbs answer the questions *Where? When? In what way?* and *To what extent?* about the words they modify. You can often make descriptions more meaningful by using adverbs. Look at these examples:

Modifying a Verb:	The audience listened to the speech *attentively*. (*Attentively* modifies the verb *listened*.)
Modifying an Adjective:	Dr. King made an *extremely* eloquent speech. (*Extremely* modifies the adjective *eloquent*.)
Modifying an Adverb:	Dr. King used language *very* persuasively. (*Very* modifies the adverb *persuasively*.)

A. PRACTICE: *Read the following passages from "I Have a Dream" and "First Inaugural Address." On the lines provided, write the adverb(s) in each sentence and the word that each adverb modifies. Then, in parentheses, tell whether the word modified by each adverb is a verb, an adjective, or another adverb.*

1. We must forever conduct our struggle on the high plane of dignity and discipline.

   _____

2. I say to you today, my friends, that in spite of the difficulties of today and tomorrow, I still have a dream. It is a dream deeply rooted in the American dream.

   _____

3. Nature still offers her bounty and human efforts have multiplied it.

   _____

4. We may now restore that temple to the ancient truths.

   _____

B. WRITING APPLICATION: *Write a brief paragraph focusing on a national issue that you think is important. Use at least three adverbs in your writing, and underline each adverb that you use.*

_____

_____

_____

_____

_____

_____

_____

_____

Name _____ Date _____

"I Have a Dream" by Dr. Martin Luther King, Jr.
"First Inaugural Address" by Franklin Delano Roosevelt
Integrated Language Skills: Support for Writing a Proposal

Use the chart below to make prewriting notes for your proposal.

Issues That Concern Students	Possible Speakers and Topics
1. _____ _____ _____ _____	1. _____ _____ _____ _____
2. _____ _____ _____ _____	2. _____ _____ _____ _____
3. _____ _____ _____ _____	3. _____ _____ _____ _____
4. _____ _____ _____	4. _____ _____ _____
5. _____ _____ _____	5. _____ _____ _____

My Choice of Speaker: _____
_____

Why This Speaker Can Inspire Students: _____
_____
_____
_____

Now use your notes to write your proposal.

"**I Have a Dream**" by Dr. Martin Luther King, Jr.
"**First Inaugural Address**" by Franklin Delano Roosevelt

Integrated Language Skills: Support for Extend Your Learning

Listening and Speaking

Use the following chart to make prewriting notes for your radio news report and commentary.

Background Information: _____

_____

_____

_____

_____

_____

_____

_____

_____

Notable Excerpts From the Speech: _____

_____

_____

_____

_____

_____

_____

_____

Effect of the Speech on the Crowd: _____

_____

_____

_____

_____

_____

_____

_____

Name _____ Date _____

"First Inaugural Address" by Franklin Delano Roosevelt
Open-Book Test

Short Answer *Write your responses to the questions in this section on the lines provided.*

1. In the second paragraph of his first inaugural address, Franklin Roosevelt says that the times call for the truth to be spoken, "the whole truth, frankly and boldly." Why might Roosevelt have begun his speech by suggesting that he is about to speak openly and to make bold statements?

   _____

   _____

   _____

2. The most famous part of Franklin Roosevelt's first inaugural address is the bold assertion at the beginning: "The only thing we have to fear is fear itself." What rhetorical device makes those words so memorable and so compelling?

   _____

   _____

   _____

3. In the opening paragraphs of his first inaugural address, Franklin Roosevelt speaks of fear, terror, and a "dark hour." Why does Roosevelt use such negative language? Cite one detail from the speech to support your response.

   _____

   _____

   _____

   _____

4. Read aloud the following sentence from Franklin Roosevelt's first inaugural address, and notice its emotional impact. What emotionally charged language is contained in the sentence?

   Practices of the unscrupulous money changers stand indicted in the court of public opinion, rejected by the hearts and minds of men.

   _____

   _____

Unit 3 Resources: Types of Nonfiction
© Pearson Education, Inc. All rights reserved.
196

5. Read the following passage from Franklin Roosevelt's first inaugural address. Then, complete the diagram to analyze and evaluate Roosevelt's use of one persuasive technique.

"Happiness lies not in the mere possession of money; it lies in the joy of achievement, in the thrill of creative effort."	→	**Technique:**		**Effect:**
		↓		
		Purpose:	→	

6. In his first inaugural address, Franklin Roosevelt refers to "the mad chase of evanescent profits." By *mad*, Roosevelt means foolish or unreasonable. Why does he use that word to describe "evanescent profits"? *Base your answer on the glossary definition of evanescent.*

_____

_____

7. Midway through his first inaugural address, Franklin Roosevelt refers to "the American spirit of the pioneer." In American history, the term *pioneer* usually describes the hardy people who settled the Midwest and the West during the nineteenth century. What is the point of referring to the pioneer spirit?

_____

_____

_____

8. In his first inaugural address, Franklin Roosevelt says that the American people must become "a trained and loyal army." What rhetorical device is Roosevelt using in this passage? Explain.

_____

_____

9. At the beginning of his first inaugural address, Franklin Roosevelt speaks frankly about the nation's economic condition. Toward the end, he talks about the measures he plans to take to meet the economic challenge facing the nation. Throughout the speech, his primary audience is the American people. What is Roosevelt's most important aim in this speech?

_____

_____

10. The following passage is from the next to last paragraph of Franklin Roosevelt's first inaugural address. What two rhetorical devices does it illustrate? Explain your answer.

They have asked for discipline and direction under leadership. They have made me the present instrument of their wishes.

_____

_____

_____

Essay

Write an extended response to the question of your choice or to the question or questions your teacher assigns you.

11. A persuasive speech often focuses on a problem and proposes a solution to it. In an essay, identify the problem that confronts Franklin Roosevelt when he delivers his first inaugural address. Then, describe the manner in which Roosevelt approaches the problem, and identify two solutions he proposes.

12. One of the most powerful weapons of a persuasive speaker is emotionally charged language. In an essay, show how Franklin Roosevelt uses such language in his first inaugural address. Cite three examples of such language, and state whether each instance was likely to stir negative emotions or positive emotions. Finally, evaluate Roosevelt's use of emotional language. Provide a well-reasoned argument to support your evaluation.

13. In his first inaugural address, Franklin Roosevelt does not devote much space to spelling out the programs and measures he intends to use to lead the nation's economy from depression to recovery. Why might Roosevelt have remained silent about the details of his plan? In an essay, analyze the ways in which Roosevelt appeals to his listeners by invoking broad, general ideals and principles rather than describing specific methods.

14. **Thinking About the Big Question: Is knowledge the same as understanding?** In his first inaugural address, does Franklin Roosevelt demonstrate that he has both knowledge (the possession of information) and understanding (the ability to make sense of information)? Does he appear to have more of one than the other? Answer this question in a brief essay. Support your opinion by referring to the speech.

Oral Response

15. Go back to question 3, 4, or 10 or to the question your teacher assigns you. Take a few minutes to expand your answer and prepare an oral response. Find additional details in Franklin Roosevelt's first inaugural address to support your points. If necessary, make notes to guide your oral response.

Name _____ Date _____

"First Inaugural Address" by Franklin Delano Roosevelt
Selection Test A

Critical Reading *Identify the letter of the choice that best answers the question.*

____ 1. Which of the following is the most important issue facing the nation at the time that Franklin D. Roosevelt delivers his "First Inaugural Address"?
A. the outbreak of World War II
B. the Vietnam War
C. the Great Depression
D. the need for a better transportation system

____ 2. At the beginning of "First Inaugural Address," how does President Roosevelt describe the way in which he will speak to the American people?
A. prudently and cautiously
B. honestly and decisively
C. intelligently and soberly
D. humorously

____ 3. Which persuasive technique can you identify in this sentence from President Roosevelt's speech?

Practices of the unscrupulous money changers stand indicted in the court of public opinion, rejected by the hearts and minds of men.

A. parallelism
B. rhythm and repetition
C. emotionally charged language
D. restatement

____ 4. In "First Inaugural Address," which of the following groups does President Roosevelt say needs ethical reform?
A. banking and business
B. medicine
C. law enforcement
D. politicians and the bureaucracy

____ 5. According to President Roosevelt, what is the nation's "greatest primary task"?
A. to increase the food supply
B. to put people to work
C. to create a great army
D. to revise the Constitution

_____ 6. Overall, which of the following best states President Roosevelt's most important aim in "First Inaugural Address"?

    A. to restore the confidence of the American people

    B. to propose major reforms in the banking system

    C. to warn foreign powers that aggression against America will never succeed

    D. to reassure ordinary Americans that economic difficulties are not their fault

_____ 7. Which of the following is the best definition of *parallelism*?

    A. the use of extended similes

    B. the repetition of a grammatical structure

    C. the use of emotionally charged language

    D. the repetition of a question or command

_____ 8. Read this sentence from President Roosevelt's "First Inaugural Address":

> Our Constitution is so simple and practical that it is possible always to meet extraordinary needs by changes in emphasis and arrangement without loss of essential form.

According to President Roosevelt, why does the U.S. Constitution deserve to be admired?

    A. It provides for a strong presidency.

    B. It ensures political and legal equality.

    C. It has proved extremely flexible over time.

    D. It has been imitated by many foreign nations.

_____ 9. In his speech, why does Franklin D. Roosevelt stress "the American spirit of the pioneer"?

    A. to gain support in the West

    B. to show his knowledge of history

    C. to emphasize the value of interdependence

    D. to encourage a spirit of sacrifice

_____ 10. In the following excerpt from "First Inaugural Address," to what does President Roosevelt compare the "unity of duty" in response to the crisis facing the nation?

> This I propose to offer, pledging that the larger purposes will bind upon us all as a sacred obligation with a unity of duty hitherto evoked only in time of armed strife.

    A. an annual ceremony

    B. a war

    C. a universal tax

    D. a plague

_____ 11. Which of the following is a helpful method of identifying persuasive devices in a text such as an essay or a speech?

  A. Read the text aloud to hear the effects of rhythm and momentum.

  B. Use library resources to check the author's literary and historical references.

  C. Interview classmates or friends about their impressions of the text.

  D. Compare the concluding paragraph of the text with the opening paragraph.

Vocabulary and Grammar

_____ 12. Which of the following is the best synonym for *abdicated?*

  A. called by name   C. gave up formally

  B. swore to   D. recommended

_____ 13. Which of the following best describes an *arduous* task?

  A. gentle   C. welcome

  B. difficult   D. impossible

_____ 14. Which word is the adverb in the following sentence from "First Inaugural Address"?

  With this pledge taken, I assume unhesitatingly the leadership of this great army of our people, dedicated to a disciplined attack upon our common problems.

  A. pledge   C. dedicated

  B. unhesitatingly   D. disciplined

Essay

15. A persuasive speech often focuses on a problem and proposes a solution to it. In an essay, identify the problem that confronted Franklin D. Roosevelt when he delivered his "First Inaugural Address." Describe the manner in which he approached this problem. Then, identify two of the solutions that he put before the American people.

16. One of the most powerful weapons of a persuasive speaker is emotionally charged language. Such language has built-in emotional associations, which stir people's emotions either positively or negatively. In an open-book essay, show how Franklin D. Roosevelt uses emotionally charged language in his "First Inaugural Address." After reviewing and analyzing some examples of this type of language, evaluate President Roosevelt's use of this persuasive technique.

17. **Thinking About the Big Question: Is knowledge the same as understanding?** Franklin Delano Roosevelt's first presidential speech in 1933 contains no hard facts about the nation's difficult economic conditions. Yet the speech contains great emotional appeal to the hearts and minds of the people. Does President Roosevelt use knowledge or understanding or both in his address to the nation? Support your response in a brief essay. Remember to refer to the "First Inaugural Address" in your answer.

Name _____ Date _____

"First Inaugural Address" by Franklin Delano Roosevelt
Selection Test B

Critical Reading *Identify the letter of the choice that best completes the statement or answers the question.*

_____ 1. At the beginning of his "First Inaugural Address," what does Franklin D. Roosevelt say that his fellow Americans expect of him?
A. a tax cut
B. thorough consultation with Congress
C. candor and decision
D. an end to hard times

_____ 2. According to President Roosevelt in his "First Inaugural Address," what is the only thing Americans have to fear?
A. fear itself
B. foreign attack
C. a further decrease in stock prices
D. a decline in corporate profits

_____ 3. Which of the following best defines the literary term *rhetorical devices*?
A. imaginative metaphors that cause the audience to consider the topic in a fresh way
B. the use of repetition and refrain to emphasize a speaker's or writer's main idea
C. complex symbolism that considers a topic from many different perspectives
D. special patterns of words and ideas that create emphasis and stir emotion

_____ 4. Which of the following does President Roosevelt strongly criticize in his "First Inaugural Address"?
A. striking workers who have crippled industry
B. bankers accused of unscrupulous greed
C. politicians who have deceived voters
D. journalists who have criticized Roosevelt

_____ 5. Which of the following rhetorical devices expresses the same idea in different words in order to clarify and stress key points?
A. parallelism
B. restatement
C. repetition
D. emphasis

_____ 6. Which of the following rhetorical devices does this passage from "First Inaugural Address" illustrate?

It is the way to recovery. It is the immediate way. It is the strongest assurance that the recovery will endure.

A. rhyme
B. symbolism
C. simile
D. parallelism

_____ 7. On the whole, which of the following best expresses the way President Roosevelt wants his audience to think?
  A. aggressively
  B. confidently
  C. gratefully
  D. politically

_____ 8. Which of the following devices does this passage from "First Inaugural Address" illustrate?
  > In the field of world policy I would dedicate this nation to the policy of the good neighbor— the neighbor who resolutely respects himself and, because he does so, respects the rights of others—the neighbor who respects his obligations and respects the sanctity of his agreements in and with a world of neighbors.

  A. exaggeration
  B. metaphor
  C. repetition
  D. symbolism

_____ 9. According to President Roosevelt, the U.S. Constitution deserves admiration because of its
  A. brevity.
  B. eloquence.
  C. flexibility.
  D. popularity.

_____ 10. Read this passage from President Roosevelt's "First Inaugural Address":
  > Primarily, this is because the rulers of the exchange of mankind's goods have failed through their own stubbornness and their own incompetence, have admitted that failure and abdicated. Practices of the unscrupulous money changers stand indicted in the court of public opinion, rejected by the hearts and minds of men.

  Which of the following persuasive techniques does this passage notably illustrate?
  A. symbolism
  B. emotionally charged language
  C. parallelism
  D. repetition

_____ 11. According to President Roosevelt in his speech, which of the following is long overdue in banking and business?
  A. a change in accounting practices
  B. an improvement in training programs
  C. a change in ethics
  D. a reduction in corporate taxes

_____ 12. In his speech, President Roosevelt invokes the spirit of the American pioneer in order to stress the importance of which of the following?
  A. interdependence
  B. curiosity
  C. courage
  D. self-sufficiency

_____ 13. Which rhetorical device does this passage from "First Inaugural Address" illustrate?
They have asked for discipline and direction under leadership. They have made me the present instrument of their wishes.

   A. symbolism
   B. restatement
   C. figurative language
   D. emotionally charged language

_____ 14. In order to analyze and evaluate persuasive techniques in a text, which of the following is a helpful strategy?
   A. Read aloud to hear the effect of the text.
   B. Use an encyclopedia to check allusions.
   C. Compare the text with another work by the same author.
   D. Consult a reliable biography of the author.

Vocabulary and Grammar

_____ 15. If a leader *abdicated* responsibility, what did he or she do?
   A. increased it   C. decreased it
   B. gave it up   D. fulfilled it

_____ 16. Which of the following is the best antonym for *feasible*?
   A. impractical   C. convenient
   B. difficult   D. realistic

_____ 17. Which word is the adverb in the following sentence?
I am convinced that you will again give that support to leadership in these critical days.

   A. convinced   C. support
   B. again   D. critical

_____ 18. In the sentence "We may now restore that temple to the ancient truths," which word or phrase does the adverb *now* modify?
   A. We   C. that temple
   B. may restore   D. ancient truths

Essay

19. In an essay, write a précis, or summary, of President Roosevelt's "First Inaugural Address." In your précis, identify the main ideas and the principal details he uses to support these ideas persuasively to convince his audience.

20. In "First Inaugural Address," Franklin D. Roosevelt does not devote much space to spelling out the specific programs or measures that he intends to use in order to turn the economy around from depression to recovery. Why do you think he adopted this strategy? In an essay, analyze the ways in which President Roosevelt appeals to his listeners by invoking broad, general ideals and principles, rather than specific methods to recharge the economy.

21. **Thinking About the Big Question: Is knowledge the same as understanding?** In his "First Inaugural Address," does Franklin D. Roosevelt demonstrate that he has both knowledge (the possession of information) and understanding (the ability to make sense of information)? Does he appear to have more of one than the other? Answer this question in a brief essay. Support your opinion by referring to the speech.

Vocabulary Warm-up Word Lists

Study these words from the selection. Then, complete the activities.

Word List A

bundle [BUN dul] *n.* a group of things that are held together or piled up
Lamont carried the large <u>bundle</u> of laundry to the basement.

churning [CHURN ing] *v.* shaking or mixing vigorously
The farmer worked hard <u>churning</u> milk into butter.

frail [FRAYL] *adj.* weak, delicate, or fragile
As she grew older, the cat was so <u>frail</u> that she could no longer climb onto the couch.

nudge [NUJ] *v.* to give a gentle push to get someone's attention
Standing in the crowd, I felt someone <u>nudge</u> me and looked up to see my cousin grinning.

plucked [PLUKT] *v.* picked out; pulled off
Just in time, Meghan <u>plucked</u> the ring out of the drain.

recite [re SYT] *v.* to tell or to read something out loud, especially from memory
We were all impressed that Malcolm could <u>recite</u> the entire Declaration of Independence.

restless [REST lis] *adj.* fidgety; moving constantly; uneasy
Anar grew <u>restless</u> sitting in the house all morning, so she took a walk.

twined [TWYND] *v.* twisted or braided together; wound around
With the vine <u>twined</u> around it, the lamppost looked as if it were sprouting leaves.

Word List B

breathlessly [BRETH lus lee] *adv.* in a manner that seems out of breath
Her face glowing, Sheree <u>breathlessly</u> told the others her amazing news.

gangly [GANG lee] *adj.* tall and thin; often awkward or clumsy
Almost overnight, Ron grew from a <u>gangly</u> teen into a sturdy young man.

ford [FORD] *n.* a shallow place in a stream or river where one can safely cross
When we came to the <u>ford</u>, we led the horses across the creek.

hoarsely [HORS lee] *adv.* in a gruff or husky voice
Even after her cough went away, Nina spoke <u>hoarsely</u> for weeks.

receding [ruh SEED ing] *v.* moving back or away; growing distant
We continued to wave as we watched the train <u>receding</u> into the tunnel.

scowling [SKOW ling] *v.* frowning in an angry manner
When Mr. Lee heard about the broken window, he could not stop himself from <u>scowling</u>.

unshapely [un SHAYP lee] *adj.* not in a pleasing shape; out of proportion
The jacket was three sizes too large, and it gave Jay an <u>unshapely</u> appearance.

wavered [WAY verd] *v.* swayed or moved back and forth; fluctuated
The stack of dishes <u>wavered</u> for a moment, then crashed to the floor.

"**Talk**" retold by Harold Courlander and George Herzog
"**The Talk**" by Gary Soto
Vocabulary Warm-up Exercises

Exercise A *Fill in the blanks, using each word from Word List A only once.*

The old man looked thin and [1] _____, but he must have been stronger than he appeared, for he carried a heavy [2] _____ on his back as he walked down the street. He stopped in front of Bertie and me. After brushing the dust off his trousers, he [3] _____ a bit of lint from his sleeve. Then, to our sur-prise, he began to [4] _____ his life story in great detail. His told us that he had worked in a dairy and had spent many hours [5] _____ milk in a giant pot. We listened for a long time, but we began to grow [6] _____, so I decided to [7] _____ Bertie with my elbow to let him know I was ready to get away from this odd gentleman. We politely said goodbye, but as we turned to leave, he drew from his pocket two long silver chains that were [8] _____ together. Without another word, he handed one to Bertie and the other to me, and then he contin-ued on his way.

Exercise B *Decide whether each statement below is true or false. Explain your answers.*

1. A person who is <u>gangly</u> would be expected to do very well at ballet or gymnastics.
   _____

2. After cheering loudly at a football game, a fan will often speak <u>hoarsely</u>.
   _____

3. A sight that is <u>receding</u> seems to be growing larger as you watch.
   _____

4. The angrier people become, the more likely they are to be <u>scowling</u>.
   _____

5. Fashion models often have <u>unshapely</u> physical features.
   _____

6. A pile of books that <u>wavered</u> before it fell was likely on an unsteady table.
   _____

7. The most dangerous place to cross a river is at a <u>ford</u>.
   _____

8. Someone with exciting news will often tell it <u>breathlessly</u>.
   _____

"**Talk**" retold by Harold Courlander and George Herzog
"**The Talk**" by Gary Soto
Reading Warm-up A

Read the following passage. Pay special attention to the underlined words. Then, read it again, and complete the activities. Use a separate sheet of paper for your written answers.

Just about every group of people throughout the world has a storytelling tradition. These stories might be folk tales, myths, or legends, but they all serve some purpose for that culture. Sometimes stories are a way of passing on information about religious beliefs, history, or practices to the next generation. Adult members of a community may <u>recite</u> folk tales to teach lessons about proper behavior. The stories may also be used as warnings about what can happen when people step outside of what is expected.

Folk tales are especially important in societies that do not have a written language. When the storyteller is an elderly person, whether strong or <u>frail</u>, children see the wisdom of the older generation. Even the most wiggly, <u>restless</u> child will pay attention when these stories are told aloud. If there are children who disturb the story session, someone will <u>nudge</u> the children to quiet them. This respect for older members of the community is often lost in many modern societies that use television to tell their stories.

Often, folk tales start with a situation that is common in that culture. This might be a maid <u>churning</u> milk into butter, a fisherman repairing his net, or a farmer trying to sell a chicken that has just been <u>plucked</u>. After that, the details depend on the lesson the storyteller wants to teach. In that way, listeners can see themselves in the story's main character.

We may not recognize parts of our own culture that began as folk tales. For example, Santa Claus, with his red coat and his large <u>bundle</u> of toys, has been part of Christian traditions across Europe for centuries. He appeared under a variety of different names and had different habits. Today, his story has become <u>twined</u> with the interests of toy makers and stores. It is hard to think of them separately. The lessons that the Santa tale once taught have now all but disappeared.

1. Underline the phrases that tell the goals of the folk tales that adults <u>recite</u>. Give a synonym for **recite**.

2. Circle the antonym that is a clue for <u>frail</u>. Describe what **frail** means.

3. Underline the word that is a clue for <u>restless</u>. Give an antonym for **restless.**

4. Underline the phrase that tells who is getting <u>nudged</u>. For what purpose do we **nudge** someone?

5. Circle the word that tells who is <u>churning</u> something. Underline what the passage says is the result of that person's **churning**.

6. Circle the word that tells what has been <u>plucked</u>. Explain the difference between **plucked** and **put into.**

7. Underline the word that tells what is in the <u>bundle</u>. Use **bundle** in a new sentence.

8. Circle a word that helps to explain the meaning of <u>twined</u>. Underline the two phrases that tell which things are **twined**.

"Talk" retold by Harold Courlander and George Herzog
"The Talk" by Gary Soto
Reading Warm-up B

Read the following passage. Pay special attention to the underlined words. Then, read it again, and complete the activities. Use a separate sheet of paper for your written answers.

Washington Irving is remembered as one of the most vivid American storytellers. Born in 1783, Irving was named for the nation's first president. As a young man he studied law, but he preferred traveling around Europe and interacting socially with friends to working. With his brother and a friend, he published a satiric magazine about society. Later, he turned to writing short stories.

Two of Irving's most celebrated stories are "The Legend of Sleepy Hollow" and "Rip Van Winkle." "Sleepy Hollow" features a character named Ichabod Crane, a tall, <u>gangly</u> schoolteacher with long arms. One night, as Ichabod is riding his horse, he believes he is being followed by a rider without a head. As he reaches a rough bridge that has been built across the <u>ford</u> of a stream, he is terrified by a sudden noise. He <u>hoarsely</u> asks who is there, but he receives no response. Then, in the darkness, he sees the bulky, <u>unshapely</u> form of the headless horseman.

The original tale does not end well for Ichabod, although writers of movies and cartoons based on the story have often changed the ending. These versions are still frightening, even though the time in which they were written is <u>receding</u> further into history.

"Rip Van Winkle" has also been translated into film. Rip is amiable but extremely lazy. Everyone in his village enjoys his company except his wife, who is portrayed as either nagging or <u>scowling</u> angrily at him. To escape her, he wanders into the mountains, where he encounters some oddly dressed men. Then, he falls asleep. When he awakens, twenty years have elapsed, but he remains unchanged. Rip returns to his village. Finally, he realizes what has happened and runs around <u>breathlessly</u> looking for his family and friends.

Washington Irving's stories were widely read and appreciated in his own day. Although his popularity has <u>wavered</u> since then, these stories remain a part of American folklore.

1. Underline the phrase that is a clue for <u>gangly</u>. How does the character's name also make him seem **gangly**?

2. Circle the word that tells where the <u>ford</u> is. Explain what **ford** means.

3. Explain why the character was speaking <u>hoarsely</u>. Give another reason a person might speak **hoarsely.**

4. Underline the word(s) that gives a clue for <u>unshapely</u>. Why might being **unshapely** make the horseman more frightening?

5. Underline what is <u>receding</u> in this sentence. Give a word or phrase that means the same as **receding.**

6. Circle the word that is a clue for <u>scowling</u>. What is an antonym for **scowling**?

7. Underline the phrase that is a clue for <u>breathlessly</u>. Write a sentence using the word **breathlessly.**

8. Underline the words that tell what has <u>wavered</u>. Give a word or phrase that means the same as **wavered.**

Name _____ Date _____

"The Talk" by Gary Soto
"Talk" retold by George Herzog and Harold Courlander

Writing About the Big Question

Is knowledge the same as understanding?

Big Question Vocabulary

ambiguous	clarify	comprehend	concept	connection
fact	feeling	information	insight	instinct
interpret	research	senses/sensory	sources	statistics

A. *Use one or more words from the list above to complete each sentence.*

1. Jamie and Mike make a strong _____ by talking about all the things that happen in their lives.

2. If you _____ the conversation in "The Talk," you will understand much about the lives of the two boys.

3. Hannah thought her _____ were deceiving her when her chair began to speak.

4. When the fish trap talked, it gave the fisherman new _____ into the information the farmer gave him.

B. *Follow the directions in responding to each of the items below.*

1. List one or two people you like to talk to.

   _____

2. How does talking to someone help you clarify your feelings and ideas? Use at least two of the Big Question vocabulary words.

   _____

   _____

C. *Complete the sentence below. Then, write a short paragraph in which you connect this experience to the big question.*

Each of these selections builds our knowledge and understanding with facts and other details. Complete this sentence:

When a writer presents facts in a humorous way, _____ .

_____

_____

_____

_____

Name _____ Date _____

"**Talk**" retold by Harold Courlander and George Herzog
"**The Talk**" by Gary Soto
Literary Analysis: Comparing Humorous Writing

A **humorous essay** is a form of nonfiction writing intended to make the reader laugh. Some humorous writing, often described as harsh or biting, ridicules its subjects. Other humorous writing, often described as gentle, treats its subjects with affection even as it makes fun of them.

Humorous writers often include one or more of the following figures of speech:

- **hyperbole:** intentional (and often outrageous) overstatement, or exaggeration
- **understatement:** the presentation of something in a restrained or subtle manner; the opposite of hyperbole

In addition to these techniques, the comic writer's **diction,** or word choice, may include funny names, slang, or other examples of verbal humor.

Although humorous writing is meant to entertain, it can have other purposes as well. For example, humor can be used to convey a serious message.

DIRECTIONS: *Write your answers to the following questions on the lines provided.*

1. Read this passage from "The Talk" by Gary Soto:

   The eyes stayed small as well, receding into pencil dots on each side of an unshapely nose that cast remarkable shadows when we turned sideways.

   What humorous technique does the passage exemplify? Briefly explain your answer.

   _____

   _____

2. What serious issue concerning childhood and adolescence does "The Talk" raise? How does the writer's tone in the essay help you to gain perspective on that issue?

   _____

   _____

3. What examples of the authors' diction stand out to you in the folk tale "Talk"? How does the diction contribute to the humor of the story?

   _____

   _____

4. What important message is conveyed in "Talk"?

   _____

   _____

5. Which story, "The Talk" or "Talk," makes the most use of hyperbole? Of understatement? Explain your answer and give examples.

   _____

   _____

Name _____ Date _____

"Talk" retold by Harold Courlander and George Herzog
"The Talk" by Gary Soto
Vocabulary Builder

Word List

bulging   feisty   refrain   renegade   wheezed

A. DIRECTIONS: *Revise each sentence so that the underlined vocabulary word is used logically. Be sure not to change the vocabulary word.*

1. We worried about the laziness of the <u>feisty</u> dog.

   _____

2. The group of <u>renegade</u> fans loyally cheered the home team whenever it scored.

   _____

3. The <u>bulging</u> balloon grew smaller and smaller before our eyes.

   _____

4. She could not <u>refrain</u> from leaving the luscious dessert untouched.

   _____

5. The runner <u>wheezed</u> loudly and smiled as he thought how strong he felt after this race.

   _____

B. DIRECTIONS: *On the line, write the letter of the choice that is the best answer for each analogy question.*

___ 1. RENEGADE : DISLOYAL ::
    A. prudent : cautious
    B. honest : deceptive
    C. reckless : cautious
    D. rude : loyal

___ 2. FEISTY : LAZY ::
    A. hostile : unfriendly
    B. nimble : athletic
    C. aggressive : peaceful
    D. talkative : chatty

___ 3. BULGING : STUFFED ::
    A. thin : narrow
    B. relaxed : zealous
    C. deprived : privileged
    D. willful : stubborn

___ 4. WHEEZED : GASPED ::
    A. shuddered : shivered
    B. perspired : panted
    C. lunged : withdrew
    D. restricted : extended

___ 5. PERSIST : REFRAIN ::
    A. identify : recognize
    B. unite : isolate
    C. resist : achieve
    D. sacrifice : resistant

Name _____ Date _____

"Talk" retold by Harold Courlander and George Herzog
"The Talk" by Gary Soto

Support for Writing to Compare Literary Works

Use a chart like the one shown to make prewriting notes for your essay analyzing why the authors chose to discuss their subjects in a humorous fashion.

	"The Talk"	"Talk"
Characters' current challenges		
Contributing circumstances		
Clues that challenges can be overcome		
Why authors chose to use humor		

Name _____ Date _____

"**The Talk**" by Gary Soto
"**Talk**" by Harold Courlander and George Herzog
Open-Book Test

Short Answer *Write your responses to the questions in this section on the lines provided.*

1. Hyperbole is deliberate exaggeration for effect. Identify one example of hyperbole from the beginning of "The Talk."

   _____

   _____

   _____

2. In "The Talk," the narrator imagines that he and his wife will "throw a slipper at our feisty dog at least a hundred times." How would a feisty dog respond to such behavior? Base your answer on the definition of *feisty*.

   _____

   _____

3. Tone in literature can be defined as the attitude an author displays toward the subject matter, the characters, or the audience. What is the tone of "The Talk"?

   _____

   _____

   _____

4. In "Talk" a farmer grows angry in the first part of the story. What causes his anger?

   _____

   _____

   _____

5. In "Talk," the farmer, the fisherman, the weaver, and the bather pay the village chief an urgent visit. What is the reason for their visit?

   _____

   _____

   _____

6. "Talk" ends with a joke. The chief's stool says, "Imagine, a talking yam!" Why is that remark funny?

   _____

   _____

   _____

7. Consider the setting and the main characters of the "The Talk" and "Talk."
   Complete this diagram by identifying similarities and differences in the two
   selections. Then, on the lines below, name the selection with the more vivid setting
   and characters. Briefly explain your answer.

Setting and Characters

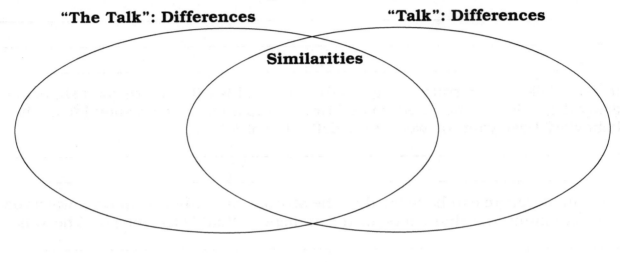

"The Talk": Differences   "Talk": Differences

Similarities

_____

_____

_____

8. An author's purpose is his or her reason for writing a work of literature. What
   appears to be the main purpose of the authors of both "The Talk" and "Talk"?

_____

_____

_____

9. Consider the subject matter of "The Talk" and "Talk." In particular, think about
   what the characters in each selection talk about. What is similar about the
   conversations in the two selections?

_____

_____

_____

10. Both "The Talk" and "Talk" are humorous. Which selection did you find funnier?
    Briefly explain your answer.

_____

_____

_____

Essay

Write an extended response to the question of your choice or to the question or questions your teacher assigns you.

11. Hyperbole, or intentional exaggeration, is a common device in humorous writing. In an essay, identify and analyze two examples of hyperbole in "The Talk." Be sure to explain what makes the hyperbole funny in each case.

12. Both "The Talk" and "Talk" contain humorous remarks and humorous situations. Which remarks and situations did you find especially entertaining? In a brief essay, discuss two funny passages. Choose two passages from one selection or one passage from each selection. Tell why each passage is funny. Also tell whether each passage employs hyperbole.

13. Although humorous writing is primarily intended to entertain, writers also use humor to convey serious messages. In an essay compare and contrast the serious messages underlying "The Talk" and "Talk." Briefly state the serious message each selection conveys. Then, comment on the success of each selection in using humor to convey its message.

14. **Thinking About the Big Question: Is knowledge the same as understanding?** Both "The Talk" and "Talk" use humor to suggest a difference between knowledge and understanding. In a brief essay, discuss one of the two selections. If you choose "The Talk," show how the essay presents a contrast between young people's knowledge and the deeper understanding that maturity usually brings to adults. If you choose "Talk," discuss how the tale suggests a contrast between people's surface knowledge of their surroundings and a deeper understanding of their environment. Cite at least two details from the selection to support your ideas.

Oral Response

15. Go back to question 3, 4, or 10 or the question your teacher assigns you. Take a few minutes to expand your answer and prepare an oral response. Find additional details in the selections to support your points. If necessary, make an outline to guide your oral response.

"**Talk**" retold by Harold Courlander and George Herzog
"**The Talk**" by Gary Soto
Selection Test A

Critical Reading *Identify the letter of the choice that best answers the question.*

____ 1. Which of the following best defines *diction*?
   A. simile
   B. symbolism
   C. word choice
   D. dialogue

____ 2. Which of the following quotations from "The Talk" illustrates hyperbole, or intentional overstatement?
   I. "My best friend and I knew that we were going to grow up to be ugly."
   II. "First, our heads got large, but our necks wavered, frail as crisp tulips."
   III. "I could hammer, saw, lift beams into place, and see the work I got done at the end of the day."
   IV. "My gangly arms nearly touched my kneecaps."

   A. I and III
   B. III and IV
   C. I, II, and IV
   D. II, III, and IV

____ 3. In "The Talk," what subject does Scott, the writer's friend, plan to study in trade school?
   A. refrigeration
   B. engineering
   C. carpentry
   D. plumbing

____ 4. Which of the following is the *opposite* of hyperbole?
   A. inverted word order
   B. slang
   C. understatement
   D. exaggeration

____ 5. In "Talk," why does the farmer get angry at his dog?
   A. He didn't like the tone of the dog's voice.
   B. His dog didn't try to protect him from the talking yam.
   C. The dog informed him that the yam was talking, not the cow.
   D. The dog ran away as soon as the yam started talking.

____ 6. How does the fisherman respond when the farmer first tells him the story?
  A. He throws away the fish trap and cries "Wah!"
  B. He reacts calmly and asks "Is that all?"
  C. He jumps out of the river and races toward the village.
  D. He listens carefully and tries to calm the farmer.

____ 7. Why do the men go to see the chief?
  A. They want permission to move into the village where it is safer.
  B. They want to protect him from things that talk.
  C. They want him to fix the problem of the talking things.
  D. They want to warn him about the talking yam.

____ 8. Which of the following do "The Talk" and "Talk" have in common?
  A. Both selections focus on challenges related to growing up.
  B. Both selections leave the main conflict unresolved.
  C. Both selections are set in a faraway location.
  D. Neither selection uses ordinary people as the main characters.

____ 9. Which of the following identifies a difference, or point of contrast, between "The Talk" and "Talk"?
  A. Soto uses diction to create humor, but Courlander and Herzog do not.
  B. "The Talk" includes serious underlying issues, but "Talk" does not.
  C. The main characters in "The Talk" are common people, whereas the main characters in "Talk" are fantastic characters.
  D. "The Talk" describes ordinary occurrences, whereas "Talk" describes fantastic occurrences.

____ 10. Which of the following is the writer's main purpose in both "The Talk" and "Talk"?
  A. to inform
  B. to persuade
  C. to entertain
  D. to complain

Vocabulary

____ 11. Which one is a synonym for *feisty* in this sentence from Soto's essay?

> In the evenings, we would drink Kool-Aid and throw a slipper at our feisty dog at least a hundred times before we went inside. . . .

    A. energetic   **C.** unfriendly

    B. lazy   **D.** independent

____ 12. Which of the following means the opposite of *renegade*?

    A. humorous   **C.** serious

    B. loyal   **D.** scarce

____ 13. When the authors of "Talk" say the bather's eyes were "bulging," what do they mean?

    A. His eyes were swelling.   **C.** He was squinting.

    B. His eyes were watering.   **D.** His eyes were closed.

Essay

14. What humorous remarks or situations did you find especially entertaining in "The Talk" and "Talk"? In a brief essay, discuss two funny passages from each selection. Be sure to tell which devices the writer uses to achieve humor in these passages.

15. "The Talk" is an essay and is nonfiction; "Talk" is a folk tale and is fiction. Does being fiction or nonfiction make the message of one more "serious" than the other? Explain your answer.

16. **Thinking About the Big Question: Is knowledge the same as understanding?** In "The Talk" by Gary Soto, the young people's knowledge is different from the deeper understanding of the adults. In "Talk" by Harold Courlander and George Herzog, the people have a surface knowledge of their surroundings, yet they may or may not have a deeper understanding of the environment. Choose either "The Talk" or "Talk" and, in an essay, use at least two details from the selection to explain and support one of the statements above.

"Talk" retold by Harold Courlander and George Herzog
"The Talk" by Gary Soto
Selection Test B

Critical Reading *Identify the letter of the choice that best completes the statement or answers the question.*

_____ 1. In "The Talk" by Gary Soto, how old are the two boys, Gary and Scott?
   A. eight
   B. twelve
   C. fourteen
   D. eighteen

_____ 2. In "The Talk," what is the cause of the boys' anxiety?
   A. their grades in school
   B. their clumsiness at sports
   C. their physical appearance
   D. their parents' disapproval

_____ 3. Which of the following best defines the figure of speech called *hyperbole*?
   A. overstatement for effect
   B. understatement for effect
   C. implied metaphor
   D. multiple layers of symbolism

_____ 4. Which of the following passages from "The Talk" illustrates hyperbole?
   I. "Since our town was made with what was left over after God made hell, there was money in air conditioning, he reasoned."
   II. "I would need only a stepladder to hand a fellow worker on the roof a pinch of nails."
   III. "In the evenings, we would drink Kool-Aid and throw a slipper at our feisty dog at least a hundred times before we went inside for a Pop-Tart and hot chocolate."
   IV. "I turned onto my stomach, a stalk of grass in my mouth."
   A. I and II
   B. I and III
   C. II and III
   D. II and IV

_____ 5. In "The Talk," what profession does Gary say he will follow when he grows up?
   A. law enforcement officer
   B. architect
   C. doctor
   D. carpenter

_____ 6. In "The Talk," what is the beautiful girl doing as the boys watch her?
   A. cooking
   B. exercising
   C. reading
   D. watching television

____ 7. After things begin talking, what event finally prompts the farmer in "Talk" to run away?
   A. The stone says, "Hey, take that thing off me!"
   B. The palm tree says, "Put that branch down!"
   C. The dog says, "It wasn't the cow who spoke to you."
   D. The palm branch says, "Man, put me down softly!"

____ 8. In "Talk," what does each man think when he first hears the story that the farmer tells?
   A. He thinks the farmer is lying.
   B. He thinks it is a frightening event.
   C. He thinks he had better leave for the village.
   D. He thinks that it is not important.

____ 9. What happens after the chief sends the men away in "Talk"?
   A. The men run off and begin sharing the stories with other people.
   B. The chief worries that the normal order of nature is changing.
   C. The stool tells the chief that the story is fantastic.
   D. The villagers gather round and demand that the chief do something.

____ 10. Why does the chief in "Talk" begin scowling as the men tell him their story?
   A. He is worried that more things will begin talking.
   B. He thinks the men are needlessly upsetting the villagers.
   C. He is frightened by the story.
   D. He dislikes it because the men are not working.

____ 11. A central truth or message of "Talk" is that
   A. people don't worry much about other people's problems.
   B. no one likes to hear stories of talking animals.
   C. chiefs do not have all the answers.
   D. people feel better when others share their anxiety.

____ 12. One difference between "The Talk" and "Talk" is
   A. "The Talk" is meant to be funny but "Talk" is not.
   B. events in "The Talk" are believable, but events in "Talk" are not.
   C. the characters in "The Talk" are humorous, but those in "Talk" are not.
   D. the setting of "The Talk" is realistic, but the setting of "Talk" is not.

____ 13. Which of the following devices appears in the writers' diction in both "Talk" and "The Talk"?
   A. hyperbole
   B. foreshadowing
   C. verbal humor
   D. slang

____ 14. On the whole, both Courlander and Herzog's and Soto's tone in these essays might best be described as
   A. light.
   B. sarcastic.
   C. skeptical.
   D. nostalgic.

_____ 15. One similarity between "The Talk" and "Talk" is that
  A. both selections take place in the United States.
  B. both selections are told from the third-person point of view.
  C. both stories are meant to entertain and to communicate a message.
  D. both selections relate the real-life experiences of the authors.

Vocabulary

_____ 16. What kind of behavior might be expected from someone with a *renegade* attitude?
  A. scrupulous   C. excitable
  B. disloyal   D. solemn

_____ 17. Which of the following adjectives best describes a *feisty* dog?
  A. sleepy   C. energetic
  B. alert   D. hostile

_____ 18. Which of the following best defines *refrain*?
  A. make decisions immediately   C. a humorous phrase
  B. do something very quickly   D. hold back from doing something

Essay

19. Writers use various devices to create humor in writing. In an essay, identify and analyze at least two examples of humorous devices used in each of the selections—"The Talk" and "Talk." Be sure to explain what makes the hyperbole funny in each case.

20. Although humorous writing is intended primarily to entertain, writers can use humor to convey a serious message as well. In an essay, compare and contrast "The Talk" and "Talk" with respect to the underlying serious issues that the authors include. In your essay, comment on how effectively you think the writers use humor to deal with serious themes.

21. **Thinking About the Big Question: Is knowledge the same as understanding?** Both "The Talk" and "Talk" use humor to suggest a difference between knowledge and understanding. In a brief essay, discuss one of the two selections. If you choose "The Talk," show how the essay presents a contrast between young people's knowledge and the deeper understanding that maturity usually brings to adults. If you choose "Talk," discuss how the tale suggests a contrast between people's surface knowledge of their surroundings and a deeper understanding of their environment. Cite at least two details from the selection to support your ideas.

Writing Workshop
Persuasion: Editorial

Prewriting: Gathering Details

As you gather evidence from a wide variety of sources, collect information that both supports as well as contradicts your position. Use the following graphic organizer to record the evidence.

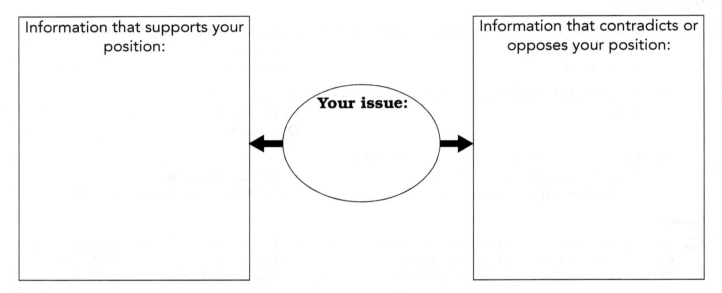

Drafting: Creating a Structure

Use the following outline to rank your arguments from the least important to the most important point.

I. Your thesis statement:
II. Your least important point:
III. Your next important point:
IV. Your most persuasive point:
V. Address your counterarguments:
VI. Make a closing statement:

Writing Workshop
Editorial: Integrating Grammar Skills

Revising to Create Parallelism

Parallelism is the use of similar grammatical forms or patterns to express similar ideas. Effective use of parallelism strengthens the connections of your ideas, and makes what you say more powerful.

Parallel Construction	Nonparallel	Parallel
Nouns	We donated blankets, clothing, and what people could eat.	We donated blankets, clothing, and food.
Adjectives	The blankets were thick and warm, and they were able to resist fires.	The blankets were thick, warm, and fire resistant.
Verbs	The volunteers gave blood and wrapped bandages, and they had a collection of money.	The volunteers gave blood, wrapped bandages, and collected money.
Prepositional Phrases	People slept on desktops and in chairs, and there were also cots.	People slept on desktops, in chairs, and on cots.
Noun Clauses	Volunteers went to the places needed when they were needed.	Volunteers went where they were needed when they were needed.

Identifying Nonparallel Constructions

A. DIRECTIONS: *Underline the words that you would change to create parallelism. On the line before the sentence, identify the part of speech or construction that you would use instead.*

<u>gerunds</u>   Our family really enjoys camping, fishing, and <u>to hunt</u>.

_____ 1. We bring food, water, and what we need to repel insects.

_____ 2. The places we camp and when we camp are family decisions.

_____ 3. We pitch our tent on the ground in a clearing, and there is a brook nearby.

Fixing Nonparallel Constructions

B. DIRECTIONS: *On the lines, rewrite these sentences using parallelism.*

1. Daily exercise, a sensible diet, and following a sleep schedule can improve your health.

   _____

2. Try aerobics to improve circulation, to build stamina, and for breathing better.

   _____

3. In yoga, you bend and stretch, with breathing through your nose.

   _____

Unit 3 Vocabulary Workshop—1
Words With Multiple Meanings

Many words have multiple meanings, or more than one meaning. To understand which meaning applies in a particular situation, you need to consider the word's context, or surroundings. For example, study the word *arms* in this sentence:

The warring nations tried to buy *arms* from the gun manufacturer.

Arms can mean "parts of the body between the shoulders and hands" or "weapons." However, the context of this sentence mentions "warring nations" and "gun manufacturers," indicating that *arms* here must mean "weapons."

DIRECTIONS: *Each italic word below has multiple meanings. Study the context in which the word appears. Then, circle the letter of its meaning in that sentence.*

1. She was the *sole* survivor of a plane crash in which ninety others perished.

   A. the bottom surface of a shoe or foot

   B. a flat fish used as food

   C. only

2. The soldiers on horseback *charged* down the hill.

   A. asked for a certain price or fee

   B. added electrical capacity

   C. attacked vigorously by moving forward

3. Eben left home *bound* for school, but then he made a detour.

   A. headed

   B. tied together with a rope, a band, or another fastener

   C. to leap

4. We divided the small pizza into *quarters* and each ate two of the pieces.

   A. any of the four equal parts of something

   B. coins worth twenty-five cents

   C. a place where someone lives temporarily; lodgings

5. Walking into the room, the empress *bore* herself with grace and dignity.

   A. drilled a hole

   B. carried

   C. to make weary by being dull or uninteresting

Unit 3 Vocabulary Workshop—2
Multiple-Meaning Words: Homonyms

Multiple-meaning words have definitions that vary greatly. For example, *block* can mean "a large chunk of something," "a child's toy brick," "an area bounded by streets on four sides," or "to prevent passage or progress." When using a multiple-meaning word, be sure the context, or surroundings, makes clear which meaning you intend.

Unclear: Randall examined the *block*.

Clear: Baby Randall examined the *block* and used it to build a toy house.

DIRECTIONS: *For each multiple-meaning word in parentheses, write a single sentence that clearly illustrates two meanings of the word. Also list the two meanings you have used.*

Example: (block) The bully tried to <u>block</u> Charles from walking around the <u>block</u>.

Meanings: to prevent passage; an area bounded by streets on four sides

1. (board)

   _____

   _____

   _____

2. (tense)

   _____

   _____

   _____

3. (might)

   _____

   _____

   _____

4. (second)

   _____

   _____

   _____

5. (nursery)

   _____

   _____

   _____

Name _____ Date _____

Communications Workshop
Delivering a Persuasive Speech

After choosing a position on a current local or national issue, fill out the following chart. Use your notes to plan and organize your speech to the class.

Position on a current local or national issue: _____

What is your position on this issue?
List your arguments in order of importance.
What facts are you using to support your opinions?
What questions do you anticipate from your audience?
How might the audience benefit from your presentation?

© Pearson Education, Inc. All rights reserved.
226

Unit 3: Types of Nonfiction
Benchmark Test 6

Literary Analysis: Rhetorical Devices Used in Persuasion *Read the selection. Then, answer the questions that follow.*

1. Statements such as *always*, *everybody*, and *never* are cue words for which of the following?
   A. emotional appeals
   B. overgeneralizations
   C. ethical concerns
   D. logical appeals

2. Why do writers of persuasion use rhetorical devices such as repetition?
   A. to link ideas or emphasize main points
   B. to show technical knowledge
   C. to obscure the underlying meaning
   D. to promote audience participation

3. How can readers best analyze and evaluate persuasive appeals?
   A. by testing the author's logic and reasoning
   B. by outlining the author's main points
   C. by examining the author's diction and syntax
   D. by discounting the author's rhetorical devices

4. Which of the following is an example of an emotional appeal?
   A. Many organizations have offered recommendations.
   B. It will have global impact in the near future.
   C. It will be the greatest environmental tragedy.
   D. Over 90% of the scientists agreed that it is probable.

5. Which of the following would be the most effective evidence?
   A. the results of a scientific study
   B. the author's thoughts and concerns
   C. a summary of the public's opinions
   D. an ethically compelling argument

Literary Analysis: Humorous Essays

6. What is the main purpose of a humorous essay?
   A. to inform
   B. to explain
   C. to persuade
   D. to entertain

7. Which technique is frequently used in humorous essays?
   A. bandwagon appeal   C. symbolism
   B. hyperbole   D. analysis

8. Which of the following is a characteristic of diction in a humorous essay?
   A. technical vocabulary   C. puns
   B. formal language   D. foreign words

Reading Skill: Persuasive Techniques *Read the selection. Then, answer the questions that follow.*

The dress code at our school is too rigid and restricts individual style and preference. Furthermore, it is ridiculously outdated. Everyone knows that students are happier and more productive when they feel good about their appearance. Corporations learned long ago that people work better when they are comfortable with their appearance, and dress codes for business are flexible. Most students have jobs and pay for their own clothes; why should the school board dictate what they can and cannot wear? Besides, the current code is nearly impossible to enforce. Teachers and administrators are spending far too much time telling students to change clothes when, surely, they have far more important tasks at hand.

9. Which of the following describes the main persuasive appeal that the author uses?
   A. logical   C. ethical
   B. reasonable   D. emotional

10. What idea is the speaker trying to convince the audience to accept?
    A. Teachers and administrators are too busy.
    B. The dress code should be changed.
    C. The school board is well aware of the problem.
    D. Students are happier when they choose what to wear.

11. Which of the following is an emotionally charged phrase?
    A. more productive   C. ridiculously outdated
    B. far more important   D. too much time

12. Which of the following is an example of an opinion?
    A. The school board establishes the dress code.
    B. Administrators must try to enforce this code.
    C. All students are happier when they have a choice.
    D. Some students work to pay for their own clothes.

13. Which of the following is an example of a fact?
    A. Administrators and teachers are too busy.
    B. Students are happier when they have a choice.
    C. The dress code is ridiculously outdated.
    D. The school board establishes the dress code.

14. The sentence "I ask, I beg, no, I demand that you consider our petition" contains an example of which persuasive device?
   A. parallelism
   B. repetition
   C. negative connotation
   D. emotionally charged language

15. Which of the following is an example of an appeal to reason?
   A. "all the students feel strongly . . ."
   B. "common sense should tell us . . ."
   C. "not one person truly believes . . ."
   D. "we know deep in our hearts . . ."

Read the following excerpt from Abraham Lincoln's "Gettysburg Address." Then, answer the questions that follow.

"But, in a larger sense, we cannot dedicate—we cannot consecrate—we cannot hallow—this ground. The brave men, living and dead, who struggled here, have consecrated it, far above our power to add or detract. The world will little note, nor long remember what we say here, but it can never forget what they did here. It is for us the living—to be dedicated here to the unfinished work which they who fought here have thus far so nobly advanced."

16. What does Lincoln want his audience to do?
   A. join the soldiers in active battle there
   B. withdraw from any participation in the struggle
   C. dedicate themselves to the unfinished work
   D. consecrate the ground where so many have died

17. The lines "we cannot dedicate—we cannot consecrate—we cannot hallow" are an example of which rhetorical device?
   A. parallelism
   B. generalization
   C. metaphor
   D. rationalization

18. Lincoln's primary appeal is to the audience's
   A. reason.
   B. intellect.
   C. mood.
   D. emotion.

19. The phrase "The brave men, living and dead . . ." contains an example of which persuasive device?
   A. parallelism
   B. restatement
   C. negative connotation
   D. emotionally charged language

20. Which of the following questions would *not* help the reader evaluate credibility?
   A. Does the author successfully convince the reader?
   B. Does the author use sound reasoning, or only emotional appeals?
   C. Does the author present a clear argument?
   D. Is the argument supported by evidence?

Grammar

21. In the following sentence, which word is an adjective?

    The gloriously beautiful afternoon drifted slowly into evening.

    A. gloriously
    B. beautiful
    C. drifted
    D. evening

22. In the following sentence, which word is an adjective?

    After training in the martial arts school, Manny's attitude changed dramatically.

    A. martial arts
    B. training
    C. dramatically
    D. changed

23. Which sentence has three adjectives?
    A. The fast car sped up and down the street.
    B. The brown-haired girl bought three shampoos at the beauty salon.
    C. Tobey's mother went to the store to buy five different desserts for the party.
    D. John quickly realized he had made a big mistake.

24. In the following sentence, which word is an adverb?

    The loud music interrupted the man who was quietly reading in the park.

    A. loud
    B. music
    C. reading
    D. quietly

25. In the following sentence, which word is an adverb?

    The football players were quite tired after the lengthy practice.

    A. football
    B. quite
    C. lengthy
    D. practice

26. Which sentence has three adverbs?
    A. He walked slowly but quite steadily despite his illness.
    B. Everyone kept talking after the teacher asked for silence.
    C. My mother cheerfully greeted her guests at the front door.
    D. Surely, a grinning student is a contented student.

27. What is the best way to fix this nonparallel sentence?

    She has glossy black hair, a tinkly laugh, and is also smart.

    A. She has glossy black hair, a tinkly laugh, and a quick wit.
    B. She is pretty, funny, and smart.
    C. She has glossy black hair, likes to laugh, and is also smart.
    D. She has glossy black hair, a tinkly laugh, and she is a smart person.

28. What purpose is achieved by using parallelism in writing?
  A. Parallelism is the mark of an educated person.
  B. Parallelism makes writing more fun to read.
  C. Parallelism strengthens connections between ideas.
  D. Parallelism shows that the writer understands grammar.

Vocabulary: Word Roots

29. In the following sentence, what is the meaning of the word *curtailed*?

Debt and new financial responsibility are the reasons Jon curtailed his poor spending habits.

  A. ended   C. increased
  B. reduced   D. continued

30. In the following sentence, what does the word *presumed* mean?

Lilly presumed her airline tickets had been confirmed, so she was shocked to find no reservation in her name when she arrived at the airport.

  A. took for granted   C. was told
  B. imagined   D. decided

31. In the following sentence, what does the word *consumed* mean?

The fire had started in the basement, but had consumed much of the second and third floors as well.

  A. spread to   C. destroyed
  B. affected   D. absorbed

32. In the following sentence, what does the word *creed* mean?

The fourth line of *The Soldiers Creed* reads: "I will never accept defeat."

  A. direction   C. guidelines
  B. set of beliefs   D. instructions

33. What is the meaning of the word formed by combining *de-* and *-duct-*?
  A. to combine   C. to take away
  B. to complete   D. to put back

34. In which of the following sentences is the word *induce* used correctly?
  A. Calming music, a peaceful thought, or meditation may be used to induce a state of hypnosis.
  B. Police gather clues and information to induce how crimes were committed.
  C. Slowly cooking tomatoes will induce them to a liquid state.
  D. Bill needed to induce the money missing from the cash register by Saturday or he would be fired.

Spelling *For each of the following sentences, choose the letter of the word that is spelled incorrectly.*

35. I will have to save *mony* if I *want* to *purchase* any new *clothes*.
                      A   B   C   D

    A. A   **C.** C
    B. B   **D.** D

36. The *costume* store has *many* unusual and *intresting outfits* for rent.
                 A   B   C   D

    A. A   **C.** C
    B. B   **D.** D

37. He went to the art *supplie* store to *purchase canvases* and *pastels*.
                       A   B   C   D

    A. A   **C.** C
    B. B   **D.** D

ESSAY

Writing

38. Write a proposal for a new fundraiser at your school. You want to convince your principal that your idea would be the most effective way to raise money.

39. Ideally, historical facts are presented objectively. Yet, historical facts can also be selectively used to support an emotional point of view. Using the following historical facts, write a paragraph that is slanted toward viewing these events positively or negatively. Before you begin, write a sentence stating how you are slanting this information. Use persuasive techniques to accomplish your writing goal. Underline the parts of your work that use a persuasive technique.
    1. It took the Union army nearly four days to march the 25 miles to Manassas.
    2. Lack of training and discipline contributed to the soldiers' slow pace.
    3. General P.G.T. Beauregard and the small Confederate force were camped along Bull Run.
    4. The Union army was accompanied by a huge crowd of reporters, politicians, and other civilians from Washington planning to picnic and watch the battle.
    5. During the four days Confederate troops were sped to the scene by train.

40. Describe an abstract. What does it include? What is its purpose?

Vocabulary in Context 3—Part 1

Identify the answer choice that best completes the statement.

1. When I reached under the bushes for the lost ball, the _____ cut my arms.
   A. thorns
   B. hook
   C. tangles
   D. prickly

2. Just before I heard thunder, I saw a _____ of lightning.
   A. iridescent
   B. flash
   C. beaming
   D. glistening

3. There was a scent of flowers in the air on this warm and _____ summer night.
   A. lilacs
   B. stifled
   C. impenetrable
   D. balmy

4. He quickly took the basketball to the hoop and _____ it.
   A. battered
   B. deferred
   C. dunked
   D. slam

5. The cat crept into the room, as _____ as a shadow.
   A. sprightly
   B. soundlessly
   C. boldly
   D. equally

6. The wrinkles were ironed out of the shirt, and it was heavily _____ .
   A. shaded
   B. squinch
   C. starched
   D. startled

7. The arrows had _____ the target in many places.
   A. baffled
   B. wavered
   C. rifled
   D. pierced

8. We hiked among the tall trees and granite _____ .
   A. boulders
   B. tumbleweed
   C. grandeur
   D. undergrowth

9. My mother didn't believe that the dog had followed me home _____ .
   A. intention
   B. unbidden
   C. ungainly
   D. abandonment

10. Sometimes I enjoy walking peacefully in the woods in _____ .
    A. servitude
    B. oblivion
    C. solitude
    D. commotion

11. My dad limps when he walks because his leg was _____ in a serious car accident.
    A. unwillingly
    B. pried
    C. maimed
    D. slain

12. As an adult, he still expects to get whatever he wants because he was so _____ as a child.
    A. indulged
    B. befriended
    C. disciplined
    D. delightfully

13. It is our hope that good will always _____ over evil.
    A. immovable
    B. outmaneuvered
    C. menace
    D. prevail

14. Her singing voice is so pleasant and _____ .
    A. melodious
    B. haughty
    C. childishness
    D. phenomena

15. The tree outside our house was bent over by the strong wind_____ .
   A. tosses
   B. gusts
   C. rebounds
   D. aeronautics

16. Both teams were physically drained, so the contest turned into a_____ game.
   A. united
   B. mental
   C. social
   D. triumphant

17. While I often disagree with Bruce's views, I seldom_____ him.
   A. define
   B. negotiate
   C. confront
   D. enforce

18. I am rather shy, although I wish I could be more_____ .
   A. offensive
   B. imperial
   C. impassive
   D. outgoing

19. When she has extra money, she carefully considers only_____ investments.
   A. excessive
   B. significantly
   C. unreasoning
   D. conservative

20. He received a medal for showing courage and_____ on the job.
   A. valor
   B. tragedy
   C. censure
   D. potential

Diagnostic Tests and Vocabulary in Context
Use and Interpretation

The Diagnostic Tests and Vocabulary in Context were developed to assist teachers in making the most appropriate assignment of *Prentice Hall Literature* program selections to students. The purpose of these assessments is to indicate the degree of difficulty that students are likely to have in reading/comprehending the selections presented in the *following* unit of instruction. Tests are provided at six separate times in each grade level—a *Diagnostic Test* (to be used prior to beginning the year's instruction) and a *Vocabulary in Context,* the final segment of the Benchmark Test appearing at the end of each of the first five units of instruction. Note that the tests are intended for use not as summative assessments for the prior unit, but as guidance for assigning literature selections in the upcoming unit of instruction.

The structure of all Diagnostic Tests and Vocabulary in Context in this series is the same. All test items are four-option, multiple-choice items. The format is established to assess a student's ability to construct sufficient meaning from the context sentence to choose the only provided word that fits both the semantics (meaning) and syntax (structure) of the context sentence. All words in the context sentences are chosen to be "below-level" words that students reading at this grade level should know. All answer choices fit *either* the meaning or structure of the context sentence, but only the correct choice fits *both* semantics and syntax. All answer choices—both correct answers and incorrect options—are key words chosen from specifically taught words that will occur in the subsequent unit of program instruction. This careful restriction of the assessed words permits a sound diagnosis of students' current reading achievement and prediction of the most appropriate level of readings to assign in the upcoming unit of instruction.

The assessment of vocabulary in context skill has consistently been shown in reading research studies to correlate very highly with "reading comprehension." This is not surprising as the format essentially assesses comprehension, albeit in sentence-length "chunks." Decades of research demonstrate that vocabulary assessment provides a strong, reliable prediction of comprehension achievement— the purpose of these tests. Further, because this format demands very little testing time, these diagnoses can be made efficiently, permitting teachers to move forward with critical instructional tasks rather than devoting excessive time to assessment.

It is important to stress that while the Diagnostic Tests and Vocabulary in Context were carefully developed and will yield sound assignment decisions, they were designed to *reinforce*, not supplant, teacher judgment as to the most appropriate instructional placement for individual students. Teacher judgment should always prevail in making placement—or indeed other important instructional—decisions concerning students.

Diagnostic Tests and Vocabulary in Context
Branching Suggestions

These tests are designed to provide maximum flexibility for teachers. Your *Unit Resources* books contain the 40-question **Diagnostic Test** and 20-question **Vocabulary in Context** tests. At *PHLitOnline,* you can access the Diagnostic Test and complete 40-question Vocabulary in Context tests. Procedures for administering the tests are described below. Choose the procedure based on the time you wish to devote to the activity and your comfort with the assignment decisions relative to the individual students. Remember that your judgment of a student's reading level should always take precedence over the results of a single written test.

Feel free to use different procedures at different times of the year. For example, for early units, you may wish to be more confident in the assignments you make—thus, using the "two-stage" process below. Later, you may choose the quicker diagnosis, confirming the results with your observations of the students' performance built up throughout the year.

The **Diagnostic Test** is composed of a single 40-item assessment. Based on the results of this assessment, make the following assignment of students to the reading selections in Unit 1:

Diagnostic Test Score	Selection to Use
If the student's score is 0–25	more accessible
If the student's score is 26–40	more challenging

Outlined below are the three basic options for administering **Vocabulary in Context** and basing selection assignments on the results of these assessments.

1. For a one-stage, quicker diagnosis using the *20-item* test in the *Unit Resources:*

Vocabulary in Context Test Score	Selection to Use
If the student's score is 0–13	more accessible
If the student's score is 14–20	more challenging

2. If you wish to confirm your assignment decisions with a *two-stage* diagnosis:

Stage 1: Administer the 20-item test in the *Unit Resources*	
Vocabulary in Context Test Score	**Selection to Use**
If the student's score is 0–9	more accessible
If the student's score is 10–15	(Go to Stage 2.)
If the student's score is 16–20	more challenging

Stage 2: Administer items 21–40 from *PHLitOnline*	
Vocabulary in Context Test Score	**Selection to Use**
If the student's score is 0–12	more accessible
If the student's score is 13–20	more challenging

3. If you base your assignment decisions on the full 40-item **Vocabulary in Context** from *PHLitOnline:*

Vocabulary in Context Test Score	Selection to Use
If the student's score is 0–25	more accessible
If the student's score is 26–40	more challenging

Unit 3 Resources: Types of Nonfiction

Name _____ Date _____

Grade 9—Benchmark Test 5
Interpretation Guide

For remediation of specific skills, you may assign students the relevant Reading Kit Practice and Assess pages indicated in the far-right column of this chart. You will find rubrics for evaluating writing samples in the last section of your Professional Development Guidebook.

Skill Objective	Test Items	Number Correct	Reading Kit
Literary Analysis			
Author's Style	1, 2, 3, 4, 5		pp. 102, 103
Expository Essay	6, 7, 8		pp. 104, 105
Biographical Writing	9, 10, 11		pp. 106, 107
Reading Skill			
Main Idea and Supporting Details	12, 13, 14, 15, 16, 17, 18		pp. 108, 109
Generate Relevant Questions	19, 20, 21		pp. 110, 111
Vocabulary			
Roots -viv-, -dur-, -temp-, -fus-	31, 32, 33, 34, 35, 36		pp. 112, 113
Grammar			
Direct and Indirect Objects	22, 23, 24		pp. 114, 115
Predicate Nominative and Predicate Adjectives	25, 26, 27		pp. 116, 117
Combine Choppy Sentences	28, 29, 30		pp. 118, 119
Writing			
Radio Advertisement (script)	37	Use rubric	pp. 122, 123
Book Jacket Copy	38	Use rubric	pp. 120, 121
Business Letter	39	Use rubric	pp. 124, 125

Name _____ Date _____

Grade 9—Benchmark Test 6
Interpretation Guide

For remediation of specific skills, you may assign students the relevant Reading Kit Practice and Assess pages indicated in the far-right column of this chart. You will find rubrics for evaluating writing samples in the last section of your Professional Development Guidebook.

Skill Objective	Test Items	Number Correct	Reading Kit
Literary Analysis			
Persuasive Essay and Persuasive Speech	1, 2, 3, 4, 5		pp. 126, 127, 128, 129
Humorous Essay	6, 7, 8		pp. 130, 131
Reading Skill			
Analyze Persuasive Appeals	9, 10, 11, 14, 15, 16, 17		pp. 132, 133
Evaluate Credibility	12, 13, 18,19, 20		pp. 134, 135
Vocabulary			
Roots -tail-, -sum, -cred-, -duc-	29, 30, 31, 32, 33, 34		pp. 136, 137
Grammar			
Adjectives	21, 22, 23		pp. 138, 139
Adverbs	24, 25, 26		pp. 140, 141
Parallelism	27, 28		pp. 142, 143
Spelling			
Tools for Checking Spelling	35, 36, 37		pp. 144, 145
Writing			
Proposal	38	Use rubric	pp. 148, 149
Editorial	39	Use rubric	pp. 150, 151
Abstract	40	Use rubric	pp. 146, 147

ANSWERS

Big Question Vocabulary—1, p. 1

Sample Answers

1. I do not **comprehend** your meaning. Please **clarify**.
2. This **concept** seems **ambiguous**. I think I need more **information**.
3. I do not **comprehend** math at all.

Big Question Vocabulary—2, p. 2

Sample Answers

1. First, gather your **facts** and **statistics** from the Internet or books.
2. Make sure to **research** your topic completely.
3. Use **sources** that are reliable. Take special care when using the Internet.
4. **Interpret** your data. Figure out what it all means so that you know what to write in your report.

Big Question Vocabulary—3, p. 3

Sample Answer

I am making a **connection** here. I have a **feeling** I met that girl before. The smell of her perfume is bringing back a **sensory** memory. Oh, no, she is coming this way. My **instinct** is to run. I am backing away. And sure enough, my **instinct** was correct. She spilled her soda everywhere!

"Before Hip-Hop Was Hip-Hop"
by Rebecca Walker

Vocabulary Warm-up Exercises, p. 8

A.
1. communicate
2. united
3. local
4. sagging
5. cultural
6. formula
7. rotation
8. significant

B. Sample Answers

1. True; Creativity takes imagination, so using your imagination can strengthen your *creativity*.
2. False; Approximate means "to do or reproduce in a similar way but not exactly," so you could use anything, including your own voice, to *approximate* the sound of a siren.
3. True; Apiece means "each," so each ticket is no more than $10.
4. True; Bravado means "to show real or false courage," so if judgment is more important, showing *bravado* could lead to problems.
5. True; Dynamic means "exciting and full of energy," so a *dynamic* game would be very exciting to watch.
6. False; A realm is an area of interest or activity, so the *realm* of science encompasses all scientific activity

and it is not a place like a country with borders and rules for entering.

7. True; Outrageous means "shocking or unreasonable," so an *outrageous* error is a serious mistake and could have serious consequences.
8. False; Someone with a violent temper may use physical force and be very angry and destructive when mad, so self-control is likely to be a problem.

Reading Warm-up A, p. 9

Sample Answers

1. (set approach); It was also unplanned.
2. (neighborhood); Fishing is a *local* activity where I live because there is a lake nearby.
3. (major); *Unimportant* is an antonym for *significant*.
4. (loose); *Drooping* is a synonym for *sagging*.
5. One dancer performed, and then another took over. *Regular* is a clue, because a *rotation* of people or activities follows a regular sequence or cycle.
6. sent the message; Music and dancing can *communicate* strong emotions, such as anger and joy.
7. (compete); A group that is *united* would get along and basically agree on things and make decisions that are best for everyone.
8. music world and society in general; Reality shows on television are a *cultural* sensation today because they are popular and lots of people watch them and talk about them.

Reading Warm-up B, p. 10

Sample Answers

1. the area of music; (area)
2. (genius and imagination); recording artists; production companies; movie studios; musicians
3. (exciting); *Lively* is a synonym for *dynamic*.
4. not exactly the same; The clips showed cartoon characters singing a song and were used to help sell a movie.
5. (shocking); *Disgraceful* is a synonym for *outrageous*.
6. (Each); Nine Soundies would be viewed because three people watching three each equals nine.
7. (Explosive); *Peaceful* is an antonym for *violent*.
8. (courage); Someone showing *bravado* might talk tough and swagger or use other body language that says that he or she is not afraid.

Rebecca Walker

Listening and Viewing, p. 11

Sample Answers

Segment 1: Books were friends to Rebecca Walker as a child. When she got older, she realized she wanted to tell her story and introduce herself to other people through words, just as she had met the characters and writers of books in childhood. Students should name a literary piece and explain why it is meaningful to them.

Segment 2: Music can influence writing by encouraging people to explore their creativity. Students may answer that hip-hop has not only changed the face of pop culture but also the books that are being written and are popular. Students may answer that books about different cultures will be more widely read in the future due to the influence of hip-hop.

Segment 3: Students should suggest one of Rebecca Walker's methods and explain why it would be an effective writing method for them to adopt.

Segment 4: She wants young people to speak out, to create their own future, to be aware of what is going on around them, and to challenge boundaries. Students may suggest that it is important to read about current events and social issues to be aware of the society around them and to actively take steps to improve it.

Unit 3: Learning About Nonfiction, p. 12

1. A; 2. A; 3. B; 4. B; 5. B; 6. A; 7. C; 8. B

"Before Hip-Hop Was Hip-Hop"
by Rebecca Walker

Model Selection: Nonfiction, p. 13

Sample Answers

1. This passage is descriptive and helps show the kids in Walker's school in a distinct way. It is a reflective passage.

2. The tone of this passage is serious, almost eloquent, and emphasizes one of the author's main ideas.

3. Repetition of the phrase "I hope" highlights Walker's message to today's youth. The tone is serious, but not formal.

Open-Book Test, p. 14

Short Answer

1. It is an essay.
   Difficulty: *Easy* **Objective:** *Literary Analysis*

2. You are focusing on tone, the author's attitude toward the subject or his or her audience.
   Difficulty: *Easy* **Objective:** *Literary Analysis*

3. Students should list at least three of these purposes: to inform, to persuade, to entertain, to reflect, to honor, to explain, or to warn.
   Difficulty: *Easy* **Objective:** *Literary Analysis*

4. In a descriptive essay, the writer describes something by presenting details of sight, hearing, smell, touch, or taste. In a reflective essay, the writer presents his or her thoughts about a personal experience or an idea.
   Difficulty: *Average* **Objective:** *Literary Analysis*

5. It would be difficult to join an entrenched clique because its membership would be firmly established and newcomers would not be welcome.
   Difficulty: *Average* **Objective:** *Vocabulary*

6. Walker's school was ethnically diverse. Students should cite one of the many details of ethnic diversity in the essay.
   Difficulty: *Challenging* **Objective:** *Interpretation*

7. She uses a great many words that are specific to the world of hip-hop.
   Difficulty: *Average* **Objective:** *Vocabulary*

8. She is praising loyalty. She is talking about friends who will support her under any circumstances.
   Difficulty: *Average* **Objective:** *Interpretation*

9. Students might note that Walker liked popular music, was interested in stylish clothing, and enjoyed parties and dancing. They should support their answers with two details from the essay.
   Difficulty: *Easy* **Objective:** *Interpretation*

10. It is a reflective essay. In it Walker expresses her thoughts in response to a personal experience.
    Difficulty: *Challenging* **Objective:** *Literary Analysis*

Essay

11. Students should recognize that Walker is concerned with informing her audience about the origins of hip-hop. She wants readers to know that hip-hop was not originally commercial and that it sprang up among a diverse group of young people living in the city. In Walker's experience, hip-hop allowed young people to cross boundaries and form a common culture. Walker discovered the values of loyalty, community, and self-confidence in hip-hop. By contrast, she sees contemporary hip-hop as a commercially marketed global industry that has lost the authenticity and spontaneity of its origins.
    Difficulty: *Easy* **Objective:** *Essay*

12. Students should recognize that Walker's treatment focuses on the origins of hip-hop culture and on the life lessons she learned during her year at P.S. 141 in the Bronx. They should cite examples of the ways in which that year opened Walker to the diversity, energy, and self-expression of her friends and classmates. They might note that it taught her that music and dance were ways of forging a community.
    Difficulty: *Average* **Objective:** *Essay*

13. Students should focus on the elements of style and explain how they affect their own reaction to Walker's essay.
    Difficulty: *Challenging* **Objective:** *Essay*

14. In their essays, students should highlight Walker's emphasis on values such as loyalty, community, and energy.
    Difficulty: *Average* **Objective:** *Essay*

Oral Response

15. Oral responses should be clear, well organized, and well supported by appropriate details from the essay.
    Difficulty: *Average* **Objective:** *Oral Interpretation*

Selection Test A, p. 17

Learning About Nonfiction

1. ANS: A	DIF: Easy	OBJ: Literary Analysis
2. ANS: B	DIF: Easy	OBJ: Literary Analysis
3. ANS: C	DIF: Easy	OBJ: Literary Analysis

Critical Reading

4. ANS: D	DIF: Easy	OBJ: Comprehension
5. ANS: B	DIF: Easy	OBJ: Comprehension
6. ANS: A	DIF: Easy	OBJ: Interpretation
7. ANS: C	DIF: Easy	OBJ: Interpretation
8. ANS: B	DIF: Easy	OBJ: Comprehension
9. ANS: C	DIF: Easy	OBJ: Interpretation
10. ANS: C	DIF: Easy	OBJ: Interpretation
11. ANS: C	DIF: Easy	OBJ: Literary Analysis
12. ANS: C	DIF: Easy	OBJ: Interpretation
13. ANS: B	DIF: Easy	OBJ: Literary Analysis

Essay

14. Students should point out that Walker believes she learned valuable life lessons from her exposure to original hip-hop during her seventh-grade year at school in the Bronx. Hip-hop allowed kids from all kinds of different ethnic backgrounds to cross boundaries and form a common culture. Walker discovered the values of loyalty, community, and self-confidence. By contrast, she sees today's hip-hop as an expensively marketed global industry; it has lost some of the authenticity and spontaneity of original hip-hop.
    Difficulty: *Easy*
    Objective: *Essay*

15. Students should identify and discuss specific examples of the elements listed. Many students will say that Walker seems well informed, enthusiastic, outgoing, and positive. She puts a premium on values like loyalty, community, self-confidence, and creativity. As reflected by her writing, her personality seems both lively and likable.
    Difficulty: *Easy*
    Objective: *Essay*

16. Students should recognize that the author's knowledge leads readers to an understanding about life and human nature or human behavior. Walker also puts an emphasis on values such as loyalty, community, and energy.
    Difficulty: *Average*
    Objective: *Essay*

Selection Test B, p. 20

Learning About Nonfiction

1. ANS: C	DIF: Average	OBJ: Literary Analysis
2. ANS: D	DIF: Average	OBJ: Literary Analysis
3. ANS: B	DIF: Average	OBJ: Literary Analysis
4. ANS: A	DIF: Average	OBJ: Literary Analysis
5. ANS: D	DIF: Average	OBJ: Literary Analysis
6. ANS: A	DIF: Average	OBJ: Literary Analysis

Critical Reading

7. ANS: B	DIF: Average	OBJ: Literary Analysis
8. ANS: C	DIF: Average	OBJ: Comprehension
9. ANS: A	DIF: Average	OBJ: Comprehension
10. ANS: B	DIF: Average	OBJ: Literary Analysis
11. ANS: C	DIF: Average	OBJ: Comprehension
12. ANS: D	DIF: Average	OBJ: Comprehension
13. ANS: C	DIF: Challenging	OBJ: Literary Analysis
14. ANS: A	DIF: Average	OBJ: Comprehension
15. ANS: D	DIF: Challenging	OBJ: Interpretation
16. ANS: B	DIF: Average	OBJ: Comprehension
17. ANS: B	DIF: Challenging	OBJ: Interpretation
18. ANS: A	DIF: Average	OBJ: Interpretation

Essay

19. Students should point out that Walker's treatment focuses on the original days of hip-hop and on the life lessons she learned during her seventh-grade year at P.S. 141 in the Bronx. That year opened her eyes to the diversity, energy, and self-expression of the students around her, and it taught her that music and dance were ways of forging a community where none had existed before. Evaluate students' essays based on their clarity, unity, coherence, and specific references to the text.
    Difficulty: *Average*
    Objective: *Essay*

20. Students should focus on the elements listed and should evaluate Walker's style in the essay. Evaluate students' writing based on its clarity, coherence, and specific references to the text.
    Difficulty: *Challenging*
    Objective: *Essay*

21. In their essays, students should highlight Walker's emphasis on values such as loyalty, community, and energy.
    Difficulty: *Average*
    Objective: *Essay*

"A Celebration of Grandfathers"
by Rudolfo Anaya

Vocabulary Warm-up Exercises, p. 24

A. 1. incredible
2. majestic
3. image
4. created
5. internal
6. source
7. respectful
8. lasting

B. Sample Answers

1. F; An *absurdity* is something that is illogical or unreasonable.

2. T; A *contribution* is something done to help.

3. F; People in a *culture* usually share the same basic values, customs, and beliefs.

4. F; If you hold your parents in high *esteem*, you will honor them.

5. F; Trying to help people is a good way to show your *humanity*.

6. F; If you *overcome* your problem, then you no longer have it and thus are better off.

7. F; *Revival* of an interest means making it active again, so you would have had that interest before.

8. T; A *transformation* is a change in form or condition.

Reading Warm-up A, p. 25

Sample Answers

1. when addressing his elders; He spoke in a *respectful* way because he was taught to be polite to older people and honor them.

2. (sunset); The mountains I saw on our trip were *majestic*.

3. that anyone would want to spend an entire lifetime working the soil; Watching my baby brother learn to walk was an *incredible* experience.

4. (farming); People would starve if farmers did not grow their crops, and thus farming relates to the *source* of life, or where all food comes from.

5. the soil that feeds them; True love is a *lasting* thing.

6. (pictured); An *image* is a "mental picture."

7. a great marble palace; Last year, I *created* a huge mobile for an art class.

8. somewhere deep in the pit of his stomach; The opposite of *internal* is external.

Reading Warm-up B, p. 26

Sample Answers

1. (customs); I consider myself part of the Jewish *culture*.

2. from Mexican to Mexican American; The *transformation* was completed when a treaty giving the territory to the United States was signed (with a pen).

3. Mexican Americans, foreign-born immigrants; If someone holds you in low *esteem*, he or she does not respect you and probably would not treat you justly.

4. (illogical); I consider going to war without an extremely good reason to be an *absurdity*.

5. (prejudice, discrimination); *Overcome* means "rise above."

6. (arts, sciences); I would be proud to make a *contribution* to society by discovering a cure for cancer.

7. (Mexican American communities); *Revival* means "a process by which something becomes popular or active again."

8. Day of the Dead is a remembrance of those who died and the fact that they once lived good lives. Thus, it honors their qualities of kindness and sympathy, or their *humanity*.

Writing About the Big Question, p. 27

A. 1. connection
2. interpret
3. clarify
4. feeling

B. Sample Answers

1. My father always works hard. He also likes to laugh and have a good time.

2. The **fact** that he works hard helps me understand that he has a sense of responsibility. The fact that he likes to laugh helps me **comprehend** why he is always so cheerful.

C. Sample Answer

Knowing what people do and how they live can give insight into who they are because this information says a lot about who a person really is. When you have knowledge about a person, it can help your understanding of others.

"A Celebration of Grandfathers"
by Rudolfo Anaya

Literary Analysis: Style, p. 28

Sample Answers

1. The words *web* and *design* emphasize his belief that everything in the universe is linked. The tone is serious and dignified.

2. The figurative language emphasizes the author's respect for the elders. The tone is positive and approving.

3. The syntax emphasizes the elders' concern about passing their values and outlook to younger generations. The author's dignified tone stresses the importance of continuity and tradition.

4. The simplicity of the diction mirrors the simplicity of the writer's grandfather. The tone is respectful and admiring.

5. The stripped-down diction and syntax call attention to the basic rhythms of life and death. The tone is realistic and positive.

Reading: Generate Prior Questions to Identify Main Idea and Details, p. 29

Sample Answers

A. 1. The word *celebration* suggests a party or an appreciation. I expect that the author will write positively about the contributions grandfathers make to their families and to society.

2. The greeting makes me think that elders were treated with respect and admiration. They were valued for their wisdom and for the advice they could pass on.

3. Anaya's description of himself as "an oral storyteller" leads me to expect that he will write in a conversational style, with anecdotes from his experiences.

B. Answers will vary. Examine students' responses for identification of a main idea and supporting details, as well as for specific examples.

Vocabulary Builder, p. 30

Sample Answers

A. 1. After struggling with the problem for hours, she sadly admits how much it still <u>perplexes</u> her.

2. Because their explanation seemed so illogical, we were struck by its <u>absurdity</u>.

3. The rain managed to <u>permeate</u> even the stoutest foul-weather gear, so our clothes were soaked.

4. What <u>anguish</u> she felt when her doctor told her that her dog had an incurable disease.

5. They were <u>nurturing</u> the young tree and hoped to save it from being cut down.

6. Many people visited the small town after its <u>revival</u>.

B. 1. A <u>vivid</u> description would help you visualize the details of the setting more accurately and completely.

2. I would rather spend time with <u>convivial</u> friends than sad ones because they would be laughing and in a good mood rather than unhappy and morose like my sad friends.

3. Yes, because I begin to get my strength back when I <u>survive</u> the flu.

Enrichment: Learning From Our Elders, p. 31

Suggested Responses

Advise students to prepare for their interviews and to be respectful during their meetings with their subjects. Encourage students to evaluate and analyze their experiences during a class discussion. Sample interview questions:

1. What was your most important or meaningful life experience?

2. What did you enjoy most about the world when you were a teenager? What do you enjoy most about the world now?

3. If you could relive a certain period of your life, what age would you choose? Why?

4. What invention do you remember as having a great impact upon your life?

5. What advice do you have for young people today?

Open-Book Test, p. 32

Short Answer

1. The main idea has to do with respecting one's elders.
   Difficulty: *Easy*   **Objective:** *Reading*

2. The title suggests a positive, serious attitude of respect and praise.
   Difficulty: *Easy*   **Objective:** *Literary Analysis*

3. The character Antonio appears to share Anaya's awe of nature. For him, too, time stands still.
   Difficulty: *Average*   **Objective:** *Interpretation*

4. It shows that the his grandfather's idea has influenced Anaya's attitude.
   Difficulty: *Challenging*   **Objective:** *Reading*

5. Anaya believes that a connection to the cycles of nature is an important lesson he learned from his grandfather.
   Difficulty: *Challenging*   **Objective:** *Reading*

6. Anaya's grandfather teaches him that death is part of the cycle of nature; it is only a "small transformation in life."
   Difficulty: *Easy*   **Objective:** *Interpretation*

7. Students should cite one of these details or another relevant detail from the essay: The mass media depict the typical American as young and beautiful; society praises beauty and youth; the mass media always depict older people selling something. Anaya is sorry that young people no longer respect their elders.
   Difficulty: *Average*   **Objective:** *Reading*

8. Students should mention at least one of the torments of old age that Anaya mentions: The body breaks down; people cry, curse, and forget the names of loved ones; they feel an emotional pain that few other people can understand.
   Difficulty: *Average*   **Objective:** *Vocabulary*

9. He wants to emphasize his respect for his heritage.
   Difficulty: *Average*   **Objective:** *Literary Analysis*

10. The author's syntax is formal. Many of Anaya's sentences are long; there are few if any sentences with unusual word order and few if any sentence fragments.
    Difficulty: *Challenging*   **Objective:** *Literary Analysis*

Essay

11. Students should point out that Anaya supports the statement by describing many important lessons that elders can teach the young. They might mention two of these lessons that one's elders can impart or any others in the essay: the values and traditions of their people, the value of cooperating with one another in a community, and the ways in which the forms of life are connected.
    Difficulty: *Easy*   **Objective:** *Essay*

12. Students should point out that although Anaya focuses his essay on the personality of his own grandfather, the

plural noun *grandfathers* in the title suggests that the essay applies to everyone's elders and to the elders of all cultures. Elders, Anaya asserts, should be respected for their vision and for the traditions and values they can pass on to young people. Some students may note that Anaya discusses the wisdom and power of other elders, such as the *curandera* Ultima and the hunter Cruz. Anaya celebrates the way in which the elders lived and the lessons and approach to life that they shared with the younger generation.

Difficulty: *Average* **Objective:** *Essay*

13. Students should choose three of the following anecdotes: Anaya's encounter with the anthill, his wish for rain, his friend's tragic death, his struggle to learn English, his caring for his grandfather toward the end of the old man's life, and his return to Puerto de Luna. Students should derive a lesson or moral from each brief story and then evaluate the effectiveness of each anecdote in terms of the essay's main idea.

Difficulty: *Challenging* **Objective:** *Essay*

14. Students should demonstrate an understanding of knowledge (they might cite, for example, the *ancianos'* knowledge of how to dance in celebration of good times and how to prepare food for a fiesta) and understanding (they should cite as an example a lesson learned from an experience, such as Anaya's understanding of "the cycles that brought the rain or kept it from us"). They might conclude that for Anaya, both knowledge and understanding are essential to a culture and are passed from generation to generation.

Difficulty: *Average* **Objective:** *Essay*

Oral Response

15. Oral responses should be clear, well organized, and well supported by appropriate details from the essay.

Difficulty: *Average* **Objective:** *Oral Interpretation*

Selection Test A, p. 35

Critical Reading

1. ANS: B	DIF: Easy	OBJ: Reading
2. ANS: C	DIF: Easy	OBJ: Interpretation
3. ANS: C	DIF: Easy	OBJ: Literary Analysis
4. ANS: A	DIF: Easy	OBJ: Comprehension
5. ANS: C	DIF: Easy	OBJ: Interpretation
6. ANS: C	DIF: Easy	OBJ: Interpretation
7. ANS: C	DIF: Easy	OBJ: Reading
8. ANS: A	DIF: Easy	OBJ: Literary Analysis
9. ANS: C	DIF: Easy	OBJ: Comprehension
10. ANS: D	DIF: Easy	OBJ: Comprehension
11. ANS: A	DIF: Easy	OBJ: Comprehension

Vocabulary and Grammar

12. ANS: C	DIF: Easy	OBJ: Vocabulary

13. ANS: D	DIF: Easy	OBJ: Vocabulary
14. ANS: B	DIF: Easy	OBJ: Grammar

Essay

15. Students should point out that Anaya supports the statement by telling the many important things that elders can teach the young. They can teach young people the values and traditions of their people, so they will continue. They can teach the value of cooperating with one another in a community. They can also teach young people that all forms of life are connected.

Difficulty: *Easy*

Objective: *Essay*

16. Students should point out that, while Anaya centers his essay on his own grandfather, he uses the plural "grandfathers." This suggests that what he says about his grandfather can apply to elders (grandfathers and grandmothers) in any culture or group. Anaya celebrates the way the elders lived and also the lessons they shared with the younger generation. Some students may note that Anaya discusses the wisdom and power of other elders in his community, such as the *curandera* Ultima and the hunter Cruz.

Difficulty: *Easy*

Objective: *Essay*

17. Students should demonstrate an understanding of *knowledge* by citing, for example, the *ancianos'* knowledge of how to dance in celebration of good times and how to prepare food for a fiesta. For *understanding,* they might cite the example of a lesson learned from an experience, such as Anaya's understanding of "the cycles that brought the rain or kept it from us."

Difficulty: *Average*

Objective: *Essay*

Selection Test B, p. 38

Critical Reading

1. ANS: B	DIF: Average	OBJ: Reading
2. ANS: B	DIF: Average	OBJ: Interpretation
3. ANS: C	DIF: Average	OBJ: Literary Analysis
4. ANS: A	DIF: Average	OBJ: Comprehension
5. ANS: C	DIF: Challenging	OBJ: Literary Analysis
6. ANS: C	DIF: Average	OBJ: Interpretation
7. ANS: C	DIF: Average	OBJ: Interpretation
8. ANS: C	DIF: Average	OBJ: Reading
9. ANS: B	DIF: Average	OBJ: Reading
10. ANS: D	DIF: Average	OBJ: Interpretation
11. ANS: B	DIF: Challenging	OBJ: Interpretation
12. ANS: A	DIF: Average	OBJ: Literary Analysis
13. ANS: C	DIF: Average	OBJ: Comprehension
14. ANS: D	DIF: Average	OBJ: Comprehension
15. ANS: A	DIF: Average	OBJ: Comprehension

Vocabulary and Grammar

16. **ANS:** C   **DIF:** Average   **OBJ:** Vocabulary
17. **ANS:** D   **DIF:** Challenging   **OBJ:** Vocabulary
18. **ANS:** B   **DIF:** Average   **OBJ:** Grammar
19. **ANS:** C   **DIF:** Average   **OBJ:** Grammar

Essay

20. Students should point out that, while Anaya centers his essay on the personality of his own grandfather, the plural "grandfathers" suggests that the essay applies to the elders of all cultures. Elders, he says, should be respected for their wisdom and for the traditions and values they can pass on to young people. Some students may note that Anaya also discusses the wisdom and power of other "old people," such as the *curandera* Ultima and the hunter Cruz. Anaya celebrates the way the elders lived and also the lessons and approach to life that they shared with the younger generation.

    Difficulty: *Average*

    Objective: *Essay*

21. Students should discuss at least two of the following anecdotes: the boy's injury from the anthill, the boy's wish for rain, the death of the young man dragged by his horse, Rudolfo's struggle to learn English, Rudolfo's caring for his grandfather toward the end of the grandfather's life, and the writer's return to Puerto de Luna. Students should derive a lesson or moral from each brief story and then evaluate the effectiveness of the anecdotes for the essay as a whole.

    Difficulty: *Average*

    Objective: *Essay*

22. Students should demonstrate an understanding of knowledge (they might cite, for example, the *ancianos'* knowledge of how to dance in celebration of good times and how to prepare food for a fiesta) and understanding (they should cite as an example a lesson learned from an experience, such as Anaya's understanding of "the cycles that brought the rain or kept it from us"). They might conclude that for Anaya, both knowledge and understanding are essential to a culture and are passed from generation to generation.

    Difficulty: *Average*

    Objective: *Essay*

"On Summer" by Lorraine Hansberry

Vocabulary Warm-up Exercises, p. 42

A.
1. originally
2. traditional
3. bias
4. radical
5. features
6. delightfully
7. courageous

8. commitment

B. Sample Answers
1. I *invariably* brush my teeth every morning.
2. My seventh-grade social studies teacher has been a good *influence* on me.
3. I am *acutely* aware of the problem of world hunger.
4. I would suggest listening to some quiet music to feel *mellow*.
5. I *associate* the excitement of starting a new school year with autumn.
6. I sometimes feel as if I cannot express my *viewpoint* in school.
7. I would not be *absolutely* comfortable at a party where I did not know anyone.
8. Thinking about a relative who is ill gives me a feeling of *melancholy*.

Reading Warm-up A, p. 43

Sample Answers
1. in the early days of the twentieth century; *Originally* means "at first."
2. If you lived in the neighborhood, you were welcome to join in the fun. I am aware of a *bias* in my neighborhood against people who have pit bulls.
3. (to becoming real Americans); I feel a *commitment* to helping my family.
4. (play in the middle of city traffic); *Courageous* means "brave in the face of danger."
5. Games that involved clapping and rhyming; Puzzles or the game of chess might be described as *delightfully* difficult.
6. (immigrant parents); I am familiar with the *traditional* game of tag.
7. easy; The *features* of the games had to be easy so new-comers could learn them quickly and play them.
8. The idea that expensive equipment or special skills might be needed to have fun; I would consider it a *radical* notion that the president should be elected for a ten-year term.

Reading Warm-up B, p. 44

Sample Answers
1. relaxing; I like to play sports with my friends in the neighborhood when the weather is *mellow*.
2. (Fall); The sequence of the seasons is *always* the same. It never changes.
3. My *viewpoint* is mixed; I miss the freedom of summer, but I am glad to get back to a regular daily routine.
4. ice-skating, skiing, and other cold-weather fun; I *associate* the celebration of Kwanzaa with winter.
5. (the arrival of winter); A synonym for *absolutely* is *totally*.
6. short days and freezing temperatures; Opposites of *melancholy* include *cheerfulness* and *joy*.

7. (weather); The track coach has a positive *influence* on me because she encourages me to always do my best.

8. <u>the fact that school will not be over for three more hours</u>; I am *acutely* aware of the sirens from the fire trucks that are whizzing past the school.

Writing About the Big Question, p. 45

A. 1. information, senses
   2. connection
   3. comprehend
   4. fact, interpret

B. Sample Answer

I spent a month each of the last two summers with my grandfather. He used to be a commercial fisherman. We talked a lot about his work and how hard it was. The **insight** I gained has helped me **comprehend** how much he sacrificed so my dad could get an education.

C. Sample Answer

Learning the facts of people's lives may change how we comprehend them because it may give us insight into why people do the things that they do. In this case, knowledge is the same as understanding.

"On Summer" by Lorraine Hansberry

Literary Analysis: Style, p. 46

Sample Answers

1. The informal phrase suggests a lightly self-mocking tone about the trials and tribulations of adolescence.
2. The author's exaggerated diction matches her description of summer days and creates a light, amusing tone.
3. The writer's use of sensory details creates a pleasant, almost enchanting tone.
4. The colorful simile and other details emphasize the gap between the author's expectations and reality; the tone is down-to-earth and realistic.
5. The simple but dignified diction creates a serious tone.

Reading: Generate Prior Questions to Identify Main Idea and Details, p. 47

Sample Answers

A. 1. I expect that the essay will consider summer from a number of different angles.
   2. The opening sentence suggests that the essay will be organized chronologically and will cover various different stages in the development of her ideas about summer.
   3. I think her struggle with cancer may have caused Hansberry to value time and the seasons as very precious.

B. Answers will vary. Examine students' responses for identification of a main idea and supporting details, as well as for specific examples.

Vocabulary Builder, p. 48

Sample Answers

A. 1. Because she keeps apart from her classmates, she has a reputation for <u>aloofness</u>.
   2. The team's unexpected defeat created intense feelings of <u>melancholy</u> in the stands.
   3. Thoroughly <u>pretentious</u>, he always dresses lavishly.
   4. He felt that this triumph was surely bound to be the <u>apex</u> of his career.
   5. The chairperson acted with clear <u>bias</u> when she refused to choose the best qualified person.
   6. I knew I was out for the <u>duration</u> of the season when the doctor said my injury was serious.

B. 1. A sculpture made of stone is more <u>durable</u> than an ice sculpture will melt when the weather turns warm.
   2. Someone with a toothache might have to <u>endure</u> having a tooth pulled.
   3. It's not fair to use <u>duress</u> to get someone to do something for you because the person should be free to make the decision he or she wants.

Enrichment: Seasonal Holidays, p. 49

Answers will vary, depending on the holiday and season selected. Evaluate students' responses on the specific examples they include to describe holiday celebrations, as well as on the connections students draw between the holiday and the season.

"A Celebration of Grandfathers" by Rudolfo Anaya
"On Summer" by Lorraine Hansberry

Integrated Language Skills: Grammar, p. 50

A. 1. anecdotes: D.O.
   2. us: I.O.; portrait: D.O.
   3. grandfather: D.O.
   4. generation: I.O.; model: D.O.

B. Examine students' paragraphs for correct usage and identification of direct and indirect objects.

Open-Book Test, p. 53

Short Answer

1. The author seems to be persuading the reader that summer is not a good season. She names the things she dislikes about it, such as the heat, the texture of sand, the "too-cold" swimming water, and the "icky" feeling of a bathing cap.

   Difficulty: *Average* **Objective:** *Interpretation*

2. *Aloofness* is usually used in reference to a person. Hansberry is comparing the coldness of winter to the coldness of an aloof person.

   Difficulty: *Average* **Objective:** *Vocabulary*

3. She most enjoyed sleeping out in the open at the park. She liked it because the adults would tell entertaining stories about their own childhood, the grass was cool and sweet, and her father talked about the stars.

   Difficulty: *Easy*   **Objective:** *Interpretation*

4. Although the topic is serious, Hansberry's tone appears to be childlike. She is viewing the memory through the eyes of a child (her young self), and for the child, there appears to be more wonder than harsh judgment or serious evaluation.

   Difficulty: *Challenging*   **Objective:** *Literary Analysis*

5. Hansberry uses anecdotes most frequently. Students should cite two of the many anecdotes in the essay.

   Difficulty: *Easy*   **Objective:** *Reading*

6. The author's syntax is formal. Many of Hansberry's sentences are long; there are few if any sentences with unusual word order and few if any sentence fragments.

   Difficulty: *Average*   **Objective:** *Literary Analysis*

7. Hansberry's tone would best be described as sympathetic. Students should recognize that Hansberry is never highly critical and is sympathetic even in describing aspects of summer she never liked.

   Difficulty: *Challenging*   **Objective:** *Interpretation*

8. The woman might be described as forceful and unyielding. She refuses to characterize her cancer as tragic. Instead, she sees it as an enemy that must be resisted and defeated.

   Difficulty: *Average*   **Objective:** *Interpretation*

9. Her attitude has changed from dislike to respect. Students might point out that she calls summer "the noblest of the seasons."

   Difficulty: *Easy*   **Objective:** *Literary Analysis*

10. Since we cannot know the future, we should live life to the fullest.

    Difficulty: *Average*   **Objective:** *Reading*

Essay

11. Students should point out that the central experience for the writer's change in attitude was her encounter with the woman in Maine who was suffering from cancer. Hansberry learned the larger lessons that every season—and time itself—has value and that life should be lived to the fullest.

    Difficulty: *Easy*   **Objective:** *Essay*

12. Students may observe that life-altering changes in attitude are rare, but the ability to change and grow is a valuable asset. Experiences that might cause such change include a life-threatening illness, as in "On Summer," the sudden loss of a relative or dear friend, or an encounter with a memorable person.

    Difficulty: *Average*   **Objective:** *Essay*

13. Students should recognize the sensory details Hansberry uses to argue against summer: "feeling very, very hot," "the too-grainy texture of sand; the too-cold coldness" of the water, the "icky-perspiry feeling of bathing caps," and the "excessive" way in which "objects always appeared in

too sharp a relief against background." For Hansberry, shadows, light, and sound were too pronounced in summer. Students should realize that although Hansberry finally calls summer "the noblest of the seasons," her descriptions of the Maine summer contain far less sensory detail than her earlier descriptions of the Chicago summers. The few sensory details in this section of the essay include the "mellow sunset" off the Maine coast, "the gentlest nights," and "the longest days." Students should explain which set of descriptions is more persuasive.

   Difficulty: *Challenging*   **Objective:** *Essay*

14. Students might point out that Hansberry probably would have equated understanding with the process of finding a balanced, meaningful approach to life. She might have regarded knowledge as a less important value, equating it with details or techniques, not with an overall approach to life. Students should cite at least two details from the essay to support their argument.

   Difficulty: *Average*   **Objective:** *Essay*

Oral Response

15. Oral responses should be clear, well organized, and well supported by details from the essay.

   Difficulty: *Average*   **Objective:** *Oral Interpretation*

Selection Test A, p. 56

Critical Reading

1. ANS: A	DIF: Easy	OBJ: Comprehension
2. ANS: B	DIF: Easy	OBJ: Interpretation
3. ANS: C	DIF: Easy	OBJ: Comprehension
4. ANS: B	DIF: Easy	OBJ: Literary Analysis
5. ANS: D	DIF: Easy	OBJ: Reading
6. ANS: C	DIF: Easy	OBJ: Comprehension
7. ANS: D	DIF: Easy	OBJ: Literary Analysis
8. ANS: D	DIF: Easy	OBJ: Interpretation
9. ANS: A	DIF: Easy	OBJ: Interpretation
10. ANS: C	DIF: Easy	OBJ: Reading
11. ANS: B	DIF: Easy	OBJ: Interpretation

Vocabulary and Grammar

12. ANS: C	DIF: Easy	OBJ: Vocabulary
13. ANS: A	DIF: Easy	OBJ: Vocabulary
14. ANS: B	DIF: Easy	OBJ: Grammar
15. ANS: B	DIF: Easy	OBJ: Grammar

Essay

16. Students should point out that the central experience in the writer's change of attitude was her encounter with the courageous woman in Maine who suffered from cancer. Hansberry learned the larger lesson that every season—and time itself in human life—has value. We should live life to the fullest.

   Difficulty: *Easy*

   Objective: *Essay*

17. Students' essays should mention one example in favor of summer and one against summer. The author argues against summer by describing the heat, the "too-grainy texture" of sand, the "too-cold coldness" of water, and the sweaty feeling of bathing caps. She says that summer's shadows, light, and sounds are too pronounced. She argues in favor of summer in her description of the Maine coast sunset and her realization that summer has gentle nights and long days. Students should tell which description (for or against) they found more persuasive, and why.

Difficulty: *Easy*
Objective: *Essay*

18. Students might point out that Hansberry regards knowledge as a less important value, equating it with details of hot, long summers spent doing ordinary things. Whereas later, she sees that the facts and events of summer help her understand an overall, meaningful approach to and place in life. Students should cite at least two details from the essay to support their response.

Difficulty: *Average*
Objective: *Essay*

appreciate summer's gentle, long nights and its warmth and to see it as "life at the apex."

Difficulty: *Average*
Objective: *Essay*

19. Students may observe that life-altering changes in attitude are rare, but the ability to change and grow is a valuable asset. Experiences that might cause such change might involve a life-threatening illness, as in "On Summer"; the sudden loss of a relative or loved one; or an encounter with a memorable personality.

Difficulty: *Average*
Objective: *Essay*

20. Students might point out that Hansberry probably would have equated understanding with the process of finding a balanced, meaningful approach to life. She might have regarded knowledge as a less important value, equating it with details or techniques, not with the overall approach to life. Students should cite at least two details from the essay to support their argument.

Difficulty: *Average*
Objective: *Essay*

Selection Test B, p. 59

Critical Reading

1. ANS: B	DIF: Average	OBJ: Comprehension
2. ANS: D	DIF: Challenging	OBJ: Literary Analysis
3. ANS: B	DIF: Challenging	OBJ: Interpretation
4. ANS: A	DIF: Average	OBJ: Comprehension
5. ANS: B	DIF: Challenging	OBJ: Literary Analysis
6. ANS: C	DIF: Challenging	OBJ: Reading
7. ANS: D	DIF: Average	OBJ: Reading
8. ANS: B	DIF: Average	OBJ: Literary Analysis
9. ANS: B	DIF: Challenging	OBJ: Interpretation
10. ANS: D	DIF: Average	OBJ: Interpretation
11. ANS: A	DIF: Average	OBJ: Interpretation
12. ANS: B	DIF: Average	OBJ: Reading

Vocabulary and Grammar

13. ANS: A	DIF: Average	OBJ: Vocabulary
14. ANS: C	DIF: Average	OBJ: Vocabulary
15. ANS: C	DIF: Average	OBJ: Vocabulary
16. ANS: B	DIF: Average	OBJ: Grammar
17. ANS: B	DIF: Average	OBJ: Grammar

Essay

18. Students' essays should note that Hansberry used to look at summer as long, boring, and uncomfortable. From the woman in Maine, the author learns to live life to the fullest and to appreciate each day. She comes to

"The News" by Neil Postman

Vocabulary Warm-up Exercises, p. 63

A.
1. journalist
2. disappearance
3. emphasizes
4. perspective
5. unthinkable
6. basic
7. permanent
8. dramatically

B. Sample Answers

1. A movie with a <u>sentimental</u> ending might have an emotional, happy ending in which the hero wins and everyone lives happily ever after.

2. No, it would not be restful because something <u>chaotic</u> is confused and crazy.

3. No, because <u>despise</u> means "to dislike strongly," and a <u>spectator</u> is someone watching a game, so you would probably not willingly watch a football game if you dislike it a lot.

4. Before making a <u>crucial</u> decision, you would take your time and carefully think through what to do because something *crucial* is very important.

5. People are at more risk of causing an accident when doing two things <u>simultaneously</u>, meaning at the same time, because their attention would be distracted.

6. No, it is not wise because an <u>assumption</u> is something that you think is true but it is not guaranteed.

If school was open the next day, you would not have your homework ready for class.

Reading Warm-up A, p. 64

Sample Answers

1. (broadcasters), (reporter); Murrow was one of the first broadcast *journalists*, and he set the standard for television news.
2. continues to be used; *Temporary* is an antonym for *permanent*.
3. (surprised); what life was like for the common soldier
4. point of view; *Viewpoint* is a synonym for *perspective*.
5. the celebrity interview; (essential part)
6. recognizes the importance of; I think television news *emphasizes* the need for people to work together to help others because it shows so many problems in the world.
7. The television networks are no longer the main source for news on television. In this sentence, *disappearance* means "no longer exists."
8. (imagine), (not have conceived of); the news limited to just a few programs daily. News is reported constantly now.

Reading Warm-up B, p. 65

Sample Answers

1. (watching); I might be a *spectator* at a sports game.
2. She had no proof, of course, but it seemed to be true from all the cards; I might make the *assumption* that tenth grade will be harder than ninth grade.
3. *Sentimental* means "something that shows so much emotion that it is over the top and could make some people uncomfortable." Yes, you can have a friend who is *sentimental* and shows a lot of emotion.
4. very much disliked; *Admire* is an antonym for *despise*.
5. Kit had a *limitation* on how much she could use her arms because she strained her muscles. *Restriction* is a synonym for *limitation*.
6. (extremely important); *Critical* is a synonym for *crucial*.
7. at the same time; No, it is not wise because you cannot completely pay attention to both, and your homework will suffer.
8. people screaming; (confusion)

Writing About the Big Question, p. 66

A. 1. fact
2. ambiguous
3. research
4. insight

B. Sample Answers

1. I get news from TV, the newspaper, and the Internet.
2. The Internet gives me lots of **information** about crime in cities across the nation. Now, when I see it in my neighborhood, I can make the **connection** to

the national scene. I know it's not just a local problem, but one that everyone has to deal with.

C. Sample Answer

We react in different ways to the presentations of news information on television and to the presentations in other media because on television, we actually see things, while in other media we may not. Seeing images can give us a better feeling for what it would be like to experience events first-hand. When reading a newspaper, for example, we have a chance to understand the facts at a more intellectual level. In this case, knowledge may not be the same as understanding.

"The News" by Neil Postman

Literary Analysis: Expository Essay, p. 67

Sample Answers

1. The topic is television newscasts.
2. Students may mention any three of the following: dramatic music; the sound of teletype machines; the world map or world clocks; the atmosphere of tension; the sight of news staff scurrying around, typing reports and answering phones; the calm and welcoming anchor.
3. The description supports Postman's main idea in the essay: that television newscasts distort and misrepresent the reality of events.
4. Television news is severely limited in coverage, compared to print media; television news cannot challenge viewers the way print media can; television news depends on the "grammar of moving pictures," which is much more limited than language in its ability to communicate.
5. The comparison supports Postman's central thesis: the public should remain skeptical about TV news because of its intrinsic limitations and flaws.
6. Local affiliate stations are unwilling to give up their profits from the game shows and situation comedies they broadcast in the half-hour following the evening news.

Reading: Reread to Identify Main Idea and Details, p. 68

Sample Answers

1. He uses these adjectives because, according to Postman, the "grammar" of moving picture images requires change. Also, viewers like to be entertained with exciting images.
2. While they watch TV, viewers may be distracted by what is happening in their living space. Also, visual changes on a small TV screen must be extreme and dramatic in order to be noticed by viewers.
3. He means that nonverbal messages (such as dramatic music and clattering teletype machines) have an emotional impact on viewers. They subtly condition viewers to view the newscast as drama, ritual, and entertainment.
4. Postman supports this claim with several arguments: time is highly restricted on television; the nature of the medium favors dynamic visual images; and the commercial pressures of TV require the news to hold

its audience above all else. Therefore, for example, a story about collapsing bleachers in South America may easily take priority over the issuance of a new federal budget in Washington.

Vocabulary Builder, p. 69

Sample Answers

A. 1. She settled her lawsuit for a substantial amount in <u>compensation</u> for her injuries.
2. The climb to the summit seemed <u>daunting</u>, and we started the hike with nervous anxiety.
3. Ray is devoted to the <u>temporal</u> realities of his job and is almost never late for work.
4. "It is because you are a <u>revered</u> expert," she said, "that we feel we must honor your opinion."
5. The only <u>medium</u> that reported the interview was the newspaper.
6. The <u>imposition</u> of a rule against leaving early limited students' freedom.

B. 1. President Washington is not a <u>contemporary</u> president because he died long ago.
2. You can tell that a situation is not <u>temporary</u> when it lasts a long time.
3. Someone would <u>temporize</u> if he were caught doing something wrong in order to gain time to think of an excuse.

Enrichment: News Analysis, p. 70

Answers will vary. Examine students' charts for specific elements listed and for comprehensive reporting on the news shows.

"The News" by Neil Postman

Open-Book Test, p. 71

Short Answer

1. This and other details support the main idea that TV newscasts are a form of theater.
   Difficulty: *Average* **Objective:** *Reading*
2. Postman believes that the journalistic achievements of anchors are less important than the image they project on television.
   Difficulty: *Average* **Objective:** *Interpretation*
3. Postman uses these details to support his point that television favors exciting, changing images over ones that neither move nor change.
   Difficulty: *Challenging* **Objective:** *Literary Analysis*
4. Postman admired Cronkite. *Revered* means "highly respected."
   Difficulty: *Average* **Objective:** *Vocabulary*
5. The quotation provides support for Postman's main idea.
   Difficulty: *Challenging* **Objective:** *Reading*
6. *Effect:* There is little or no in-depth news coverage. Newspapers do not have a need to "include everyone."
   Difficulty: *Average* **Objective:** *Literary Analysis*

7. Local affiliate stations earn more money broadcasting game shows or situation comedies in the half hour after the news than they would if that time slot were taken up by an expanded news broadcast.
   Difficulty: *Easy* **Objective:** *Literary Analysis*
8. Postman apparently believes that television news presents a distorted view of reality.
   Difficulty: *Challenging* **Objective:** *Interpretation*
9. The tone is objective. In their explanations, students should note that Postman both criticizes and praises television news.
   Difficulty: *Easy* **Objective:** *Interpretation*
10. Sample answer: Television news has serious drawbacks and limitations.
    Difficulty: *Easy* **Objective:** *Reading*

Essay

11. Students should clearly state two main points from the essay. They may mention any of the following: the tendency of television news to show dramatic, entertaining images; the symbolism and theatricality in the opening minutes of a news broadcast; the randomness in the presentation of news stories; the emphasis on the anchor as a host rather than a journalist; and the half-hour time limit and consequent lack of depth in news reports. Students should provide at least one detail to support each main point they identify.
    Difficulty: *Easy* **Objective:** *Essay*
12. In their essays, students should include some or all of the following points: considerations of space, length, and time; the ability to challenge readers; the role of theatricality; the role of the anchor; and the range and depth of stories. Students should support their main ideas with details from the reading.
    Difficulty: *Average* **Objective:** *Essay*
13. In their essays, students should present a clear argument in support of television news and then support their position with relevant details. Students may also refute points made by Postman. For example, Postman's dismissal of "talking heads" might be refuted by the popularity of the *NewsHour* on PBS, which regularly features panels of experts discussing an issue in depth.
    Difficulty: *Challenging* **Objective:** *Essay*
14. In their essays, students should demonstrate an understanding of the difference between knowledge and understanding. They should then relate both notions to the news, identifying practical methods by which people can become better informed (that is, gain more knowledge) and achieve a fuller understanding of facts.
    Difficulty: *Average* **Objective:** *Essay*

Oral Response

15. Oral responses should be clear, well organized, and well supported by appropriate details from the essay.
    Difficulty: *Average* **Objective:** *Oral Interpretation*

Unit 3 Resources: Types of Nonfiction

Selection Test A, p. 74

Critical Reading

1. ANS: C   DIF: Easy   OBJ: Reading
2. ANS: C   DIF: Easy   OBJ: Comprehension
3. ANS: A   DIF: Easy   OBJ: Comprehension
4. ANS: A   DIF: Easy   OBJ: Comprehension
5. ANS: D   DIF: Easy   OBJ: Interpretation
6. ANS: C   DIF: Easy   OBJ: Reading
7. ANS: D   DIF: Easy   OBJ: Literary Analysis
8. ANS: B   DIF: Easy   OBJ: Comprehension
9. ANS: B   DIF: Easy   OBJ: Comprehension
10. ANS: B   DIF: Easy   OBJ: Literary Analysis

Vocabulary and Grammar

11. ANS: C   DIF: Easy   OBJ: Vocabulary
12. ANS: C   DIF: Easy   OBJ: Vocabulary
13. ANS: A   DIF: Easy   OBJ: Grammar
14. ANS: C   DIF: Easy   OBJ: Grammar

Essay

15. Students' essays should clearly state two main points from the essay. Students may mention any of the following: the tendency of TV news to show dramatic, entertaining images; the symbolism and theatricality of the opening of a newscast; the chaotic lack of relationships among TV news stories; the emphasis on the TV anchor as host rather than as journalist; the half-hour time limitation and consequent lack of in-depth reporting on issues. Students' essays should provide one or two specific examples for each main point identified.

    Difficulty: *Easy*

    Objective: *Essay*

16. Students' essays should include some or all of the following: considerations of space, length, and time; the ability of the print media to challenge readers; freedom in the print media from distractions like dramatic music; the presence vs. the absence of the anchorperson; and the ability of the print media to cover a far broader range of stories. Students should support their main ideas with specific details and examples.

    Difficulty: *Easy*

    Objective: *Essay*

17. Students might cite the example that a picture of an aircraft carrier needs to be accompanied with language to help the viewer understand where the carrier is, where it is headed, and when and why. On the other hand, language about an earthquake that is unaccompanied by pictures would lack the impact and interest that moving pictures of devastation and destruction would give the information.

    Difficulty: *Average*

    Objective: *Easy*

Selection Test B, p. 77

Critical Reading

1. ANS: C   DIF: Average   OBJ: Reading
2. ANS: A   DIF: Average   OBJ: Comprehension
3. ANS: A   DIF: Average   OBJ: Literary Analysis
4. ANS: D   DIF: Average   OBJ: Comprehension
5. ANS: D   DIF: Challenging   OBJ: Interpretation
6. ANS: C   DIF: Average   OBJ: Reading
7. ANS: D   DIF: Average   OBJ: Literary Analysis
8. ANS: A   DIF: Challenging   OBJ: Interpretation
9. ANS: B   DIF: Average   OBJ: Comprehension
10. ANS: B   DIF: Average   OBJ: Interpretation
11. ANS: C   DIF: Average   OBJ: Reading
12. ANS: C   DIF: Average   OBJ: Literary Analysis
13. ANS: B   DIF: Challenging   OBJ: Interpretation
14. ANS: A   DIF: Average   OBJ: Literary Analysis

Vocabulary and Grammar

15. ANS: A   DIF: Average   OBJ: Vocabulary
16. ANS: B   DIF: Average   OBJ: Vocabulary
17. ANS: A   DIF: Average   OBJ: Grammar
18. ANS: D   DIF: Average   OBJ: Grammar

Essay

19. Student essays should clearly identify Postman's main idea and two of his supporting arguments, examples, and details. For example, students might mention the symbolic messages communicated by devices like music and other sounds, or the time limitations on television news programs. Students should then analyze the relationship between these arguments and Postman's main idea in the essay.

    Difficulty: *Average*

    Objective: *Essay*

20. Students' essays should clearly state a position favorable to TV news and then support this position with specific examples and arguments. Students may also refute specific points made by Postman. For example, Postman's dismissal of "talking heads" on television might be refuted by reference to the "News Hour" on PBS, which regularly features panels of experts discussing an issue under the guidance of a moderator.

    Difficulty: *Challenging*

    Objective: *Essay*

21. In their essays, students should demonstrate an understanding of the difference between knowledge and understanding. They should then relate both notions to the news, identifying practical methods by which people can become better informed (that is, gain more knowledge) and achieve a fuller understanding of facts.

    Difficulty: *Average*

    Objective: *Essay*

Unit 3 Resources: Types of Nonfiction

"Single Room, Earth View" by Sally Ride

Vocabulary Warm-up Exercises, p. 81

A. 1. magnificent
2. environment
3. observations
4. informal
5. drama
6. sensations
7. continually
8. circular

B. Sample Answers
1. T; *Murky* means the hallway is dark and hard to see in and might make you uneasy.
2. F; *Similarly* means "alike," so the athletes would have about the same skill level.
3. T; A *sophisticated* idea would be one that is good but also complicated, and some people would find a complicated idea hard to follow.
4. T; An *abrupt* rainstorm would be sudden and unexpected, and that could quickly end a picnic.
5. F; An *intriguing* movie would be interesting and could be mysterious, and both qualities would hold most people's attention.
6. T; *Fascination* is a strong interest, and a mechanic who fixes cars would likely have a strong interest in them.
7. F; Wood that is left to *smolder* would still be burning even though there are no flames, so it would not be safe to touch.
8. F; A problem that grows *significantly* gets larger in size and scope and would be harder to solve, not easier.

Reading Warm-up A, p. 82

Sample Answers
1. (excitement); powerful; It is *powerful* because drama is full of power and an experience that has a strong impact.
2. (setting); If I were concerned about the *natural environment*, I would describe *environment* as the land, air, and water around us.
3. no break; *Constantly* is a synonym for *continually*.
4. around Earth; Something *circular* in the classroom is the round wall clock or the round wastebasket.
5. use expert data from scientific equipment; add to it their own informal field notes; *Observations* are records and information that come from study.
6. (casual); I would be jotting down ideas or something I might see but not in an organized, serious way, such as for class.
7. heart-pounding; You can feel your heart beating fast when you are excited or scared, so *sensations* would be connected with how your body experiences something.

8. The lights are *magnificent* because there are so many of them, created by the many people living on Earth. In the context, *magnificent* means "amazing, especially in size."

Reading Warm-up B, p. 83

Sample Answers
1. wondering with great interest; I have a *fascination* for flowers and can learn more by tending a garden.
2. (shadow), (darkened); *Clear* is an antonym for *murky*.
3. provides information that is . . . accurate and complex; Advanced computers and telescopes are examples of *sophisticated* equipment that astronauts might use.
4. For thousands of years they placed Earth at the center of the universe. *Significantly* means "in a noticeable way."
5. (strange); I find science *intriguing* because the natural world is interesting but also can be bizarre.
6. (sudden); I would feel surprised because *abrupt* means "sudden and unexpected."
7. not extinguished; The fire is low but can still flame. Yes, your temper can *smolder*, though not in a real way like a fire. You can be angry about something but not yell, just as a fire can burn without a flame.
8. (other discoveries), (same idea); Two friends might behave *similarly* by having friendly personalities, enjoying sports, or being leaders in school. They would act in ways that are alike, but not exactly alike.

Writing About the Big Question, p. 84

A. 1. concept
2. feeling
3. clarify
4. fact

B. Sample Answers
1. We gain the technology needed to send rockets into space. We get pictures of Earth from space.
2. We get lots of **information** from the technology we create for space. We learn electronics and communication. Applying the **research** to our needs for better communication on Earth helps all of us.

C. Sample Answer

Looking at Earth from space may change how we comprehend the world because it might give us a different perspective. Things that seemed important might not be anymore. In this case, knowledge would be the same as understanding.

"Single Room, Earth View" by Sally Ride

Literary Analysis: Expository Essay, p. 85

Sample Answers
1. She discusses spaceflight.

2. Ride says that trying to describe spaceflight is like trying to describe airplane travel to someone who has never flown. Spaceflight differs from airplane travel because it is a "giant step" farther away from Earth. Space travelers have a different perspective and different feelings, impressions, and insights.

3. This discussion relates to the main idea because it signals how difficult it is to convey the wonder and spectacular splendor of spaceflight.

4. She mentions oil slicks on the Persian Gulf, pollution-damaged trees in the forests of central Europe, and air pollution in some cities.

5. For part—perhaps half—of each orbit, the space shuttle flies above the dark nighttime side of Earth. She could see the twinkling lights of the cities.

6. In the conclusion, Ride says that spaceflight cannot be compared to airplane travel. She emphasizes the uniqueness of the perspective, environment, and unknown elements of spaceflight.

Reading: Reread to Identify Main Idea and Details, p. 86

Sample Answers

1. She finds the "maplike" appearance of Hawaii from space both logical and extremely surprising.

2. If you glance away or stop concentrating for a second, the speed of flight makes identifying your location difficult.

3. She became a believer because the sharp relief of landforms made it easy for her to imagine the dynamic upheavals and collisions of the plate tectonics theory.

4. "The signatures of civilization" are such things as bridges, runways, cities, and cultivated areas of land. They are the imprint (signature) of human life on Earth.

Vocabulary Builder, p. 87

Sample Answers

A. 1. B; 2. C; 3. D; 4. B; 5. C; 6. D; 7. A
B. 1. The novelty of the situation comedy is that it was not like any others.

2. The novice mechanic had not been working on cars very long.

3. Before the renovation, the house was in bad need of repairs.

Enrichment: Plate Tectonics, p. 88

Sample Answers

1. Earth's surface layer consists of a dozen large and several smaller plates that very slowly move toward, under, away from, and alongside each other. Plate movements cause earthquakes, volcanoes, and mountains.

2. The Arabian and African plates are divergent, or moving away from each other.

3. The plate on which India rests is converging with the Eurasian Plate. Therefore, India appears to be crashing into the Asian continent.

4. She can see mountain ranges, volcanoes, and land masses—geological formations that mark plate boundaries.

"The News" by Neil Postman
"Single Room, Earth View" by Sally Ride

Integrated Language Skills: Grammar, p. 89

Answers

A. 1. Linking verb: *is*; predicate adjective: *smaller*
2. Linking verb: *is*; predicate adjective: *different*
3. Linking verb: *are*; predicate nominative: *symbols*
4. Linking verb: *is*; predicate nominative: *time*
5. Linking verb: *became*; predicate nominative: *believer*
6. Linking verb: *is*; predicate nominative: *object*
7. Linking verb: *is*; predicate adjective: *black*
8. Linking verb: *is*; predicate nominative: *element*

B. Examine students' paragraphs to make sure they have used and correctly identified two predicate adjectives and two predicate nominatives. You might have students read their paragraphs aloud in small groups.

Open-Book Test, p. 92

Short Answer

1. The space shuttle circles the Earth once every 90 minutes, or at a rate of 5 miles per second, so in just a few minutes the view changes dramatically.

   Difficulty: *Easy* **Objective:** *Literary Analysis*

2. A novice geologist is inexperienced.

   Difficulty: *Average* **Objective:** *Vocabulary*

3. From the moon, the Earth appears to be a "blue marble." From the shuttle, the entire globe cannot be seen in one view.

   Difficulty: *Average* **Objective:** *Literary Analysis*

4. Students should name the oil slicks on the Persian Gulf, trees in central Europe damaged by pollution, or the haziness and muted colors that indicate the pollution in some cities.

   Difficulty: *Average* **Objective:** *Reading*

5. Some features of the ocean are so large that they can be viewed in full only from the vantage point of space. Students should mention the vast circular and spiral eddies, the huge standing waves, or "the spiral eddies that sometimes trail into one another."

   Difficulty: *Average* **Objective:** *Interpretation*

6. Students are likely to say that the description evokes feelings of uncertainty and suspense. They should point to the repetition of *very* and the word *black* to support their response.

   Difficulty: *Challenging* **Objective:** *Literary Analysis*

7. *Full Moon:* Earth is lit by an eerie light; clouds look "ghostly"; moonlight on water creates bright reflections. *No Moon:* City lights twinkle; it can be hard to distinguish the Earth from the sky. Ride uses

comparison and contrast to provide support for her essay in this discussion.

Difficulty: *Average* **Objective:** *Literary Analysis*

8. Ride says that this idea is "not true." She uses the anecdote as evidence of what space flight is not. That is, she uses it to support her idea that space flight is unlike anything else.

Difficulty: *Challenging* **Objective:** *Reading*

9. Students might call the tone friendly or serious. The reference at the beginning of the essay to the "wide-eyed, ten-year-old girls" suggests a friendly tone, but the anecdote at the end about space flight's not being like an airline flight shows that she is also serious.

Difficulty: *Challenging* **Objective:** *Interpretation*

10. Space travel offers a unique view of Earth.

Difficulty: *Easy* **Objective:** *Reading*

Essay

11. Students should explain that viewing Earth from outer space has allowed scientists to see things they would not otherwise have seen. Students might mention, for example, the huge eddies and standing waves, which have contributed to scientists' understanding of ocean dynamics. Students might also mention the photographs and sensors that have been used to document and measure pollution on Earth.

Difficulty: *Easy* **Objective:** *Essay*

12. Students should point out that Ride groups together related observations. Each observation is an idea, and it is supported by details. Some students may realize that the essay begins and ends with remarks about laypersons' attempts to understand space flight and that the essay's main idea—that there is nothing else like space flight—is expressed at the end. Students are likely to appreciate Ride's straightforward presentation.

Difficulty: *Average* **Objective:** *Essay*

13. Students should cite examples of description (there are many), comparison and contrast (for example, between an airline flight and space flight, between the dark side of the planet when there is no moon and the dark side when there is a full moon), and cause and effect (for example, observable changes on Earth as a result of pollution). They should recognize that Ride's essay is meant to give a general audience a sense of what space flight is like and what can be learned from outer space. Students will probably conclude that Ride's essay is effective because it uses vivid, well-described details to support her main point; it is likely to engage its intended audience.

Difficulty: *Challenging* **Objective:** *Essay*

14. Students should point out that astronauts' observations and measurements increase knowledge and that scientists can use that knowledge to reach a greater understanding of Earth's environment and the solar system.

Difficulty: *Average* **Objective:** *Essay*

Oral Response

15. Oral responses should be clear, well organized, and well supported by appropriate details from the essay.

Difficulty: *Average* **Objective:** *Oral Interpretation*

Selection Test A, p. 95

Critical Reading

1. **ANS:** B	**DIF:** Easy	**OBJ:** Reading
2. **ANS:** D	**DIF:** Easy	**OBJ:** Literary Analysis
3. **ANS:** A	**DIF:** Easy	**OBJ:** Interpretation
4. **ANS:** A	**DIF:** Easy	**OBJ:** Reading
5. **ANS:** D	**DIF:** Easy	**OBJ:** Interpretation
6. **ANS:** A	**DIF:** Easy	**OBJ:** Interpretation
7. **ANS:** D	**DIF:** Easy	**OBJ:** Literary Analysis
8. **ANS:** C	**DIF:** Easy	**OBJ:** Reading
9. **ANS:** A	**DIF:** Easy	**OBJ:** Interpretation

Vocabulary and Grammar

10. **ANS:** B	**DIF:** Easy	**OBJ:** Vocabulary
11. **ANS:** B	**DIF:** Easy	**OBJ:** Vocabulary
12. **ANS:** D	**DIF:** Easy	**OBJ:** Grammar
13. **ANS:** C	**DIF:** Easy	**OBJ:** Grammar

Essay

14. Students may point out that the author organizes the essay by grouping types of observations together and describing examples of each. Each observation is a main point, and the examples are supporting evidence. Students may say that it is easy to identify main points and supporting evidence since the author describes the observations one after another. Or they may say that it is hard to tell when one observation is finished and a new one begins.

Difficulty: *Easy*

Objective: *Essay*

15. Students may mention any of the following as evidence of human life: smoke from fires along the east coast of Africa, city lights sparkling at night, the straight lines of bridges and runways, the sharp delineations from desert to irrigated land, oil slicks on the Persian Gulf, pollution-damaged trees in Europe, and pollutant haze over cities. Students may compare the African fires to the city lights of the eastern United States to show the extremes of human existence on Earth. The straight lines and sharp delineations may show how humans have ignored nature's way in the pursuit of progress. The pollution shows the carelessness with which humans have treated their home, planet Earth.

Difficulty: *Easy*

Objective: *Essay*

16. Students should point out that knowledge, or information, is gathered through astronauts' informal observations and precise scientific measurements. Scientists can use that knowledge to reach a greater understanding of Earth, Earth's environment, and the solar system. For example, astronaut observations over time revealed that pollution was having a negative effect on the ability to see Earth from space.

Difficulty: *Average*
Objective: *Essay*

Selection Test B, p. 98

Critical Reading

1. ANS: B	DIF: Average	OBJ: Reading
2. ANS: D	DIF: Average	OBJ: Literary Analysis
3. ANS: A	DIF: Average	OBJ: Interpretation
4. ANS: D	DIF: Average	OBJ: Literary Analysis
5. ANS: C	DIF: Average	OBJ: Comprehension
6. ANS: A	DIF: Average	OBJ: Reading
7. ANS: D	DIF: Average	OBJ: Interpretation
8. ANS: A	DIF: Average	OBJ: Interpretation
9. ANS: B	DIF: Average	OBJ: Literary Analysis
10. ANS: C	DIF: Challenging	OBJ: Reading
11. ANS: C	DIF: Challenging	OBJ: Comprehension
12. ANS: A	DIF: Average	OBJ: Interpretation
13. ANS: C	DIF: Challenging	OBJ: Comprehension

Vocabulary and Grammar

14. ANS: B	DIF: Average	OBJ: Vocabulary
15. ANS: D	DIF: Average	OBJ: Vocabulary
16. ANS: D	DIF: Average	OBJ: Grammar
17. ANS: C	DIF: Average	OBJ: Grammar

Essay

18. Students' essays should point to Ride's geographical references, such as a page torn from Rand-McNally or her naming of well-known places. Students might also note Ride's comparisons to everyday objects, such as biscuits rising in an oven, twinkling lights, or exploding fireworks.

Difficulty: *Average*
Objective: *Essay*

19. Students' essays should note how the change in perspective when viewing Earth from orbit has allowed astronauts to see things not otherwise possible. They might mention such sights as huge eddies and standing waves in oceans, which have contributed to scientists' knowledge of ocean dynamics. Students might also discuss the use of photographs and sensors from the space shuttle to measure and document various types of pollution on Earth.

Difficulty: *Average*
Objective: *Essay*

20. Students' essays should recognize that Ride's writing style is informal and geared toward an educated, although not specifically scientific, audience. Her writing flows naturally from factual, detailed descriptions of scenes to personal descriptions of her feelings about her observations. As support, students might include Ride's description of the Hawaiian Islands and her feelings about their surreal appearance, or her comparison of the moon's reflection on the Mississippi to Huck Finn's lantern and the strange feelings she experiences as she views it.

Difficulty: *Challenging*
Objective: *Essay*

21. Students should point out that astronauts' observations and measurements increase knowledge and that scientists can use that knowledge to reach a greater understanding of Earth's environment and the solar system.

Difficulty: *Average*
Objective: *Essay*

from A Lincoln Preface by Carl Sandburg
"Arthur Ashe Remembered" by John McPhee

Vocabulary Warm-up Exercises, p. 102

A. 1. baffled
2. betray
3. mirth
4. cunning
5. massive
6. unexpected
7. existence
8. unpredictable

B. Sample Answers
1. Our victorious team is a source of pride for our school.
2. They were so different that they were a study in contrasts.
3. A matchless friend is the best person to have around because you cannot have a better friend.
4. We received the news prematurely, before everyone else knew.
5. It was a tragedy for the old couple when the storm destroyed their house.
6. Before she started the marathon, she wavered and almost dropped out.
7. A favorable response to my vacation request will make me very happy.

Reading Warm-up A, p. 103

Sample Answers
1. (Some of these kids had probably been babies together in the local hospital.); *Life* is a synonym for *existence* in this passage.

2. (happy); Someone *full of mirth* is laughing and very happy and full of joy.

3. (not understanding); *Confused* is a synonym for *baffled*.

4. (huge number); She describes her experience with changing schools as *massive* because she has done it so many times.

5. (without warning, surprise); <u>this move, her grand-mother had a stroke</u>

6. (never would have predicted); Yes, they are similar words because they both refer to not being able to plan or know what will happen next. Something *unexpected* is not expected, and something *unpredictable* cannot be predicted.

7. (dishonesty); What was *cunning* about her plan was not showing her honest feelings of being afraid that others would not like her. A word I would use to describe her plan is *clever*.

8. (her fears about whether others would like her); *Reveal* is an antonym for *betray*. Yes, I agree with her logic because if you act friendly and confident, people are more likely to be friendly in return.

Reading Warm-up B, p. 104

Sample Answers

1. (early and unexpected); She lost her parents at a younger age than most people do.

2. <u>She showed by her willingness to get involved to help others that she believed in herself and what she could do.</u> She went from being very withdrawn and insecure to more confident and involved.

3. (sad and shocking event); *Disaster* is a synonym for *tragedy*.

4. (determination); If Franklin Roosevelt had *wavered*, he would have shown uncertainly about being able to overcome his disability and might have stopped trying.

5. <u>Eleanor constantly pushed the President to develop programs that would benefit the poor.</u> (benefit)

6. (very best); My mother is *matchless* because I think she is the best in the world!

7. <u>She was deeply shy as a girl. Yet she grew up to be one of the most outspoken women of her time.</u> *Differences* is a synonym for *contrasts*, and *similarities* is an antonym.

8. (winners); *Triumphant* is a synonym for *victorious*, which describes her life because she overcame so much and did so much.

Writing About the Big Question, p. 105

A. 1. comprehend

2. information or research; interpret

3. statistics

4. ambiguous

B. Sample Answers

1. I got lost in the woods when I was hiking. Somehow I got turned around and didn't have a clue which way to go.

2. I didn't trust any of the **information** I had because I was so confused. My **instincts** told me which way to walk and I trusted them. In fifteen minutes, I had found my way again.

C. Sample Answer

he or she helps us understand the life of the person described.

The facts tell us what people did, but they also give us insight into why they did certain things and maybe how they felt about those things. We may have to read between the lines, but the facts lead us to an understanding we could never get otherwise.

Literary Analysis: Biographical Writing, p. 106

Sample Answers

1. Lincoln enjoyed the public's idea of him as an independent, sometimes unconventional, leader with a sense of humor.

2. Sandburg describes Lincoln as complex and multifaceted, living life to the fullest and combining "work, thought, laughter, tears, hate, [and] love."

3. Supporting details include direct quotations from Ashe and detailed descriptions of Ashe's actions.

4. McPhee uses direct quotations from Ashe's father and from Ashe himself and anecdotes and detailed descriptions of the actions and reactions of Ashe and other people.

Vocabulary Builder, p. 107

A. Sample Answers

1. Most of the people detested their ruler's use of despotic power.

2. Mary's personality is an enigma, so it is hard for us to discover her true motives.

3. A successful athlete typically needs a lithe body.

4. The movie was so droll that we practically fell out of our seats with laughter.

5. In our opinion, the team leader's disgraceful conduct deserves censure.

6. The ancient temple is a legacy from a bygone civilization.

B. 1. C; 2. B; 3. A; 4. D

Open-Book Test, p. 109

Short Answer

1. The author writes about the life and personality of another person.

   Difficulty: *Easy*   **Objective:** *Literary Analysis*

2. Sandburg wants to show that Lincoln was a skilled politician who knew how to get what he wanted.

   Difficulty: *Challenging*   **Objective:** *Interpretation*

3. No, a person whose actions receive censure would be strongly disapproved of.

   Difficulty: *Average*   **Objective:** *Vocabulary*

Unit 3 Resources: Types of Nonfiction

4. Sandburg wants to show Lincoln's many-sided personality before describing the specifics of his life.
   Difficulty: *Challenging*   **Objective:** *Interpretation*

5. Appropriate adjectives include *admiring, enthusiastic, complimentary,* and *laudatory.*
   Difficulty: *Easy*   **Objective:** *Interpretation*

6. Students should recognize that the most forceful impression McPhee creates is of a man who was in control, who would not let others know what he was thinking.
   Difficulty: *Challenging*   **Objective:** *Literary Analysis*

7. Both selections are biographical.
   Difficulty: *Easy*   **Objective:** *Literary Analysis*

8. Lincoln often openly displayed his emotions, whereas Ashe was usually reserved.
   Difficulty: *Challenging*   **Objective:** *Literary Analysis*

9. The biographers wish to illustrate their subjects' personalities.
   Difficulty: *Average*   **Objective:** *Literary Analysis*

10. 1. They possessed courage and determination.
    2. They died young, perhaps without having accomplished everything they might have accomplished. Readers are likely to admire both men and feel an emotional connection to them.
    Difficulty: *Average*   **Objective:** *Interpretation*

Essay

11. In their essays, students should identify one anecdote, explain its importance, and describe what it reveals about the subject.
    Difficulty: *Easy*   **Objective:** *Essay*

12. Students may point out that both Lincoln and Ashe were extraordinary achievers both died young, both admiration caused pepoles the feel puzzlement and or resentment; and both possessed courage and a strong determination to succeed. One important difference is that Lincoln expressed his emotions freely, whereas Ashe controlled his feelings.
    Difficulty: *Average*   **Objective:** *Essay*

13. In their essays, students should recognize that Sandburg covers a wide range of personality traits by using a variety of anecdotes and quotations whereas McPhee focuses on a single overall impression of Arthur Ashe.
    Difficulty: *Challenging*   **Objective:** *Essay*

14. Students should point out that the purposes of biographical writing include interpreting the subject's personality and achievements and revealing the significance of his or her life in the wider world. Students will probably say, therefore, that an experienced biographer would hold the view that understanding goes further than a knowledge of mere facts and events. Students should support their ideas with details from one or both selections.
    Difficulty: *Average*   **Objective:** *Essay*

Oral Response

15. Oral responses should be clear, well organized, and well supported by appropriate details from the selection or selections.
    Difficulty: *Average*   **Objective:** *Oral Interpretation*

Selection Test A, p. 112

Critical Reading

1. **ANS:** D	**DIF:** Easy	**OBJ:** Interpretation
2. **ANS:** A	**DIF:** Easy	**OBJ:** Comprehension
3. **ANS:** A	**DIF:** Easy	**OBJ:** Literary Analysis
4. **ANS:** A	**DIF:** Easy	**OBJ:** Comprehension
5. **ANS:** B	**DIF:** Easy	**OBJ:** Interpretation
6. **ANS:** D	**DIF:** Easy	**OBJ:** Interpretation
7. **ANS:** B	**DIF:** Easy	**OBJ:** Interpretation
8. **ANS:** B	**DIF:** Easy	**OBJ:** Literary Analysis
9. **ANS:** C	**DIF:** Easy	**OBJ:** Comprehension
10. **ANS:** A	**DIF:** Easy	**OBJ:** Interpretation
11. **ANS:** D	**DIF:** Easy	**OBJ:** Interpretation

Vocabulary

12. **ANS:** A	**DIF:** Easy	**OBJ:** Vocabulary
13. **ANS:** A	**DIF:** Easy	**OBJ:** Vocabulary
14. **ANS:** B	**DIF:** Easy	**OBJ:** Vocabulary

Essay

15. In their essays, students should identify two favorite anecdotes from the selections and include an explanation of why they chose each one. The discussion should represent details accurately. Students should also explain what the anecdote reveals about the subject.
    Difficulty: *Easy*
    Objective: *Essay*

16. Evaluate students' essays for the scope and applicability of their thesis statements and for detailed supporting references to each selection. In general, students may describe Lincoln as complex and many-sided and Ashe as cool and enigmatic. Other descriptions are acceptable, provided they are well supported by references to the text.
    Difficulty: *Easy*
    Objective: *Essay*

17. Students should use the definitions of *knowledge* and *understanding* as provided in the question to judge whether the biographer they chose provides knowledge and understanding about his subject. Essays should include relevant details from the selection they chose.
    Difficulty: *Average*
    Objective: *Essay*

Selection Test B, p. 115

Critical Reading

1. ANS: B   DIF: Average   OBJ: Literary Analysis
2. ANS: B   DIF: Average   OBJ: Comprehension
3. ANS: D   DIF: Average   OBJ: Comprehension
4. ANS: D   DIF: Challenging   OBJ: Literary Analysis
5. ANS: C   DIF: Challenging   OBJ: Interpretation
6. ANS: A   DIF: Average   OBJ: Interpretation
7. ANS: D   DIF: Average   OBJ: Interpretation
8. ANS: A   DIF: Average   OBJ: Interpretation
9. ANS: A   DIF: Average   OBJ: Interpretation
10. ANS: A   DIF: Average   OBJ: Comprehension
11. ANS: C   DIF: Average   OBJ: Literary Analysis
12. ANS: B   DIF: Challenging   OBJ: Interpretation
13. ANS: B   DIF: Average   OBJ: Interpretation
14. ANS: D   DIF: Average   OBJ: Literary Analysis

Vocabulary

15. ANS: B   DIF: Average   OBJ: Vocabulary
16. ANS: A   DIF: Average   OBJ: Vocabulary
17. ANS: C   DIF: Challenging   OBJ: Vocabulary
18. ANS: A   DIF: Average   OBJ: Vocabulary

Essay

19. Students may point out that both Lincoln and Ashe were extraordinary achievers, both died prematurely, both inspired a mixture of admiration and puzzlement or resentment, and both possessed courage and a strong determination to succeed. One important difference is that Lincoln expressed his emotions freely, whereas Ashe controlled his feelings and was unreadable, or enigmatic.

    Difficulty: *Average*
    Objective: *Essay*

20. In their essays, students should cite specific examples of Sandburg's use of anecdotes and quotations to illustrate Lincoln's wide range of emotions and personality traits. Students should also analyze McPhee's essay for specific details that contribute to an overall impression: Ashe's enigmatic, unpredictable style as a brilliant tennis player.

    Difficulty: *Average*
    Objective: *Essay*

21. Students should point out that the purposes of biographical writing include interpreting the subject's personality and achievements and revealing the significance of his or her life in the wider world. Students will probably say, therefore, that an experienced biographer would hold the view that understanding goes further than a knowledge of mere

facts and events. Students should support their ideas with details from one or both selections.

    Difficulty: *Average*
    Objective: *Essay*

Writing Workshop—Unit 3, Part 1

Business Letter: Integrating Grammar Skills, p. 119

A.   2. compound subject; 3. compound direct object; 4. compound predicate adjective

B. Sample Answers

1. The swim team meets on Tuesdays and Thursdays.
2. The swim coach is strict but fair.
3. Todd belongs to the swim team and also works as an after-school lifeguard.
4. Harry may join the swim team or another team.

Benchmark Test 5, p. 120

MULTIPLE CHOICE

1. ANS: B
2. ANS: C
3. ANS: C
4. ANS: B
5. ANS: D
6. ANS: D
7. ANS: B
8. ANS: B
9. ANS: C
10. ANS: D
11. ANS: A
12. ANS: A
13. ANS: B
14. ANS: A
15. ANS: B
16. ANS: D
17. ANS: C
18. ANS: C
19. ANS: D
20. ANS: A
21. ANS: C
22. ANS: B
23. ANS: A
24. ANS: B
25. ANS: C
26. ANS: A
27. ANS: A

28. ANS: B

29. ANS: A

30. ANS: C

31. ANS: B

32. ANS: C

33. ANS: D

34. ANS: B

35. ANS: A

36. ANS: C

ESSAY

37. Students should make their main idea and supporting details clear to the reader.

38. I have always admired my father because he is a teacher. He teaches his students what they need to know to succeed in life. He has also taught me a lot about myself. He has led an interesting life, including serving in the army and traveling around the world. In this autobiography, many of his adventures are included.

39. Letters should follow business letter format and include all the parts of a business letter. Language should be appropriate for a business letter and arguments should be logical.

"Carry Your Own Skis" by Lian Dolan

Vocabulary Warm-up Exercises, p. 128

A. 1. typical
2. assignment
3. applying
4. involves
5. painful
6. concept
7. occasional
8. attitude

B. Sample Answers

1. I will feel that I have achieved *adulthood* when I can live on my own without help from my parents.
2. To me, the worst part of *cleanup* would be scrubbing the grill.
3. If you *commit* to something, you have accepted an obligation, so you would be letting people down if you changed your mind.
4. If you have a *deadline*, you have to start working early enough to finish on time.
5. No, if you have an *option*, you can either attend or not attend.
6. They might *participate* because they are interested in the project or because they want credit for an extra-curricular activity.
7. Yes, a *paycheck* is money paid for doing a job.

8. If you already have something, you would not be in *pursuit* of it unless it is something that you are trying to get more of.

Reading Warm-up A, p. 129

Sample Answers

1. (Norway); The *concept* of getting a pet is fun, but the reality of taking care of it is work.
2. (downhill racing, ski jumping, cross-country racing); *Involves* means "includes."
3. (brave, hardy); A *typical* ninth-grader likes hanging out with friends and keeping busy.
4. (Learning to ski); Getting in trouble for something I did not do would be a *painful* experience.
5. (a lot of fun); The proper *attitude* would be to think of it as an exciting adventure, to not give up, and to listen respectfully to the instructor.
6. (once in a while); I take an *occasional* trip to Florida to visit my great-grandmother.
7. task; I was given an *assignment* to take photographs for the school yearbook.
8. for a job as a ski instructor; I expect to be *applying* to college in the future.

Reading Warm-up B, p. 130

Sample Answers

1. His homework was never ready when it was supposed to be; I had to meet a *deadline* to earn a Girl Scout badge.
2. any kind of project; I was asked to *commit* to showing up for soccer practice twice a week.
3. (a good time); *Pursuit* means "the act of going after or achieving something."
4. (after the meal); Randy was probably too lazy to do the work involved in the *cleanup*.
5. (play); I was given the *option* to take French or Spanish, and I chose Spanish.
6. (a car wash); I like to *participate* in choral concerts.
7. (childhood); *Adulthood* might begin when you get a full-time job.
8. (weekly); I planned to use part of my first *paycheck* to buy my dad a birthday present.

Writing About the Big Question, p. 131

A. 1. concept
2. feeling
3. comprehend
4. clarify

B. Sample Answers

1. I worked for my uncle last summer in his landscaping business. I hauled dirt in wheelbarrows and planted trees and carried rock for landscaping. It was really hard work.
2. At first, I thought the **fact** that I'd be working outside would be great. Plus, I didn't have to think too hard.

My **instinct** now tells me to get an education so I don't have to work that hard all my life.

C. Sample Answer

Personal responsibility is a concept that many people do not understand because they do not take responsibility for their own actions. Having knowledge about personal responsibility and understanding it are totally different.

"Carry Your Own Skis" by Lian Dolan

Literary Analysis: Persuasive Essay, p. 132

Sample Answers

1. Individuals need to act responsibly and take care of their own needs.
2. These details show that skiing was a challenging, sometimes uncomfortable activity that involved hard work and shared effort as well as enjoyment.
3. Words and phrases with strong negative associations include *riddled, blame-shifters, no-RSVPers,* and *painful.*
4. Dolan's use of repetition appeals primarily to emotion. Students' paragraphs should identify some of the repeated phrases ("carry your own skis," "to the lodge and back," "be responsible for yourself and your stuff or you miss out") and then show how Dolan uses repetition to build up emotional support for her point of view.

Reading: Reread to Analyze and Evaluate Persuasive Appeals, p. 133

A. Sample Answers

1. Dolan begins her essay this way because it lets her show how hard her mother and aunt worked to accomplish their goal and why. Paragraph 3 ends with the valuable "life lesson" the author learned as a child.
2. The consequences include missing fun, being unpopular, and letting people down. She gives specific examples to support her argument, such as being left all day at the ski lodge, not being invited to go on camping trips, and missing a deadline at work.
3. Dolan draws an analogy between her responsibilities in adult life (husband, children, house, friends, radio show) and the skis, boots, and poles she carried in childhood. Most students will say that the analogy is effective.

B. Students should identify two appeals. They might point out that Dolan could have given several more specific instances from her current life—perhaps from conflicts that have arisen in connection with her radio show. She might also have mentioned feelings of independence, satisfaction, and pride that come from being self-sufficient. Examine students' responses for relevance and plausibility.

Vocabulary Builder, p. 134

A. 1. B; 2. A; 3. A; 4. A; 5. C; 6. D

B. Sample Answers

1. You can determine the <u>potency</u> of a medicine by reading its label or asking your doctor.

2. A king might believe he has <u>omnipotence</u> because he has supreme power over the country that he rules.
3. If a talent scout claimed I had the <u>potential</u> to become a big star, I would work very hard to make this dream a reality.

Enrichment: Decisive Experiences, p. 135

Answers will vary. Examine students' charts to make sure that they have identified three specific events/experiences and have briefly noted the long-term significance of each one.

Open-Book Test, p. 136

Short Answer

1. She means that skiers then did not enjoy the conveniences that they enjoy now. There was a great deal more physical labor involved in reaching the top of a slope than there is today.
   Difficulty: *Easy* **Objective:** *Interpretation*
2. The tone is playful but critical. The author is being a little funny, but she also seems to be making fun of people who enjoy some of the luxuries of modern ski resorts.
   Difficulty: *Challenging* **Objective:** *Interpretation*
3. She is saying that something was certain to go wrong with the car, and the drive home would always be difficult and uncomfortable.
   Difficulty: *Average* **Objective:** *Vocabulary*
4. The essay strongly suggests that the elder Dolan stressed responsibility and self-sufficiency. Those are the values that the phrase "carry your own skis" represents.
   Difficulty: *Average* **Objective:** *Interpretation*
5. She means that you should be responsible for yourself.
   Difficulty: *Easy* **Objective:** *Interpretation*
6. She means that there are a lot of those kinds of people, and they can be found throughout the world.
   Difficulty: *Average* **Objective:** *Vocabulary*
7. *Evidence:* People shift blame, fail to respond to invitations, and avoid taking part in events unless they will benefit directly. *Evaluation:* Most students will say that Dolan sufficiently supports her claim; a few may point out that the evidence is not factual and is therefore insufficient to support the claim.
   Difficulty: *Average* **Objective:** *Reading*
8. She is appealing to emotion. The passage includes words with strong negative associations.
   Difficulty: *Challenging* **Objective:** *Literary Analysis*
9. Dolan is appealing to emotion. The repetition is meant to persuade reader to share her feelings on the subject of personal responsibility.
   Difficulty: *Average* **Objective:** *Literary Analysis*
10. She is trying to persuade readers to be responsible for themselves.
    Difficulty: *Easy* **Objective:** *Literary Analysis*

Essay

11. Students should cite the author's numerous repetitions of and variations on "carry your own skis." They may also note Dolan's repetition of *responsible* and the phrase "the lodge and back, baby." They should recognize that the repetition in Dolan's essay appeals to emotion by emphasizing the ideas of personal responsibility and self-reliance. Finally, students should provide valid reasons to support their opinion of the effectiveness of the repetition in this essay.

    Difficulty: *Easy*   **Objective:** *Essay*

12. Students should recognize that the main idea of Dolan's essay is the importance of personal responsibility and self-reliance. "Carry your own skis," a phrase she repeats numerous times, becomes a metaphor for taking charge of one's life and fulfilling one's obligations. There is little or no evidence in the essay that can be classified as an appeal to reason; virtually all of the evidence is an appeal to emotion: the repetition of key phrases, such as "carry your own skies," and criticism of people the writer finds lazy, selfish, immature, or overly dependent on others.

    Difficulty: *Average*   **Objective:** *Essay*

13. Students should explain that Dolan uses her family's experience with skiing as a metaphor for her message. Dolan goes to considerable lengths to show that skiing was not a luxurious experience for her family and that it taught the children in her family a valuable lesson about life. She uses clever language to describe the kinds of people who are not self-reliant and who do not take responsibility for their obligations. Students should provide valid reasons to support their opinions of Dolan's success in making her writing fresh and forceful.

    Difficulty: *Challenging*   **Objective:** *Essay*

14. Students might point to Dolan's remark that before she had a name for it, she had recognized that some people were not showing personal responsibility. This suggests that on a certain level, the understanding preceded the knowledge. Alternatively, students might say that Dolan learned her lesson first: that she must carry her own skis. From the knowledge, she came to understand the larger meaning of that lesson.

    Difficulty: *Average*   **Objective:** *Essay*

Oral Response

15. Oral responses should be clear, well organized, and well supported by appropriate details from the essay.

    Difficulty: *Average*   **Objective:** *Oral Interpretation*

Selection Test A, p. 139

Critical Reading

1. ANS: C	DIF: Easy	OBJ: Comprehension	
2. ANS: B	DIF: Easy	OBJ: Interpretation	
3. ANS: C	DIF: Easy	OBJ: Interpretation	
4. ANS: D	DIF: Easy	OBJ: Comprehension	
5. ANS: A	DIF: Easy	OBJ: Interpretation	

6. ANS: A	DIF: Easy	OBJ: Literary Analysis	
7. ANS: B	DIF: Easy	OBJ: Interpretation	
8. ANS: D	DIF: Easy	OBJ: Literary Analysis	
9. ANS: B	DIF: Easy	OBJ: Literary Analysis	
10. ANS: C	DIF: Easy	OBJ: Reading	
11. ANS: A	DIF: Easy	OBJ: Interpretation	

Vocabulary and Grammar

12. ANS: C	DIF: Easy	OBJ: Vocabulary	
13. ANS: B	DIF: Easy	OBJ: Vocabulary	
14. ANS: D	DIF: Easy	OBJ: Grammar	
15. ANS: B	DIF: Easy	OBJ: Grammar	

Essay

16. Students should mention the author's numerous repetitions and variations on the title "carry your own skis." Students may also note Dolan's repetition of words like *responsible* and phrases like "the lodge and back, baby." Students will probably agree that the repetition of these words and phrases appeals to emotion rather than to reason.

    Difficulty: *Easy*
    Objective: *Essay*

17. Students' essays should note that Dolan uses her mother's rule, "carry your own skis," as a metaphor for being responsible for oneself and one's actions. Students should provide two examples from the text (for example, making peanut butter sandwiches at camp, doing her work at college, juggling work and home responsibilities as an adult). Look for some statement of Dolan's goal: to persuade readers to be responsible for themselves and their actions.

    Difficulty: *Easy*
    Objective: *Essay*

18. Students might say that as a young girl skiing with her family, Dolan learned her lesson: She must carry her own skis or sit in the lodge all day and miss out on the fun and challenge of skiing. From this knowledge, she came to understand the larger meaning of that lesson, that in life you need to be responsible for yourself, your family, your job, and your finances, or you miss out on your life.

    Difficulty: *Average*
    Objective: *Essay*

Selection Test B, p. 142

Critical Reading

1. ANS: B	DIF: Average	OBJ: Interpretation	
2. ANS: B	DIF: Average	OBJ: Interpretation	
3. ANS: D	DIF: Average	OBJ: Comprehension	
4. ANS: A	DIF: Average	OBJ: Interpretation	
5. ANS: C	DIF: Average	OBJ: Reading	
6. ANS: B	DIF: Average	OBJ: Literary Analysis	

Unit 3 Resources: Types of Nonfiction

7. ANS: B	DIF: Average	OBJ: Interpretation
8. ANS: C	DIF: Challenging	OBJ: Interpretation
9. ANS: D	DIF: Average	OBJ: Literary Analysis
10. ANS: B	DIF: Average	OBJ: Literary Analysis
11. ANS: C	DIF: Challenging	OBJ: Reading
12. ANS: A	DIF: Challenging	OBJ: Literary Analysis
13. ANS: B	DIF: Average	OBJ: Reading

Vocabulary and Grammar

14. ANS: C	DIF: Challenging	OBJ: Vocabulary
15. ANS: C	DIF: Average	OBJ: Grammar
16. ANS: C	DIF: Challenging	OBJ: Grammar

Essay

17. Students should point out that Dolan's theme is the necessity for individual responsibility. "Carry your own skis," a phrase that she repeats numerous times, becomes a metaphor for taking charge of one's life and fulfilling one's obligations. Dolan supports the theme with a mixture of appeals. For example, she appeals to reason when she points out that none of the children wanted to spend the day left in the lodge. She appeals to emotion when she criticizes irresponsible people who are lazy, selfish, immature, or overdependent on others.
Difficulty: *Average*
Objective: *Essay*

18. Students' essays should note that Dolan selects skiing as a background for her message. Although many people might think of skiing as an expensive, elitist sport, Dolan goes to considerable lengths to shape the setting so that it fits her central theme. For example, she contrasts the "hard work" of skiing when she was young to the luxurious conditions of today. Dolan also contrasts responsible attitudes with irresponsible ones, providing a variety of examples of laziness and selfishness. Although it might be difficult in theory to dispute her proposition, Dolan's examples show that many people do not take responsibility for themselves in practice.
Difficulty: *Challenging*
Objective: *Essay*

19. Students might point to Dolan's remark that before she had a name for it, she had recognized that some people were not showing personal responsibility. This suggests that on a certain level, the understanding preceded the knowledge. Alternatively, students might say that Dolan learned her lesson first: that she must carry her own skis. From the knowledge, she came to understand the larger meaning of that lesson.
Difficulty: *Average*
Objective: *Essay*

"Libraries Face Sad Chapter" by Pete Hamill

Vocabulary Warm-up Exercises, p. 146

A.
1. civilization
2. presumed
3. recited
4. illustrations
5. volumes
6. powerful
7. combined
8. reduced

B. Sample Answers
1. F; An *aura* of excitement would prevent people from being bored.
2. F; *Circulating* books are passed from person to person.
3. T; Congress passes laws and therefore is responsible for their *establishment.*
4. T; A good writer needs to have new and interesting ideas to create new *imaginative* works.
5. F; Everyone should be concerned with behaving properly and living a *moral* life.
6. T; A *pledge* is a promise that should be taken seriously.
7. T; The oceans are full of, or *teeming* with, fish.
8. F; If dues are *voluntary,* people can decide whether or not to pay them.

Reading Warm-up A, p. 147

Sample Answers
1. lined the library shelves; *Volumes* might be found in boxes or on shelves of a bookstore or on a coffee table in someone's home.
2. the way he thought about things; A novel I read about the First World War had a *powerful* influence on my way of thinking about war.
3. that he was in the middle of a dream; I incorrectly *presumed* that I could wear shorts to the graduation party, but dress was a bit more formal.
4. eating a pepperoni pizza and staying up much too late to finish the new fantasy novel he had borrowed the week before; *Combined* means "two or more things joined together."
5. (titles); I *recited* a poem I wrote in my English class last year.
6. (color, dazzling); I enjoyed the fanciful *illustrations* in *Alice in Wonderland.*
7. (world, people); A society at the highest level of *civilization* would live in peace. Everyone would get along, and people would have interesting conversations about art, music, and literature.
8. All of their wisdom and knowledge; "Treat others as you would like them to treat you."

Reading Warm-up B, p. 148

Sample Answers

1. made Alexandria, Egypt, a great center of culture and learning; The *founding* of the Alexandrian Library made Alexandria, Egypt, a great center of culture and learning.

2. information; The pond in the park is *teeming* with green algae.

3. these scrolls never left the building; The *circulating* cool air throughout the building kept us quite comfortable.

4. (wonder); An *aura* is "a quality or feeling that seems to come from a person or place."

5. philosophers and religious leaders from distant lands; *Moral* teachings deal with ideas of right and wrong. Facts are objective statements that can be proved true or false.

6. new and better ways to preserve and share the written word; *Imaginative* people have the creative ability to come up with new and original ideas.

7. to return the books to the library when they had finished reading them; I have taken a *pledge* to complete all my homework assignments on time.

8. the people who used them; A word that means the opposite of *voluntary* is *required*.

Writing About the Big Question, p. 149

A. 1. Statistics
   2. sources, information
   3. research
   4. insight

B. Sample Answers

1. I used the library to research Lincoln as a war-time leader. I used the library to research the early years of NASA.

2. I could have planned my time better. I should have thought more about the topic beforehand to **clarify** my goal and to decide how to go about my **research.**

C. Sample Answer

Libraries, as a source of information and a place for research, are still important because they house so much knowledge. Using the knowledge you can find in a library can help your understanding of the world.

"Libraries Face Sad Chapter" by Pete Hamill

Literary Analysis: Persuasive Essay, p. 150

Sample Answers

1. Hamill believes that libraries, which face hard times because of budget cuts, need the public's support. He proposes a voluntary fund to sustain libraries.

2. Students may mention any two of the following: Hamill argues that people need books more than ever in hard times because myths, heroes, moral tales, and information are necessary for human beings. He also points out that freely circulating books are a necessity at a time when books and movies are more expensive than ever.

He argues that libraries offer the chance to revive the power of the printed page for children. Finally, Hamill says that the poor, especially immigrants and their children, need access to libraries.

3. Words with strong emotional associations include *cliffs, pleasure, thrills, villainy, heroism,* and *vast.* Except for *villainy,* which has negative associations, all of these words have positive associations.

4. The debt is an obligation to our forebears, who paid taxes to support libraries and who taught their descendants to read and to respect the printed word. Hamill argues that these New Yorkers left a legacy that we must, in turn, sustain and pass on to our descendants. Most students will agree that Hamill's conclusion is an effective ending.

Reading: Reread to Analyze and Evaluate Persuasive Appeals, p. 151

A. Sample Answers

1. Hamill's memories of his childhood offer an opportunity to make the point that books provide a strong stimulus to the imaginations of young readers. Hamill selects details to support his assertion that libraries are "treasure houses."

2. Libraries are more important than ever in hard times because people need myths, heroes, and stories, which they find in books. Hamill also argues that freely circulating books are needed by people who cannot afford to buy a book or see a movie.

3. Hamill appeals to both reason and emotion in this section. Appeal to reason: He compares today's use of libraries by immigrants in Brooklyn and Queens with their use by Irish, Jewish, and Italian immigrants during his childhood. Appeals to emotion: Hamill's descriptions of his father's preparation for the citizenship test; his first hearing the language of the Bill of Rights; his appeal to readers' civic responsibility.

B. Students should point out that Hamill's stress on children's imagination and sense of discovery gives his essay an idealistic tone. He balances this idealism, however, with a practical approach to raising the funds required to maintain libraries and their services.

Vocabulary Builder, p. 152

A. Sample Answers

1. We were pleased to find out that the duration of the exam was only half an hour.

2. The championship match was curtailed by rain, leaving the spectators uncertain about the outcome.

3. Since e-mail is a rapid and cheap medium, its popularity today is easy to understand.

4. If the author wrote so many books, why are so few volumes of his work in the library?

5. We presumed he was going with us, so we waited for him to meet us.

6. Alexandra likes to <u>emulate</u> her sister, so she always wears the same kind of clothes.

B. 1. A <u>consumer</u> usually gets what he or she wants by buying it.

2. As a result of Columbus's <u>assumption</u> that the world is round, he crossed the Atlantic Ocean, searching for a sea route to the riches of the East.

3. TV programs <u>resume</u> when commercials are over.

Enrichment: The Role of Libraries, p. 153

Students' reports should contain specific descriptions of services offered along the lines of those mentioned.

"Carry Your Own Skis" by Lian Dolan
"Libraries Face Sad Chapter" by Pete Hamill

Integrated Language Skills: Grammar, p. 154

A. 1. icy, parking, small, great

2. most, freezing, my, older, faster, talented [*More* is an adverb modifying *talented*.]

3. that, two, mock-Corinthian, majestic

4. those, ancient, prehistoric, moral

B. Examine students' paragraphs for correct usage and identification of adjectives.

Open-Book Test, p. 157

Short Answer

1. This section of the essay is based on Hamill's own experience.

Difficulty: *Easy*   **Objective:** *Literary Analysis*

2. It is a bad thing: Services would be reduced or limited.

Difficulty: *Average*   **Objective:** *Vocabulary*

3. *Facts, statistics, expert testimony:* The mayor has a huge shortfall to make up. The city government cannot print money. *Words with strong connotations:* "post–September 11 austerities," "something must give" The claim appeals to both reason and emotion.

Difficulty: *Average*   **Objective:** *Literary Analysis*

4. The popularity of the Harry Potter books shows that young people make up a huge audience.

Difficulty: *Easy*   **Objective:** *Literary Analysis*

5. Hamill provides evidence, but the evidence appears to be a mixture of fact (for example, "the older people want information about . . . how to get better jobs") and speculation ("the children want to vanish into books their parents cannot afford").

Difficulty: *Average*   **Objective:** *Reading*

6. Carnegie believed that public libraries were important institutions.

Difficulty: *Easy*   **Objective:** *Interpretation*

7. Hamill points out that public libraries were established with private funds. This fact supports Hamill's arguments that private citizens should support public libraries during a budget crisis.

Difficulty: *Challenging*   **Objective:** *Interpretation*

8. Their support would serve to honor the people of the past who helped the immigrants of past generations succeed in America and whose taxes helped finance the library system.

Difficulty: *Challenging*   **Objective:** *Literary Analysis*

9. Hamill wants the children of today's immigrants to have the same experiences in libraries that children of his generation had.

Difficulty: *Average*   **Objective:** *Literary Analysis*

10. Hamill's tone would best be described as serious or respectful. Practically every sentence of the essay betrays Hamill's deep respect for libraries.

Difficulty: *Average*   **Objective:** *Interpretation*

Essay

11. Students should identify Hamill's main idea: that citizens should contribute to a private fund that would maintain the public libraries at full strength during a budget crisis. Then, they should identify two of Hamill's reasons. They might mention, for example, that library books stimulate children's imagination, that immigrants and the poor use libraries to better their circumstances, and that such a fund would honor those who built and stocked the libraries. Students should identify the reasons they cite as appeals to reason or emotion and provide valid reasons for their evaluation of the effectiveness of the arguments.

Difficulty: *Easy*   **Objective:** *Essay*

12. Students should name at least some of the kinds of works Hamill mentions: children's books, a children's magazine, history books, mysteries, novels of fantasy and adventure. They might also mention some of the authors Hamill names, such as Alexandre Dumas, Robert Louis Stevenson, Arthur Conan Doyle, Mark Twain, Walt Whitman, Leo Tolstoy, James Joyce, and Marcel Proust. Finally, they should mention the book that contained the Constitution and the resources that people consult to find better jobs or to find out about obtaining citizenship or a green card. Beyond those specifics, students should show an awareness of Hamill's lively writing style, his belief that libraries help to make the immigrants of one generation the successful citizens of the next, and his deep belief in the worthiness of cultivating "the life of the mind."

Difficulty: *Average*   **Objective:** *Essay*

13. Students should recognize that Hamill's suggestion has the merit of sharing civic responsibility and showing respect for the sacrifices of the taxpayers who helped build the system of public libraries. They should also recognize that it strengthens Hamill's argument that public libraries are essential to the betterment of the lower class by suggesting a way for the libraries to stay open during a budget crisis. They might also note that Hamill shows good sense by appealing to both the

wealthy and the middle class. Finally, students should support their opinion of Hamill's argument with valid reasons and verifiable evidence.

Difficulty: *Challenging*   **Objective:** *Essay*

14. Students should draw a connection between the rich world of the imagination that Hamill describes at the beginning of his essay and the acquisition of knowledge, and they should draw a connection between understanding and the use of that knowledge by immigrants and the poor to better their circumstances. For Hamill, in other words, libraries offer the opportunity to acquire knowledge, and with that knowledge people can come to the understanding they need to improve themselves.

Difficulty: *Average*   **Objective:** *Essay*

Oral Response

15. Oral responses should be clear, well organized, and well supported by appropriate details from the essay.

Difficulty: *Average*   **Objective:** *Oral Interpretation*

Selection Test A, p. 160

Critical Reading

1. ANS: B	DIF: Easy	OBJ: Comprehension
2. ANS: D	DIF: Easy	OBJ: Literary Analysis
3. ANS: B	DIF: Easy	OBJ: Literary Analysis
4. ANS: B	DIF: Easy	OBJ: Reading
5. ANS: B	DIF: Easy	OBJ: Literary Analysis
6. ANS: C	DIF: Easy	OBJ: Interpretation
7. ANS: D	DIF: Easy	OBJ: Literary Analysis
8. ANS: A	DIF: Easy	OBJ: Reading
9. ANS: C	DIF: Easy	OBJ: Comprehension
10. ANS: A	DIF: Easy	OBJ: Reading

Vocabulary and Grammar

11. ANS: C	DIF: Easy	OBJ: Vocabulary
12. ANS: C	DIF: Easy	OBJ: Vocabulary
13. ANS: D	DIF: Easy	OBJ: Grammar

Essay

14. Students should clearly state Hamill's main idea: that the public should contribute to a private fund to maintain libraries at full strength. Then students should identify and evaluate two of Hamill's reasons. They might mention, for example, his arguments that library books stimulate the imaginations of children, that libraries are invaluable resources for immigrants and for the poor, and that such a fund would honor past New Yorkers who built and stocked the libraries and took their children there. Students' evaluations of the reasons will vary.

Difficulty: *Easy*

Objective: *Essay*

15. Students' essays should state a clear position at the outset and then proceed to support this point of view with a mixture of evidence, appeals to logic, and appropriate appeals to emotion.

Difficulty: *Easy*

Objective: *Essay*

16. Students should note that public library books gave young Hamill a rich world of imagination and the opportunity to acquire knowledge about science, geography, and history. This knowledge led to his inheriting and understanding the larger world and civilization.

Difficulty: *Average*

Objective: *Essay*

Selection Test B, p. 163

Critical Reading

1. ANS: B	DIF: Average	OBJ: Comprehension
2. ANS: D	DIF: Average	OBJ: Literary Analysis
3. ANS: B	DIF: Average	OBJ: Literary Analysis
4. ANS: C	DIF: Average	OBJ: Reading
5. ANS: B	DIF: Average	OBJ: Literary Analysis
6. ANS: D	DIF: Average	OBJ: Literary Analysis
7. ANS: B	DIF: Average	OBJ: Interpretation
8. ANS: A	DIF: Average	OBJ: Reading
9. ANS: C	DIF: Average	OBJ: Comprehension
10. ANS: A	DIF: Challenging	OBJ: Reading
11. ANS: C	DIF: Average	OBJ: Interpretation
12. ANS: C	DIF: Challenging	OBJ: Interpretation
13. ANS: D	DIF: Challenging	OBJ: Literary Analysis
14. ANS: B	DIF: Average	OBJ: Literary Analysis

Vocabulary and Grammar

15. ANS: C	DIF: Average	OBJ: Vocabulary
16. ANS: B	DIF: Average	OBJ: Grammar
17. ANS: B	DIF: Challenging	OBJ: Grammar
18. ANS: C	DIF: Challenging	OBJ: Grammar

Essay

19. Students should point out that Hamill's personal recollections create powerful emotional appeals—to family, citizenship, imagination. As examples, students may mention his father's reading the Bill of Rights and memories of how books appealed to his imagination and introduced him to the world beyond his neighborhood. These appeals help support Hamill's position that public libraries' hours and services must be maintained.

Difficulty: *Average*

Objective: *Essay*

20. Students' essays should mention a number of the references Hamill makes to specific genres of literature, such as children's books and adventure novels. Essays should also refer to a number of specific authors: for example, Alexandre Dumas, Robert Louis Stevenson, Arthur Conan Doyle, Mark Twain, Walt Whitman, Leo Tolstoy, James Joyce, and Marcel Proust. Beyond these specifics, students' essays should show an awareness of Hamill's lively writing style, the links he forges between libraries and the education and citizenship of immigrants, and his deep belief in the worthwhile cultivation of "the life of the mind."

    Difficulty: *Average*

    Objective: *Essay*

21. Students' essays should point out that Hamill's suggestion has the merit of sharing civic responsibility and of showing respect for the sacrifices of taxpayers in the past who helped build the system of public libraries. Hamill also shows practical good sense in his appeals to both the rich and the middle class. Students may also note that Hamill concludes the essay with an eloquent echo of the beginning, where he evoked kids' dreams of baseball and of *The Count of Monte Cristo*.

    Difficulty: *Challenging*

    Objective: *Essay*

22. Students should draw a connection between the rich world of the imagination that Hamill describes at the beginning of his essay and the acquisition of knowledge, and they should draw a connection between understanding and the use of that knowledge by immigrants and the poor to better their circumstances. For Hamill, in other words, libraries offer the opportunity to acquire knowledge, and with that knowledge people can come to the understanding they need to improve themselves.

    Difficulty: *Average*

    Objective: *Essay*

"I Have a Dream" by Martin Luther King, Jr.

Vocabulary Warm-up Exercises, p. 167

A. 1. peaks
   2. mighty
   3. glory
   4. difficulties
   5. faith
   6. situation
   7. character
   8. liberty

B. Sample Answers

   1. *Discords* between Marco and Elizabeth eventually led to the end of their friendship.
   2. Tim and Carlotta were *equal* partners in the business, so each received half of the profits.
   3. The *former* president of our club was reelected today.

   4. The *hamlet* we live in is one of the smallest villages in the United States.
   5. The governor vowed to fight *injustice* wherever she found it.
   6. The *oppression* of the people ended when the evil tyrant was overthrown.
   7. The tadpole is going to *transform* itself into a frog.

Reading Warm-up A, p. 168

Sample Answers

   1. problems; I have experienced *difficulties* trying to memorize my lines for the school play.
   2. that the problems could somehow be worked out; I have *faith* that my parents will always love me.
   3. (worse); My friend put me in a difficult *situation* when she kept asking me to reveal a secret.
   4. highest; People with *character* would be honest, hard-working, and idealistic.
   5. (whatever was necessary); People would want *liberty* so that they could be free to believe and behave as they pleased.
   6. in both its noble ideas and its beautiful language; A synonym for *glory* is *splendor*.
   7. (Mountains); The Guadalupe Mountains include the highest point in Texas.
   8. (British army); The *mighty* wind knocked down power lines and huge trees.

Reading Warm-up B, p. 169

Sample Answers

   1. (small); Atlanta could not be described as a *hamlet*. It is a big city.
   2. the local public schools refused to accept any African American student teachers; An *injustice* today is denying people promotions at work because of the color of their skin.
   3. all Americans regardless of their color; *Equal* means "having the same rights and chances as everyone else."
   4. African Americans; *Oppression* means "the act of treating people in an unfair and a cruel way."
   5. (Coretta Scott King); *Current* means the opposite of *former*.
   6. A *symphony* of voices is many voices blending together.
   7. tearing apart American society; There are *discords* between my older sister and her boyfriend. I think they could be resolved if they would calmly discuss their problems.
   8. many women and men; I could help *transform* the awful life of a stray cat into a good one in which it gets food, shelter, and love.

Writing About the Big Question, p. 170

A. 1. information, fact, or insight
   2. feeling

3. connection

4. statistics

B. Sample Answers

1. I heard a good speaker at our high school. He talked about the history of the city's civil right's movement.

2. The speaker gave **statistics** to show how some people were not treated fairly. He described his personal efforts in the civil rights struggle. It gave me **insight** into the risks and sacrifices people of that time made.

C. Sample Answer

The concept of equality might be ambiguous to some people because it is a hard concept to grasp, especially if you come from a place where there is no equality. Knowing about equality and truly understanding it are different.

"I Have a Dream" by Martin Luther King, Jr.

Literary Analysis: Persuasive Speech, p. 171

Sample Answers

1. Parallelism and repetition: "One hundred years later" begins each sentence; "the manacles of segregation" is parallel with "the chains of discrimination"; "a lonely island of poverty" is parallel with "a vast ocean of material prosperity."

2. Restatement: The second sentence uses different words to restate the main idea of the first sentence ("promissory note" and "This note was a promise").

3. Repetition and restatement: The second sentence uses the same metaphor ("bad check"; "a check which has come back marked 'insufficient funds'") to expand on the main idea of the first sentence. ("defaulted on this promissory note")

Reading: Analyze Persuasive Techniques, p. 172

1. A. Abraham Lincoln
   B. the Lincoln Memorial in Washington, D.C.
   C. Lincoln's Gettysburg Address, which opens with the words "Four score and seven years ago"

2. A. Both sentences begin with "Now is the time."
   B. Emotionally charged words and phrases include *promises, Democracy, dark, desolate, sunlit,* and *racial justice.*

3. A. The passage is dominated by an image of the seasons—specifically, summer and autumn.
   B. The phrase "invigorating autumn" is parallel with "sweltering summer."

Vocabulary Builder, p. 173

A. Sample Answers

1. You would consider a <u>hallowed</u> ground with respect, since it is sacred.

2. Most people take a <u>creed</u> seriously because it is a statement of beliefs.

3. You might take steps to improve the condition of a <u>degenerate</u> house.

4. People often take photographs during <u>momentous</u> occasions in their lives because it helps them remember the moment.

5. If a friend <u>defaulted</u> on his promise to pay back money he borrowed from me, I'd feel angry.

6. Many people dislike living under <u>oppression</u> because they dislike the rulers' unjust use of power over their lives.

B. 1. It's not wise to give <u>credence</u> to everything you hear on commercials because these ads are trying to persuade you to spend your money.

2. Lawyers want <u>credible</u> witnesses to support their case because they want the judge and jury to believe their witnesses.

3. Someone who is too <u>credulous</u> could get into all kinds of trouble, such as losing his or her money.

Enrichment: Timeline of an Era, p. 174

Sample Answers

Examine students' timelines to make sure that they have provided accurate dates and brief descriptions. The chronology of events listed is as follows:

Supreme Court decision of *Brown v. Board of Education* (1954)

Montgomery bus boycott (1955–1956)

Founding of the Southern Christian Leadership Conference (1957)

Lunch-counter sit-ins in such cities as Greensboro, North Carolina (1960)

King's "Letter from Birmingham City Jail" (1963)

March on Washington (1963)

Civil Rights Act (1964)

Voting Rights Act (1965)

March from Selma to Montgomery, Alabama (1965)

King's assassination (1968)

Open-Book Test, p. 175

Short Answer

1. He is referring to Abraham Lincoln.

   Difficulty: *Easy*   **Objective:** *Interpretation*

2. Students should cite "One hundred years later, the Negro" or "One hundred years later the Negro is still."

   Difficulty: *Easy*   **Objective:** *Literary Analysis*

3. King uses those documents as evidence to support his claim that African Americans are entitled to equal rights.

   Difficulty: *Challenging*   **Objective:** *Interpretation*

4. Students should identify the idea that America has promised African Americans the rights of life, liberty, and the pursuit of happiness but has not delivered on the promise.
   Difficulty: *Challenging*   **Objective:** *Literary Analysis*

5. King is delivering the speech at the Lincoln Memorial. Because Lincoln championed the freedom of African Americans, King considers the memorial a sacred place.
   Difficulty: *Average*   **Objective:** *Vocabulary*

6. Students should underline the following instances of parallelism; words that they might circle (to indicate words that were meant to be emphasized) are noted here in italics; accept any other reasonable choices: "We can *never* be satisfied as long as the Negro is the victim of the unspeakable horrors of police brutality. We can *never* be satisfied as long as our bodies . . . cannot gain lodging in . . . motels . . . and . . . hotels. . . . We can *not* be satisfied as long as the Negro's basic mobility is from a small ghetto to a larger one. No, *no*, we are *not* satisfied, and *we will not be satisfied* until justice rolls down like waters and righteousness like a mighty stream."Students should offer a reasonable explanation of the effect of the rhetorical devices used in the passage; they might note, for example, that the effect is to gradually increase the tension so that the final sentence makes the greatest emotional impact.
   Difficulty: *Average*   **Objective:** *Reading*

7. King is telling African Americans that he knows that the conditions they are living under are very poor. He does not want them to feel hopeless. Instead, he wants them to take action to improve their situation.
   Difficulty: *Average*   **Objective:** *Interpretation*

8. A person may not be discriminated against on the basis of his or her beliefs.
   Difficulty: *Average*   **Objective:** *Vocabulary*

9. The song makes the African Americans' struggle for their civil rights seem patriotic and connects it to the American tradition of fighting to achieve liberty.
   Difficulty: *Challenging*   **Objective:** *Interpretation*

10. The line is "Let freedom ring."
    Difficulty: *Easy*   **Objective:** *Literary Analysis*

Essay

11. Students will most likely focus on parallelism and restatement or repetition. They should correctly identify the examples they cite and present a plausible explanation of the effect it creates.
    Difficulty: *Easy*   **Objective:** *Essay*

12. Students should provide a reasonable definition of the American dream, in which they demonstrate an understanding that it has to do with all citizens' having equal rights, privileges, and opportunities in the social, political, and economic spheres and that it refers in particular to everyone's experiencing economic well-being (if not affluence). They should recognize that King's dream focuses in particular on racial and social

equality. They should then point out the similarities and differences between their definition and King's dream.
Difficulty: *Average*   **Objective:** *Essay*

13. Students will likely acknowledge that King was in effect preaching to an audience that shared his optimism; they would not have taken part in the demonstration (the March on Washington) if they did not. Students should also note, however, that King's references to "drinking from the cup of bitterness and hatred," his declaration that "the marvelous new militancy . . . must not lead us to a distrust of all white people," and his plea that African Americans "not wallow in the valley of despair" show that King was aware that some African Americans did not share his dream or his optimism. Students should defend their opinion of the difficulty of King's argument with a well-reasoned argument.
    Difficulty: *Challenging*   **Objective:** *Essay*

14. Students should recognize that King appears to be very knowledgeable about the injustices black Americans were facing in the early 1960s. Most students will say that King understood very well how best to persuade his listeners of the wisdom of his dream. He understood that it was important not to appear to threaten the white establishment, yet it was also important to continue to take the steps that would realize the dream. Students should cite details from the speech and well-reasoned arguments to support their opinion.
    Difficulty: *Average*   **Objective:** *Essay*

Oral Response

15. Oral responses should be clear, well organized, and well supported by appropriate details from the speech.
    Difficulty: *Average*   **Objective:** *Oral Interpretation*

Selection Test A, p. 178

Critical Reading

	ANS	DIF	OBJ
1.	A	Easy	Comprehension
2.	B	Easy	Literary Analysis
3.	C	Easy	Interpretation
4.	C	Easy	Comprehension
5.	B	Easy	Literary Analysis
6.	B	Easy	Interpretation
7.	D	Easy	Interpretation
8.	D	Easy	Reading
9.	C	Easy	Reading
10.	C	Easy	Interpretation
11.	A	Easy	Interpretation

Vocabulary and Grammar

	ANS	DIF	OBJ
12.	D	Easy	Vocabulary
13.	B	Easy	Vocabulary
14.	C	Easy	Grammar

Essay

15. Students' essays should include two specific examples of the persuasive techniques listed. Students should also explain how each example works to enhance the persuasive effect of Dr. King's speech as a whole.

    Difficulty: *Easy*

    Objective: *Essay*

16. Students' essays should give a reasonable description of the speaker's tone. For example, they may say that Dr. King is forceful and realistic in the first part of the speech, and visionary and optimistic in the second half. Students should use specific references to support their descriptions of tone. Finally, students should include a discussion of how they think the speaker's tone probably affected the audience for the speech.

    Difficulty: *Easy*

    Objective: *Essay*

17. Students should recognize that Dr. King used the knowledge of facts and events to persuade his listeners to understand that his dream was a larger American dream and to help them understand the "difficulties of today and tomorrow" that they would have to face to achieve this dream. Students should cite details from the speech and well-reasoned arguments to support their answer.

    Difficulty: *Average*

    Objective: *Essay*

Selection Test B, p. 181

Critical Reading

1. ANS: D	DIF: Average	OBJ: Comprehension
2. ANS: C	DIF: Average	OBJ: Interpretation
3. ANS: B	DIF: Average	OBJ: Literary Analysis
4. ANS: D	DIF: Average	OBJ: Interpretation
5. ANS: B	DIF: Challenging	OBJ: Literary Analysis
6. ANS: B	DIF: Average	OBJ: Comprehension
7. ANS: C	DIF: Challenging	OBJ: Interpretation
8. ANS: C	DIF: Average	OBJ: Reading
9. ANS: B	DIF: Challenging	OBJ: Interpretation
10. ANS: C	DIF: Average	OBJ: Reading
11. ANS: B	DIF: Average	OBJ: Reading
12. ANS: B	DIF: Average	OBJ: Interpretation
13. ANS: B	DIF: Average	OBJ: Literary Analysis

Vocabulary and Grammar

14. ANS: A	DIF: Average	OBJ: Vocabulary
15. ANS: D	DIF: Average	OBJ: Vocabulary
16. ANS: B	DIF: Average	OBJ: Grammar
17. ANS: B	DIF: Average	OBJ: Grammar

Essay

18. Students should first state Dr. King's dream: equality and freedom for all Americans. They should also relate this dream to the "American dream" of equality, justice, and the free pursuit of happiness and success. As students state their own dreams, they may use, for example, repetition or quotations to persuade their audience of the importance of their dreams. Students should distinguish between their individual dreams and a dream for all Americans.

    Difficulty: *Average*

    Objective: *Essay*

19. Students should cite the title of the speech, which becomes a repeated motif in the second half, as a fundamentally optimistic phrase. They may also cite such details in the closing portion as the patriotic tone of "My Country, 'Tis of Thee"; the evocations of faith and togetherness; the repeated phrase "let freedom ring"; the allusions to every geographical region in the United States; and the references to different skin colors and religious beliefs. Earlier in the speech, Dr. King has laid the groundwork for optimism with his urgent pleas and his reminder that creative protest can never be allowed to degenerate into physical violence.

    Difficulty: *Average*

    Objective: *Essay*

20. Students should recognize that Dr. King appears to be very knowledgeable about the injustices black Americans were facing in the early 1960s. Most students will say that Dr. King understood very well how best to persuade his listeners of the wisdom of his dream. He understood that it was important not to appear to threaten the white establishment, yet it was also important to continue to take the steps that would realize the dream. Students should cite details from the speech and well-reasoned arguments to support their opinion.

    Difficulty: *Average*

    Objective: *Essay*

"First Inaugural Address"
by Franklin Delano Roosevelt

Vocabulary Warm-up Exercises, p. 185

A.
1. critical
2. boldly
3. effective
4. leadership
5. primarily
6. stricken
7. recognition
8. destiny

B. Sample Answers

1. If poor grades will <u>confront</u> you, that means you are not doing well in school and need to study harder or seek extra help to improve your grades.

2. No, the friendship would not be enjoyable because <u>strife</u> means there is trouble of some kind between you and a friend, so you do not get along.

3. If you are acting <u>courageously</u>, you are showing a great deal of bravery, and that could be considered <u>extraordinary</u>, or acting in a way that is special or amazing to others.

4. If you break a school <u>policy</u>, you have done something against official rules or regulations and will have to face the consequences.

5. Yes, <u>vigorous</u> exercise requires lots of energy and would probably increase your heart rate.

6. No, you should not feel free to cancel, because an <u>obligation</u> is a commitment, and your friend would be counting on you to fulfill the commitment you made.

Reading Warm-up A, p. 186

Sample Answers

1. <u>the Great Depression</u>; (important)
2. (fear); <u>financial catastrophe</u>
3. (understanding); *Recognition* of a problem is required before you can take steps to solve it; if you do not see a problem or understand that it exists, you cannot solve it.
4. <u>the normal ups and downs of business</u>; (for the most part)
5. <u>strengthen companies and create jobs</u>; *Useful* is a synonym for *effective*.
6. (foolish); It was a mistake for Hoover to speak *boldly* because the economy was actually in very poor shape.
7. (future); Throughout history, Americans thought that the *destiny* of the United States was to be a great country that expanded from ocean to ocean.
8. <u>a take-charge president who could guide the country out of its misery</u>; People wanted stronger *leadership* because conditions in the country were getting worse and worse as the Depression went on.

Reading Warm-up B, p. 187

Sample Answers

1. (duty); An *obligation* I have to my parents is to follow family rules.
2. <u>people were troubled and angry</u>; *Conflict* is a synonym for *strife*.
3. <u>official positions and government-sponsored programs</u>; I agree with the school *policy* that requires students who play a sport to maintain a certain grade point average.
4. (extreme); I am an *extraordinary* friend because I am very loyal and always stand by my friends no matter what.

5. <u>meet them head-on</u>; FDR developed programs to *confront* and solve the problem of unemployment, which Hoover did not.
6. (energy); The New Deal jobs needed *vigorous* workers because they involved physical labor that required strength and energy.
7. <u>They never dreamed of insisting that they deserved more pay</u>; No, *arrogantly* would be an antonym for *humbly* because *arrogantly* means "to act as if you know more than others and think a lot of yourself."
8. (bravely); Lincoln behaved *courageously* during the Civil War when he faced a divided nation.

Writing About the Big Question, p. 188

A. 1. instinct
2. facts; information
3. clarify
4. insight

B. Sample Answers

1. Presidents are elected by the people, therefore they are obligated to explain to citizens why they do the things they do.
2. Roosevelt helped **clarify** the causes of the Great Depression. He also talked about how to end it. He explained that people must not give in to a **feeling** of fear or hopelessness.

C. Sample Answer

For leaders to inspire confidence, they must comprehend the wishes of the people because it will help them do what the people want. In this case, knowledge and understanding are pretty much the same.

"First Inaugural Address" by Franklin Delano Roosevelt

Literary Analysis: Persuasive Speech, p. 189

Sample Answers

1. Parallelism; Each element has the same grammatical structure.
2. Restatement; The second sentence elaborates on and varies the main idea of the first.
3. Repetition; The second sentence maintains the image of the "money changers" and the "temple." Some students may note that Roosevelt uses metaphor and biblical allusion.
4. Analogy; Roosevelt compares U.S. policy to a good neighbor.

Reading: Analyze Persuasive Techniques, p. 190

Sample Answers

1. A. Parallelism occurs in these balanced word groups: "their own stubbornness" and "their own incompetence"; "indicted in the court of public opinion" and "rejected by the hearts and minds of men."

B. Examples of emotionally charged language include *failed, stubbornness, incompetence, failure, abdicated, unscrupulous, indicted,* and *rejected.* They are all negatively charged words.

2. A. Parallelism is illustrated in the five phrases introduced by the preposition *on.*
   B. Roosevelt uses restatement in the second sentence by expressing the same idea as that in the first sentence in different words.

3. A. All of these adjectives have positive emotional associations.
   B. Answers will vary. Students may describe the rhythm as balanced or building in momentum; the word patterns beginning with the preposition *with* are parallel.

Vocabulary Builder, p. 191

A. **Sample Answers**

1. Because the task was so <u>arduous</u>, we had to work for hours to complete it.
2. The people hoped that the queen's rule would last a lifetime, so it came as a cruel disappointment that she <u>abdicated</u> the throne in the second year of her reign.
3. On my cousin's <u>induction</u> into the army, our family gathered to say goodbye to him.
4. Because she always spoke with <u>candor,</u> people always believed her.
5. The child needed <u>discipline</u> badly because she was so frightfully disobedient.
6. If you are a good student, it is quite <u>feasible</u> that you'll do very well in college.

B. 1. Many people would think it would be exciting to <u>conduct</u> a group of skilled musicians.
2. If there were a price <u>reduction,</u> the price of the CDs would be lower.
3. You should <u>deduct</u> what something costs from how much you have to see if you can pay for it.

Enrichment: The New Deal, p. 192

Answers will vary. Examine students' New Deal dictionaries to ensure that they have included a representative and accurate selection of New Deal bills, programs, and agencies in alphabetical order. Sample answers may include the following:

AAA: Agricultural Adjustment Administration (1933); farm-relief agency established to restore agricultural prosperity

CCC: Civilian Conservation Corps (1933); put young men to work planting forest land

FDIC: Federal Deposit Insurance Corporation (1933); agency created to insure the savings of bank depositors

NLRB: National Labor Relations Board (1935); agency overseeing labor negotiations

NRA: National Recovery Administration (1933); instituted industrywide codes to eliminate unfair trade practices, reduce unemployment, and establish minimum wages

SEC: Securities and Exchange Commission (1934); agency regulating stock and bond markets

TVA: Tennessee Valley Authority (1933); agency that developed electricity in rural areas of the Southeast

WPA: Works Progress Administration (1935); provided work for the unemployed

"I Have a Dream" by Martin Luther King, Jr.
"First Inaugural Address"
by Franklin Delano Roosevelt

Integrated Language Skills: Grammar, p. 193

A. 1. forever-conduct (verb)
2. today-say (verb); still-have (verb); deeply-rooted (adjective)
3. still-offers (verb)
4. now-restore (verb)

B. Examine students' paragraphs for correct usage and identification of adverbs.

"First Inaugural Address"
by Franklin Delano Roosevelt

Open-Book Test, p. 196

Short Answer

1. He wants to win the approval and support of his audience, the citizens of the United States.
   Difficulty: *Easy* **Objective:** *Interpretation*
2. Repetition of the word *fear* makes the assertion memorable.
   Difficulty: *Easy* **Objective:** *Literary Analysis*
3. Students should explain that Roosevelt has said he will speak frankly and that those words describe the mood of the times, when the Great Depression was at its worst.
   Difficulty: *Average* **Objective:** *Interpretation*
4. Students should cite "unscrupulous money changers" and perhaps "the court of public opinion."
   Difficulty: *Easy* **Objective:** *Reading*
5. Sample answer: *Technique:* Repetition; *Purpose:* To persuade the American people that they should not equate wealth with happiness and to encourage them to consider creative ways to solve the nation's problems; *Effect:* create a sense of confidence and excitement in the American people
   Difficulty: *Average* **Objective:** *Reading*
6. *Evanescent* profits tend to disappear. Roosevelt is saying that it is foolish or unreasonable to chase after profits that are temporary or short-lived.
   Difficulty: *Average* **Objective:** *Vocabulary*
7. Students might point out that the pioneer spirit is associated with a willingness to take chances and with a proud time in American history, when the country was expanding and opportunity seemed endless.
   Difficulty: *Challenging* **Objective:** *Interpretation*

8. He is using analogy: He is comparing the American people to an army.
   Difficulty: *Average* **Objective:** *Literary Analysis*

9. His most important aim is to restore the American people's confidence in the nation.
   Difficulty: *Challenging* **Objective:** *Interpretation*

10. The passage illustrates parallelism in that both sentences contain the same sentence structure. It illustrates restatement by using different words to express the same idea.
    Difficulty: *Challenging* **Objective:** *Literary Analysis*

Essay

11. Students should identify the problem as the economic hardship of the Great Depression. They should note that Roosevelt approaches the problem with confidence and honesty. Students should mention any two of the following solutions: reforming business ethics, putting people back to work, recognizing our interdependence, and supporting strong executive leadership in the effort; Roosevelt also calls on Americans to perform their duty.
    Difficulty: *Easy* **Objective:** *Essay*

12. Examples of emotionally charged language with positive associations include "the time to speak the truth, the whole truth, frankly and boldly," "a leadership of frankness and vigor," and "plenty is at our doorstep." Examples of emotionally charged language with negative associations include "fear itself," "nameless, unreasoning, unjustified terror," "in every dark hour," "the dark realities of the moment," and "false leadership." Students will most likely argue that Roosevelt used language effectively. They might note that his balance of positive and negative language supports his declaration that he will speak boldly and honestly.
    Difficulty: *Average* **Objective:** *Essay*

13. They should note that Roosevelt's main aim is to gain the people's confidence by giving them the impression that he possesses the ability to lead the nation out of the Depression. He achieves his aim by providing reasons to have hope ("the only thing we have to fear is fear itself"; "we are stricken by no plague of locusts"; "plenty is at our doorstep") and by focusing on values his audience can identify with (the dignity of work and the importance of interdependence). Students should recognize that Roosevelt most likely believed that a general appeal would be more effective at uniting the people and gaining their confidence than would a laundry list of projects, which might give the audience plenty to debate and disagree with.
    Difficulty: *Challenging* **Objective:** *Essay*

14. Students are likely to recognize that Roosevelt's speech is short on a demonstration of the new president's knowledge—the speech contains no hard facts about the nation's economic condition. In contrast, with its use of emotional appeals, it demonstrates that Roosevelt has a deep understanding of the people's emotional state and what they need to hear from their new president.
    Difficulty: *Average* **Objective:** *Essay*

Oral Response

15. Oral responses should be clear, well organized, and well supported by appropriate details from the speech.
    Difficulty: *Average* **Objective:** *Oral Interpretation*

Selection Test A, p. 199

Critical Reading

1. **ANS:** C	**DIF:** Easy	**OBJ:** Comprehension
2. **ANS:** B	**DIF:** Easy	**OBJ:** Interpretation
3. **ANS:** C	**DIF:** Easy	**OBJ:** Reading
4. **ANS:** A	**DIF:** Easy	**OBJ:** Comprehension
5. **ANS:** B	**DIF:** Easy	**OBJ:** Comprehension
6. **ANS:** A	**DIF:** Easy	**OBJ:** Interpretation
7. **ANS:** B	**DIF:** Easy	**OBJ:** Literary Analysis
8. **ANS:** C	**DIF:** Easy	**OBJ:** Comprehension
9. **ANS:** C	**DIF:** Easy	**OBJ:** Interpretation
10. **ANS:** B	**DIF:** Easy	**OBJ:** Interpretation
11. **ANS:** A	**DIF:** Easy	**OBJ:** Reading

Vocabulary and Grammar

12. **ANS:** C	**DIF:** Easy	**OBJ:** Vocabulary
13. **ANS:** B	**DIF:** Easy	**OBJ:** Vocabulary
14. **ANS:** B	**DIF:** Easy	**OBJ:** Grammar

Essay

15. Students' essays should identify the problem as the economic hardship of the Great Depression. Essays should note that President Roosevelt approaches this problem with confidence and honesty. He advises his listeners that the only thing they have to fear is fear itself. Students should mention any two of the following solutions: reforming business ethics; putting people back to work; recognizing our interdependence; supporting strong executive leadership in the effort to turn the economy around; Americans' performing their duty.
    Difficulty: *Easy*
    Objective: *Essay*

16. In their essays, students should cite a number of examples of words and phrases in the speech with strong emotional associations. Positive examples abound, such as "the truth, the whole truth"; "much to be thankful for"; "Nature still offers her bounty." Some examples of negatively charged words and phrases: "fear"; "nameless, unreasoning, unjustified terror"; "false leadership." Most students will agree that Roosevelt uses this persuasive technique skillfully and effectively.
    Difficulty: *Easy*
    Objective: *Essay*

17. Students are likely to recognize that Roosevelt's speech is short on a demonstration of the new president's knowledge, because of a lack of hard facts about the economy. In contrast, its use of emotional appeals demonstrates that he has a deep understanding of the people's emotional state and what they need to hear from their new president.

Difficulty: *Average*
Objective: *Essay*

Selection Test B, p. 202

Critical Reading

1. ANS: C	DIF: Average	OBJ: Comprehension
2. ANS: A	DIF: Average	OBJ: Comprehension
3. ANS: D	DIF: Average	OBJ: Literary Analysis
4. ANS: B	DIF: Average	OBJ: Interpretation
5. ANS: B	DIF: Average	OBJ: Literary Analysis
6. ANS: D	DIF: Average	OBJ: Literary Analysis
7. ANS: B	DIF: Challenging	OBJ: Interpretation
8. ANS: C	DIF: Challenging	OBJ: Literary Analysis
9. ANS: C	DIF: Average	OBJ: Interpretation
10. ANS: B	DIF: Challenging	OBJ: Reading
11. ANS: C	DIF: Average	OBJ: Comprehension
12. ANS: A	DIF: Challenging	OBJ: Interpretation
13. ANS: B	DIF: Average	OBJ: Reading
14. ANS: A	DIF: Average	OBJ: Reading

Vocabulary and Grammar

15. ANS: B	DIF: Average	OBJ: Vocabulary
16. ANS: A	DIF: Challenging	OBJ: Vocabulary
17. ANS: B	DIF: Average	OBJ: Grammar
18. ANS: B	DIF: Average	OBJ: Grammar

Essay

19. Students' essays should identify President Roosevelt's main ideas in the speech. Thus, students should mention some or all of the following: Roosevelt's rejection of fear, his distinction between material things and idealistic goals, his criticism of greed, his stress on the value of work, his call for confidence, his stress on interdependence, his reaffirmation of constitutional government, and his reassurance that he is prepared to take vigorous action to ensure recovery. Students should include details from the speech that support each of the main ideas they mention.

Difficulty: *Average*
Objective: *Essay*

20. Students should list a number of ideals President Roosevelt invokes—for example, the dignity of work, the value of interdependence, or the necessity to reject fear. Students should also explain why they think he decided

to stress broad, general themes in his speech rather than specific remedial measures.

Difficulty: *Average*
Objective: *Essay*

21. Students are likely to recognize that Roosevelt's speech is short on a demonstration of the new president's knowledge—the speech contains no hard facts about the nation's economic condition. In contrast, with its use of emotional appeals, it demonstrates that Roosevelt has a deep understanding of the people's emotional state and what they need to hear from their new president.

Difficulty: *Average*
Objective: *Essay*

"The Talk" by Gary Soto
"Talk" retold by Harold Courlander and George Herzog

Vocabulary Warm-up Exercises A, p. 206

A.
1. frail
2. bundle
3. plucked
4. recite
5. churning
6. restless
7. nudge
8. twined

B. Sample Answers
1. False. <u>Gangly</u> implies that a person is somewhat awkward, not graceful the way a ballet dancer or gymnast needs to be.
2. True. Cheering or shouting for a long time hurts the throat and makes a person speak <u>hoarsely</u>.
3. False. <u>Receding</u> means moving into the distance, so the sight would appear to be growing smaller, not larger.
4. True. When people are angry or upset, they are likely to be frowning or <u>scowling</u>.
5. False. Fashion models are usually attractive, so their features are unlikely to be <u>unshapely</u>.
6. True. If the pile of books <u>wavered</u>, which means swayed back and forth, it probably meant that the surface they were on was wobbling in some way.
7. False. A <u>ford</u> is a place where a river is safe, not dangerous, to cross.
8. True. Someone who is excited may have a hard time catching her breath, so she will speak <u>breathlessly</u>.

Reading Warm-up A, p. 207

Sample Answers
1. <u>to teach lessons</u>, <u>used as warnings</u>; A synonym for *recite* is *tell*.
2. (strong); *Frail* means fragile, weak, or delicate.

3. wiggly; An antonym for *restless* might be *relaxed* or *calm*.

4. children who disturb the story session; We *nudge* children to get them to be quiet and to pay attention.

5. (maid); milk into butter

6. (a chicken); *Plucked* means that something, like a feather, has been removed. *Put into* means that a person has inserted something into something else; it is the opposite of *plucked*.

7. toys; A noisy *bundle* of kittens was left on the doorstep of the vet's office.

8. (separately); his story [the Santa tale]; the interests of toy makers and stores

Reading Warm-up B, p. 208

Sample Answers

1. with long arms; The word *crane* can be either a long, thin bird or a tall piece of equipment.

2. (stream); A *ford* is a shallow place in a river or stream where you can cross.

3. He spoke *hoarsely* because he was terrified. A person might also speak *hoarsely* if he or she has a sore throat.

4. bulky; An *unshapely* headless horseman might seem more ghostlike and less like a human being.

5. the time in which they were written; A phrase that means the same as *receding* is *moving farther away*.

6. (angrily); *Smiling* is an antonym for *scowling*.

7. runs around; He answered the telephone *breathlessly* because he had just run up the stairs.

8. his popularity; *Wavered* also means *came and went*.

Writing About the Big Question, p. 209

A. 1. connection
2. interpret
3. senses
4. insight

B. Sample Answers

1. I like to talk to my friend Jeffrey.

2. Jeffrey always has a different **insight** into my experiences. He helps me see how my **feelings** are mixed up and how the **facts** can be **interpreted** in a different way.

C. Sample Answer

it helps us acknowledge truths that might otherwise be hard to accept.

The more we know the more we understand. It doesn't matter that facts are presented in a humorous way. What matters is getting people to think about them and realize what they can tell us about ourselves or others or the world in general. Whenever that happens, even if it's in a humorous way, we grow in understanding.

Literary Analysis: Comparing Humorous Writing, p. 210

Sample Answers

1. The passage exemplifies hyperbole, or deliberate exaggeration for effect. The boys' eyes cannot really have been as small as pencil dots, and their noses probably did not cast "remarkable" shadows.

2. Soto's essay touches on the agonizing self-consciousness of young people about to enter adolescence. The boys' anxiety about their awkward looks is recalled affectionately from an adult point of view, with the result that we gain a balanced perspective on what might have seemed at the time to be a distressing situation.

3. Answers will vary. Students may point out that the authors choose ordinary items with humorous names—such as *yams, fish trap, bundle,* and *stool*—to do much of the talking. They also use the unusual exclamation *Wah!* and picturesque words such as *wheezed* and *bulging* to describe characters. The diction makes the characters sound and look like the odd, simple characters in a cartoon.

4. "Talk" conveys the important message that we often regard other people as foolish and as overreacting to harmless events until those events happen to us. Then, those events take on dramatic and serious overtones.

5. "The Talk" uses hyperbole, while "Talk" uses understatement. Examples of hyperbole in "The Talk" include the narrator's description of his "gangly arms" that "nearly touched my kneecaps." An example of understatement in "Talk" is the almost casual description the writers give of the farmer's initial response to the talking yam and dog. In reality, people would be totally astounded by the event. The farmer, however, actually gets angry at his dog because of the tone of his voice.

Vocabulary Builder, p. 211

A. Sample Answers

1. We were delighted by the energy of the feisty dog.

2. The group of renegade fans cheered the opposing team whenever it scored.

3. The bulging balloon grew larger and larger before our eyes.

4. She could not refrain from eating the luscious dessert.

5. The runner wheezed loudly and grimaced as he thought how terrible he felt after this race.

B. 1. A; 2. C; 3. A; 4. A; 5. B

Open-Book Test, p. 213

Short Answer

1. Examples of hyperbole in "The Talk" include these statements by the narrator: "My best friend and I knew we were going to grow up to be ugly"; "First, our heads got large, but our necks wavered, frail as crisp tulips"; "My gangly arms

nearly touched my kneecaps"; and "we would . . . throw a slipper at our feisty dog at least a hundred times."

Difficulty: *Easy*   **Objective:** *Literary Analysis*

2. The dog would respond enthusiastically.

Difficulty: *Average*   **Objective:** *Vocabulary*

3. The tone might be described as light-hearted, nostalgic, innocent, or naive.

Difficulty: *Challenging*   **Objective:** *Interpretation*

4. A yam, his dog, a palm tree, and a stone talk to him. They complain about the way he is treating them.

Difficulty: *Easy*   **Objective:** *Interpretation*

5. They are frightened because an animal and inanimate objects have talked to them.

Difficulty: *Average*   **Objective:** *Interpretation*

6. The stool is suggesting that it is odd that a yam would talk when it is just as odd that a stool would talk.

Difficulty: *Average*   **Objective:** *Literary Analysis*

7. Sample answers: *"The Talk": Differences:* a modern town in the United States, adolescent boys
"Talk": Differences: an old-fashioned community in Ghana, grown men *Similarities:* naive characters
Students should recognize that the setting and characters of "The Talk" are more vivid. The selection includes details of the setting (for example, a lawn, a porch light) and details about the boys' appearance.

Difficulty: *Average*   **Objective:** *Literary Analysis*

8. The main purpose of the authors of both selections seems to be to entertain readers or listeners. Students might also mention that the authors of both selections use humor to explore their characters' anxieties.

Difficulty: *Easy*   **Objective:** *Literary Analysis*

9. Students should recognize that the characters are confronting fears, anxieties, or concerns.

Difficulty: *Challenging*   **Objective:** *Literary Analysis*

10. Students are likely to choose "The Talk" because the situation is realistic and most likely somewhat familiar to them. Whichever selection they choose, students should explain why they found it funnier than the other.

Difficulty: *Average*   **Objective:** *Literary Analysis*

Essay

11. Examples of hyperbole in "The Talk," as noted earlier, include these statements by the narrator: "My best friend and I knew we were going to grow up to be ugly"; "First, our heads got large, but our necks wavered, frail as crisp tulips"; "My gangly arms nearly touched my kneecaps"; and "we would . . . throw a slipper at our feisty dog at least a hundred times." Students should choose two of those or two other examples and tell what is funny about them.

Difficulty: *Easy*   **Objective:** *Essay*

12. Students should identify two passages from the selections, tell why each one is funny, and tell whether or not the passages contain hyperbole.

Difficulty: *Average*   **Objective:** *Essay*

13. Students should point out that "The Talk" deals with young people's self-image, their concerns about attracting a mate, their ideas about what their family life will be like, and their thoughts about the careers they will have. They should realize that the concerns conveyed by "Talk" are much more subtle. They might realize that the story touches on the consequences of laziness (the man's troubles start when the yam points out that the man has not weeded it), the chief's concern with community harmony, and the chief's failure to take the men's concerns seriously. Students should also comment on the effectiveness of the humor in each selection. They should recognize that "The Talk" uses humor effectively by putting in humorous terms concerns that most young people will identify with. "Talk" uses humor effectively by repeating the situation and, at the end, showing that the chief has missed the point.

Difficulty: *Challenging*   **Objective:** *Essay*

14. Students writing about "The Talk" should point out the naivete of the boys' ideas. The boys have knowledge of what their future will be like, but they do not have a mature understanding of the reality of adult life. Students writing about "Talk" should realize that none of the characters appears to possess an understanding of the situation. The tale ends by pointing out that the chief, who should possess greater understanding than the men of the village, appears to have as little understanding as the others.

Difficulty: *Average*   **Objective:** *Essay*

Oral Response

15. Oral responses should be clear, well organized, and well supported by appropriate details from the selections.

Difficulty: *Average*   **Objective:** *Oral Interpretation*

Selection Test A, p. 216
Critical Reading

1. ANS: C	DIF: Easy	OBJ: Literary Analysis
2. ANS: C	DIF: Easy	OBJ: Literary Analysis
3. ANS: A	DIF: Easy	OBJ: Comprehension
4. ANS: C	DIF: Easy	OBJ: Literary Analysis
5. ANS: A	DIF: Easy	OBJ: Interpretation
6. ANS: B	DIF: Easy	OBJ: Interpretation
7. ANS: C	DIF: Easy	OBJ: Interpretation
8. ANS: B	DIF: Easy	OBJ: Interpretation
9. ANS: D	DIF: Easy	OBJ: Interpretation
10. ANS: C	DIF: Easy	OBJ: Interpretation

Vocabulary

11. ANS: A	DIF: Easy	OBJ: Vocabulary
12. ANS: B	DIF: Easy	OBJ: Vocabulary
13. ANS: A	DIF: Easy	OBJ: Vocabulary

Essay

14. Evaluate students' essays on the specific identification and analysis of two humorous passages in each selection. Students should make appropriate mention of devices for creating humor such as hyperbole, understatement, slang, or funny names.
Difficulty: *Easy*
Objective: *Essay*

15. Students should realize that although one is nonfiction and one is fiction, the messages are equally serious.

16. Students writing about "The Talk" should point out the naivete of the boys' ideas. The boys have knowledge of what their future will be like, but they do not have a mature understanding of the reality of adult life. Students writing about "Talk" should realize that none of the characters appears to possess an understanding of the situation. The tale ends by pointing out that the chief, who should possess greater understanding than the men of the village, appears to have as little understanding as the others.
Difficulty: *Average*
Objective: *Essay*

Selection Test B, p. 219

Critical Reading

1. ANS: B	DIF: Average	OBJ: Comprehension
2. ANS: C	DIF: Average	OBJ: Comprehension
3. ANS: A	DIF: Average	OBJ: Literary Analysis
4. ANS: B	DIF: Challenging	OBJ: Literary Analysis
5. ANS: D	DIF: Average	OBJ: Comprehension
6. ANS: C	DIF: Average	OBJ: Comprehension
7. ANS: A	DIF: Average	OBJ: Comprehension
8. ANS: D	DIF: Average	OBJ: Interpretation
9. ANS: C	DIF: Challenging	OBJ: Interpretation
10. ANS: B	DIF: Challenging	OBJ: Interpretation
11. ANS: A	DIF: Average	OBJ: Interpretation
12. ANS: B	DIF: Average	OBJ: Interpretation
13. ANS: C	DIF: Challenging	OBJ: Literary Analysis
14. ANS: A	DIF: Average	OBJ: Interpretation
15. ANS: C	DIF: Average	OBJ: Interpretation

Vocabulary

16. ANS: B	DIF: Average	OBJ: Vocabulary
17. ANS: C	DIF: Average	OBJ: Vocabulary
18. ANS: D	DIF: Average	OBJ: Vocabulary

Essay

19. In their essays, students should identify two examples of humorous devices in "The Talk" and two examples in "Talk." Evaluate students' analyses on the basis of their clear, concise explanations of the humor in each case.
Difficulty: *Average*
Objective: *Essay*

20. Students should point out that Gary Soto's essay "The Talk" broaches such serious themes as young people's self-image and future careers. Courlander and Herzog's "Talk" deals with the theme of how people respond to the concerns of others. Use criteria such as clarity and coherence to evaluate students' discussions of the writers' use of humor to deal with these serious themes.
Difficulty: *Average*
Objective: *Essay*

21. Students writing about "The Talk" should point out the naivete of the boys' ideas. The boys have knowledge of what their future will be like, but they do not have a mature understanding of the reality of adult life. Students writing about "Talk" should realize that none of the characters appears to possess an understanding of the situation. The tale ends by pointing out that the chief, who should possess greater understanding than the men of the village, appears to have as little understanding as the others.
Difficulty: *Average*
Objective: *Essay*

Writing Workshop

Editorial: Integrating Grammar Skills, p. 223

A. 1. what we need to repel insects; nouns
2. The places we camp; noun clauses
3. and there is a brook nearby; prepositional phrases

B. Sample Answers
1. Daily exercise, a sensible diet, and a strict sleep schedule can all help improve your health.
2. Try aerobics to improve circulation, to build stamina, and to breathe better.
3. In yoga, you bend, stretch, and breathe through your nose.

Vocabulary Workshop—1, p. 224

Sample Answer
1. C
2. C
3. A
4. A
5. B

Vocabulary Workshop—2, p. 225

Sample Answers

1. The new board member picked up a piece of chalk and wrote her name on the board. Meanings: a group of persons who manage something; a flat surface of slate or another material on which things are written

2. Sandy grew tense when his English teacher asked him if the verb was in the past or present tense. Meanings: nervous; a verb's indication of time

3. She might lose heart, but she'll probably keep trying with all her might. Meanings: possibly can; great power or strength

4. Michelle came in first, and a second later, Rona came in second. Meanings: a sixtieth of a minute; a position immediately after first

5. Carlos grew plants at a nursery; his sister was a child care worker at a nursery. Meanings: a place where plants are raised; a school for very young children

Benchmark Test 6, p. 227

MULTIPLE CHOICE

1. ANS: B
2. ANS: A
3. ANS: A
4. ANS: C
5. ANS: A
6. ANS: D
7. ANS: B
8. ANS: C
9. ANS: D
10. ANS: B
11. ANS: C
12. ANS: C
13. ANS: D
14. ANS: B
15. ANS: B
16. ANS: C
17. ANS: A
18. ANS: D
19. ANS: D
20. ANS: A
21. ANS: B
22. ANS: A
23. ANS: B
24. ANS: D
25. ANS: B
26. ANS: A
27. ANS: A
28. ANS: C
29. ANS: B
30. ANS: A
31. ANS: C
32. ANS: B
33. ANS: C
34. ANS: A
35. ANS: A
36. ANS: C
37. ANS: A

ESSAY

38. Students should display their knowledge of the elements of persuasive writing.

39. Students should demonstrate the ability to apply basic persuasive techniques. Their work should contain one of the following: restatement, repetition, emotionally charged language, or bandwagon appeals.

40. Students should demonstrate clear understanding of an abstract and its use.

Vocabulary in Context 3, p. 233

MULTIPLE CHOICE

1. ANS: A
2. ANS: B
3. ANS: D
4. ANS: C
5. ANS: B
6. ANS: C
7. ANS: D
8. ANS: A
9. ANS: B
10. ANS: C
11. ANS: C
12. ANS: A
13. ANS: D
14. ANS: A
15. ANS: B
16. ANS: B
17. ANS: C
18. ANS: D
19. ANS: D
20. ANS: A